THE EXPERT'S GUIDE TO SUCCESS IN ALL MARKET CONDITIONS

PROPERTY AUCTIONS

REPOSSESSIONS, BANKRUPTCIES AND BARGAIN PROPERTIES

Property Auctions: Repossessions, Bankruptcies and Bargain Properties: The expert's guide to success in all market conditions

4th Edition Paperback ISBN: 978-1-7393549-4-7
ePub ISBN: 978-1-7393549-1-6

British Library Cataloguing-in-Publication data
A catalogue record for this book is available from the British Library.

Cover design and typeset by Spiffing Covers

THE EXPERT'S GUIDE TO SUCCESS IN ALL MARKET CONDITIONS

PROPERTY AUCTIONS

REPOSSESSIONS, BANKRUPTCIES AND BARGAIN PROPERTIES

DOMINIC FARRELL

Contents

About the Author

Dominic Farrell was born and bred in Liverpool and attended the Salesian High School, then the University of Bradford where he read economics. After graduation, he attended the Royal Military Academy Sandhurst and was commissioned into the King's Regiment. He served all over the world, completed a master's degree in defence administration at Cranfield University, and was decorated by HM The Queen in the Operational Honours List 2001. He was awarded the Queen's Commendation for Valuable Service (QCVS) for outstanding service on an operational tour.

Dominic also found time, in his so-called "spare time," to serve as the military script adviser on the hugely successful ITV drama Soldier Soldier, often having to remind his Army colleagues that it was, after all, a drama rather than a documentary.

He retired as a major at his first pension point to pursue property development full-time, having built a portfolio of buy-to-let properties while still serving in the army.

Dominic quickly established himself as a property developer in Cyprus in the run-up to European Union accession. This was a huge success, until the Credit Crunch and financial crisis of 2008 and its aftermath.

For many developers worldwide, the market collapsed. This period was also an opportunity, and Dominic quickly established Distressed Assets (www.distressedassets.co.uk) to seize opportunities brought about by the crisis, some examples of which are shown in this book.

He has been an active property developer and investor for decades, buying and selling hundreds of properties, but for the past 18 years has focused almost exclusively on distressed assets at property auctions, where he feels the real value is to be found.

Dominic has a very successful mentorship programme for property investors wishing to master the property auction world, as well as other forms of distressed assets. He also runs one-day property auction and distressed assets workshops four times a year in London and live online (for further details, see the end of this book).

He lives in Liverpool and is happily married with three children, two dogs and two cats.

Introduction

What is a distressed asset?

When a property owner, developer or creditor needs immediate cash and wants to sell a property, portfolio or development quickly at less than its market value, it becomes a distressed asset. These distressed assets are usually sold at auction.

There are opportunities in all market conditions for an astute investor to buy property at 'distressed values' or below-market value, and this book will show you how. It's based on extensive experience spanning decades of buying and selling hundreds of properties in both recessions and booms. I do this full-time, and live and breathe property auctions: the research, targeting, filtering and acquisition of outstanding investment opportunities, both for development and sale and traditional buy-to-let.

All of the examples in this book are real and verifiable, a sample of what we do and bring to life the theory: for without real-life results, what's the point in a book about theory? What if theory doesn't work when applied to the rough and tumble of the real world?

At Distressed Assets, we no longer buy or source properties through estate agents, as value, transparency and certainty are much better at auction.

By the end of this book, you might well agree.

Are you a retail or wholesale investor?

Retail investors generally buy through estate agents and pay the retail price, whereas wholesale investors buy at auction.

Wholesale investors buy in-built equity right from the start and a high yield, which is commensurate with a property significantly below market-value.

This book illustrates principles or methodology, and how they work in real life: principles that don't work when applied to a real market situation aren't worth having. In the army, we say that no plan survives contact with the enemy, so how effective is the applied methodology set out in this book?

A good example of applying the theory is a property acquired recently, purchased prior to auction, then refinanced six months later on a mortgage (Figure 1).

Figure 1: 47% capital gain in six months with no refurbishment required

I use this example in my workshops because it succinctly illustrates many points, not least the importance of thorough due diligence, auction tactics and moving decisively to secure the acquisition. By the time you have read this book, you will know how to do deals like this yourself.

In essence, this three-bedroom, freehold terraced house in an excellent rental area was purchased prior to auction at £75,000. Other properties – albeit smaller two-bedroom houses – were for sale with local estate agents at £110,000 and £125,000 respectively.

After six months, the property was conservatively mortgaged at 47% higher than the purchase price, without any refurbishment or renovation. By any standards, this is an exceptional acquisition, but not in the distressed assets world of property auctions. You will see further examples of outstanding property deals throughout this book stretching back to 2009, and as recent as 2026.

Armed with the knowledge in this book, hard work and perseverance, you can do it too.

Here are some further examples to illustrate this point.

Case Study
Distressed Assets: Liverpool L35 – January 2026

This transaction illustrates a key principle: properties that fail to sell at auction are not necessarily flawed, but often mispriced or overlooked.

The property had been offered at auction twice without success. As the guide price reduced and interest remained limited, a pre-auction negotiation strategy was adopted. Two offers were rejected before a third was accepted, securing the purchase ahead of a further auction.

Properties like this are frequently ignored by the wider auction crowd. Inexperienced buyers tend to follow others and focus on familiar stock, in familiar areas, often pushing prices beyond market value. Experienced investors take a different approach, targeting assets with manageable issues, or problems which can be fixed, that others overlook.

The property required relatively minor works, already had some refurbishment, and benefited from a large rear garden. In the same month, standard two-bedroom terraced houses in weaker locations with lower rental potential were selling for around £120,000.

The contrast highlights a fundamental lesson: auction success comes from understanding crowd behaviour and identifying mispriced assets. The financial breakdown is shown in Figure 2.

January 2026

Purchased Prior to Auction

Purchase Price: £135,000

Gross Yield: 13%–18%

Property Overview

- Four-bedroom house
- Two bathrooms
- 1,216 sq ft
- EPC rating: C
- Conservatory
- Off-road parking for 2–3 vehicles
- Large plot

Location

- Five-minute walk to a major hospital

Comparable Sales

- £200,000–£240,000

Wholesale acquisition prior to auction, delivering strong income with multiple exit strategies.

Figure 2: Avoid the herd or crowd to secure incredible bargains at auction

Case Study
Distressed Assets: Liverpool L4 – January 2024

A client completed on an end-of-terrace freehold house being sold by a receiver at auction. After two attempts, our pre-auction offer was finally accepted at £70,000.

The latest sales in the road – a lovely cul-de-sac – had been £135,950, £110,500 and £110,000 respectively. The client was delighted. The property is a large, 900 sq. ft tenanted family home: at the market rent, it will yield 13.6%. It also has potential for development into a five-bedroom House in Multiple Occupation (HMO), subject to permission, or could be used for serviced accommodation following the Airbnb model, given its proximity to the Liverpool FC stadium in Anfield.

The difference between buying distressed assets (wholesale) and through estate agents (retail) could not be better illustrated.

Case Study
Distressed Assets: Liverpool L15 - June 2025

This freehold house was acquired prior to auction in 2024 for £75,000 and refinanced just eight months later, in June 2025, at £120,000, without any refurbishment whatsoever. That represents a capital uplift of 60%. The property was in excellent condition throughout, benefitting from new external insulation and a new roof, and was unquestionably an outstanding bargain.

The client had attended one of my London workshops and, at the end of the session, asked for my opinion on another property they were due to exchange contracts on the following week via private treaty (estate agent). That property was in a less desirable area, in inferior condition, and priced at £108,000 - £33,000 (44%) more than this auction acquisition.

I know the area extremely well and, crucially, understand the difference between retail and wholesale pricing. I advised the client to walk away from the private treaty purchase and instead focus on securing far better opportunities in the auction market. Although withdrawing involved some costs, they took the advice, walked away, and have never looked back. This was their first purchase, and they have since gone on to acquire further properties through my mentorship programme.

Figure 3: 60% capital gain in 8 months with no refurbishment required

Lessons

There are three important lessons to take from this acquisition.

First, never assume the information in property particulars or legal pack is correct. In this case, the seller had failed to update the EPC from an E to a C, something I spotted immediately from the online photographs alone.

Second, when you identify a genuine opportunity, act decisively. I viewed the property the very next day, and the client submitted an offer that afternoon. The initial offer was rejected, but the revised offer was accepted shortly afterwards.

Finally, do not become psychologically anchored to a poor deal simply because you have already incurred legal or sourcing costs. Sometimes the correct decision is to take a small loss and walk away. Better still, avoid placing yourself in that position in the first place.

The purpose of this book is to show you where and how to find exceptional opportunities like this, and to help you approach property auctions with the mindset and discipline of a professional investor.

Whether you're new to property auctions, buy-to-let or a seasoned investor, or looking to property investment to increase your wealth or fund your retirement, this book has something for everyone. Anyone can make money in rising markets, it's very simple – but applying the techniques in this book will enable you to profit in all market conditions, whether prices are rising, falling or stagnating.

We all know that during rising markets, the opportunities to make money from property are many, whether that's investing off-plan, buying and renovating, land development or just standard buy-to-let.

What is less known is that opportunities during difficult economic times are just as good, if not better. Recessions present a unique set of circumstances, with businesses closing, property developers going into receivership or administration, and banks repossessing properties from those who can no longer meet their commitments. These 'distressed assets' can be researched, analysed and, having completed thorough due diligence, purchased – usually at significant discounts to market value. Further, at these discounts, the returns in the form of rent (yield) are excellent – the asset can work hard for you over the medium-to-long term.

Since the Covid-19 pandemic and lockdowns in the UK and other countries, property auctions have changed – but for the better, presenting an even more attractive platform for investment success. Now, the live auction room is supplemented by the facility to bid online, watching the auctioneer and action in the room via streaming services (the 'hybrid model'). Some auctions are solely online, and you can participate wherever you are in the world, just with the click of a mouse. After many years of buying property at auction, I am a convert to the online live auction (and will explain why, later in this book).

This book demystifies the acquisition of distressed properties at auction and shows you how to make money whatever the economic weather. It brings together all of the key concepts that successful property auction investors focus on which, combined, give you a solid platform on which to base investment decisions.

The first part of the book details the tools and techniques to help you identify, analyse and filter properties, shortlisting your targets. The second part takes you through the actual viewing and buying process and the tactics involved to be successful. There are chapters on raising finance and the auction legal process, which are two key components of the journey and essential to understand. The book also includes some real-life acquisitions to show how the theory works in practice.

This revised edition includes a new chapter (14) on selling or trading property at auction. I have sold many properties for myself and clients at various auctions, and for various reasons. There has been a growing interest in trading and selling at auction in general, so this new chapter is designed to share my first-hand experience and offer a few tips.

Enjoy the book, let's get started!

March 2026

Chapter 1
Economics and Market Cycles

'Economics is a choice between alternatives all the time. Those are the trade-offs.'

Paul Samuelson, economist[1]

The UK property market doesn't sit in isolation from the wider economy. It's a component of the economy, and an important one at that. As we've seen over the years, there is a strong correlation between the performance of the economy and the strength, or otherwise, of the property market. Remember, too, that both the property and construction industries contribute significantly to UK gross domestic product (GDP) in terms of revenue, employment and taxes. The economy isn't the sole factor determining property prices, but it is without doubt the most significant.

This chapter doesn't provide an economic or property market history of the UK; rather, it highlights the key factors that all property investors should be aware of when making investment decisions. These shouldn't be made in a vacuum or isolation, but in the wider context of economic and property market cycles.

The key question that buy-to-let investors need to understand in terms of economic theory and property is: 'What determines property prices and rents?'

1 P. Samuelson and W. Nordhaus (1948) *Economics*, McGraw-Hill.

Property prices and rents

Property is no different from oil, gas, food, cars, antiques, art or any other product where price is determined by interaction of demand for the item, product or service and its supply.

We've seen in the recent past how shortage of products or commodities such as oil, gas, wheat, coffee and sugar have led to a sharp rise in price, as demand is far greater than available supply. Similarly, as demand falls for a given product, due to a superior alternative or change in taste, fashion or technology, prices generally fall to attract sufficient buyers to clear inventories.

We're seeing it today, with weak prices in the second-hand diesel car market. This interaction between supply and demand determines prices in a market economy.

Rents

Recently, there has been a trend for rents to rise significantly, as inflation has resurfaced not just in the UK, but globally. There are a number of factors at play.

Supply-side

Government policies have limited the number of private sector rental properties in the market. Private, rented sector supply will need to increase by 227,000 homes per annum to meet the demand for 1.8 million new households over the next decade, according to analysis by the consultancy, Capital Economics.[2]

This simply will not happen: in fact, there is an argument that supply may fall. In the short-to-medium term, the supply of rental property is fixed – which is good news for landlords and new entrants to property development.

2 A. Evans and M. Hall-Harris (2022) 'Challenges and opportunities for the private rented sector: An assessment of the private rented sector and its role in meeting housing need in the UK. A report for the National Residential Landlords Association', Capital Economics, February. Available at: www.nrla.org.uk/capital-economics-report, accessed 5 January 2026.

Demand-side

Average UK monthly private rents increased by 4.4%, to £1,366, in the 12 months to November 2025.[3] Zoopla forecasts about 2.5% rental growth in 2026, reflecting continued but more modest demand pressure.[4]

Prices (rents)

When we apply economic theory to the real world of property and the rental market, it's easy to understand why rents are rising – significantly in some cases, as demand pushes against a fixed supply.

This underpins the private rental sector and supports strong rental returns.

Yield

The yield (ratio of rent to property price), and in particular net (after costs) income, is the key buy-to-let investors' yardstick for measuring performance. To maximise returns, we mustn't overpay for a property – and indeed, purchase it at below-market-value.

This is the entire theme of this book, and why auctions can be the best route to success and long-term wealth generation.

Prices

Many factors determine property prices, including:

- Demand, including demographics – we're also living longer
- Economic growth (GDP), inflation, deflation, exchange rates – overseas buyers are attracted by a relatively weak pound
- Property supply – the rate of housebuilding is a key factor
- Availability of finance (mortgages) – mortgage market deregulation and regulation
- Base or interest rates – low interest rates assist affordability, while rising interest can be seen as an opportunity for the astute investor

3 Office for National Statistics for the year ending December 2025.

4 Zoopla Rental Market Report, 10 December 2025

- Government policy and regulation – the abolition of Section 21 evictions[5] and withdrawal of some tax breaks for landlords have reduced property supply; as a consequence, rents have risen strongly
- Taxation – stamp duty, capital gains and mortgage interest relief
- Optimism and pessimism – sentiment.

This list is not exhaustive and will have regional variations which may be due to large infrastructure projects, job relocation from one region to another, enterprise zones and the like. Some areas of the country will be growing, while others are not as fast.

The UK economy

The UK is a member of the G7, which is a forum for the world's seven largest industrial market economies: USA, Japan, Germany, France, UK, Italy and Canada. Although its relative position in the hierarchy fluctuates from time to time, the UK economy is significant in global terms, and the UK property market and construction sector are both vital components of UK GDP. The relationship between property and the economy is two-way: the fortunes of one generally reflect those of the other.

Various key indicators highlight whether an economy is strong or not, but first it's useful to look at market cycles.

Market cycles

All markets move in cycles, with key stages (Figure 4).

5 A Section 21 eviction is a 'no fault' eviction under the Housing Act 1988, where the owner can give two months' written notice to a tenant to vacate the property. This will be abolished 1 May 2026. Guide to the Renters' Rights Act 6 November 2025. Available at: https://www.gov.uk/government/publications/guide-to-the-renters-rights-act/guide-to-the-renters-rights-act accessed 5 January 2026.

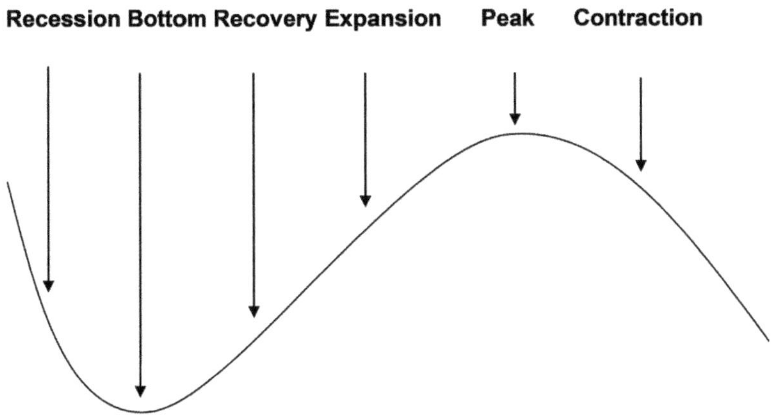

Figure 4: Market cycles

'Economic cycle' refers to economy-wide fluctuations in economic activity over time, which can be a number of months or even years. These fluctuations occur around a long-term trend, involving movement over time between phases of economic growth and stagnation or decline. They are evaluated using the rate of growth of GDP. Despite being called cycles, there is no predictable pattern.

In recent years, the UK economy has moved from recession to expansion fairly frequently. Recent recessions have occurred in:

- 1973 (three Qs; Q is a quarter or three-month period)
- 1975 (two Qs)
- 1980–1981 (five Qs)
- 1990–1991 (five Qs)
- 2008–2009 (five Qs) – the Great Recession
- 2020 (two Qs) – Covid-19 recession
- 2023 (two Qs).

A recession is defined as two consecutive quarters of negative growth. As we can note from recent recessions in the UK dating back to the oil crisis in 1973, they can last for a long time.

Multiplier effect

That a recession can last for years rather than months can be explained in part by the multiplier effect:

> The multiplier effect is an economic term, referring to the proportional amount of increase, or decrease, in final income that results from an injection, or withdrawal, of capital.[6]

Injection

In other words, if £25 billion is injected into the economy through tax cuts or increased government spending, we could expect a greater increase in GDP than the original investment. Jobs are created, and those with jobs spend their wages on goods and services in shops, online or at the car showroom. The local economy grows, more jobs are created and the upward spiral continues.

The original investment of £25 billion multiplies itself many times through the economy. Some income is saved, so the extent of the multiplier effect is affected by the savings rate. The UK gross savings rate has fluctuated over the past couple of decades, in the range of about 6% to 11%.

Leakage

Here, the converse is true. As unemployment rises, people who are no longer working have less to spend on goods and services, and increase pressure on government finances for two reasons. First, they no longer pay tax; second, they draw state benefits. As less is spent (leakage), shops, restaurants and pubs might close, for example; while those who supply these businesses (the supply chain) begin to shed staff as revenues decline.

This downward multiplier effect is very strong, as it's reinforced by fear, just as the rising multiplier effect is supported by greed (a topic we will return to later in Chapter 2).

6 A. Ganti (2025) 'What is the multiplier effect?' Investopedia, 15 June. Available at: www.investopedia.com/terms/m/multipliereffect.asp, accessed 5 January 2026.

In a recession, the government should take measures to increase the money supply through fiscal measures such as tax breaks for individuals and companies, or aggressive cuts in interest rates (although in the UK, this function has been given to the Bank of England's Monetary Policy Committee). Most governments recognise the dangers of a negative multiplier effect which, unless they take strong steps, could lead to a depression such as that experienced between 1930 and 1934 – when the UK didn't really surface from its economic malaise until the start of the Second World War, five years later.

In its most simple form, the multiplier effect is a useful tool for non-economists to understand the nature of economic growth or recession. Economists argue all day long about the effectiveness of this concept as an economic tool, but for us property investors, it encapsulates a simple truism:

If money is injected into an economy, we would expect growth.

If it's withdrawn, we should expect a slowdown (all other factors such as inflation remaining constant in this model).

There aren't many property books that discuss the wider economy and its impact on the property market, and so the investor's strategy or plan.

It's crucial to think about how you can prepare to take opportunities which may arise: for example, as an economy goes into recession and there is an increase in repossessions and bankruptcies.

As tragic as these situations are for the individuals and companies affected, assets will be sold and someone has to buy them. The people are long gone, and you are buying an empty property or properties.

By having a feel for how the economy works, investors can interpret economic data for themselves and make informed decisions.

At the time of writing, we are seeing evidence of a change in economic circumstances, as more distressed assets are sent to auction for a quick sale. Whether from overleveraged individuals (i.e. who have borrowed too much money) or companies, many are divesting some assets to reduce their borrowings and raise cash.

This is an opportunity, and we will see some real-world examples later in this book.

Property and economic growth or recession

Economic growth is the opposite of recession, although only one quarter of growth counts – unlike recession, where the definition requires two consecutive quarters.

For example, if the total output of goods and services by the UK economy were £100 and the economy were to grow by 3% in a year, it would have grown to £103. (In reality, it's actually more like £2.2 trillion which, written that way, gives you a feel for its size.)

In general terms, although there may be a time lag, property prices rise during a period of sustained economic expansion, and decline or remain stagnant during a recession. As the economy is cyclical in nature, so is the property market. Periods of expansion are interspersed with periods of contraction or stagnation, so an investment strategy for buy-to-let property should take into account the stage of the property market cycle in which we are investing.

Inflation and deflation

Inflation refers to a sustained rise in prices, while deflation is the opposite. In general, inflation is associated with strong economic growth and high employment; deflation with recession or depression and high unemployment. This is a simplistic model but, as a generalisation, helps us gain perspective on it.

However, an economy can contract while at the same time experiencing an increase in inflation. This is 'stagflation', which we have experienced from time to time in the UK, such as the early 1970s and during the 2008–2009 recession.

Inflation and deflation are the opposite sides of the same coin. I will deal with inflation here; for deflation, where you read rising prices, substitute falling prices, costs and demand. Inflation is the term we use to describe rising prices. How quickly prices go up is called the rate of inflation.

We hear a lot about inflation in the press and on TV, but how does it affect buy-to-let property investors? Inflation has two main drivers: costs and demand.

Costs

When a company experiences a rise in any part of its cost base, such as wages, rent and interest payments on loans and raw materials, it has the option to pass these increased costs onto the customer through higher prices.

The extent to which it can do this depends on consumer sensitivity to the price rise of its products, and the availability of substitutes. Inflation caused by an increase in costs is known as cost-push. In property markets, prices can be driven higher by increasing land prices, taxation, loan repayments and the rising cost of materials and labour.

Demand

As UK property investors and home buyers, we have experienced one of the greatest examples of 'demand-pull' inflation in recent years – right on our doorstep. UK property prices have been pulled up by an insatiable appetite for property since the latter part of the 1990s associated with falling interest rates, liberalisation of the financial services industry and a strong economic environment of high employment, low inflation and a growing economy.

As discussed earlier, one of the unique attributes of property as an investment is that demand always outstrips supply in the UK private rental sector.

Economists call this 'inelastic', as supply can't expand sufficiently to meet demand, and so prices (rents) rise. Further, unlike some goods and services, there is little by way of a substitution effect, as rents will be generally rising across the market and other options for renters are limited.

Inflation has been in abeyance for many years, and the Bank of England's remit in the UK is to keep it to an annual rate of 2% (as measured by the consumer price index, CPI).

The Bank of England changes interest rates in an attempt to affect the level of spending in the economy. When spending grows more quickly than the amount of goods and services produced, inflation results – in this way, the Bank changes interest rates to control inflation. The interest rate set by the Bank affects the range of interest rates set by banks and other financial institutions. Raising or lowering interest rates affects spending in the wider economy.

Lower interest rates:

- Make saving less attractive
- Make borrowing more attractive
- Improve cash flow for companies which have borrowings
- Stimulate spending
- Make buy-to-let investment more attractive, and help to present investors with cash flow
- Boost asset prices such as property and shares which leads to increasing wealth and willingness to consume (spend).

Higher interest rates have the opposite effect.

One of the most important influences on the demand for property, and so its price, is the level of interest rates. In general, falling interest rates support the property market, and rising interest rates have a negative effect.

Tip

The astute property investor recognises that rising interest rates represent an opportunity, not a threat.

The value of money

Inflation erodes the value of money. For example, if you were to purchase a buy-to-let property for £200,000 with a £150,000 mortgage, and inflation is running at 10% per annum, after two years the property may have risen in monetary terms by 20% (as well as everything else in the economy). But more importantly, the real value of the £150,000 debt has been eroded. If this continues, it will become negligible over time.

This is what happened in the UK during the post-war years. How many of our parents or grandparents bought properties for a few thousand pounds and now sit on an asset measured in £100,000s? That's inflation!

Interest rates, the mortgage industry and lessons from history

The buy-to-let mortgage was born in July 1996, following an initiative by the Association of Residential Letting Agents. During this period, there was a rapid rise in UK property prices until the Credit Crunch and recession. Since then, as the fallout from huge failures in the banking sector took hold, the number of buy-to-let mortgage products and providers reduced significantly. Low interest rates and flexible mortgages with high loan-to-values (LTVs) have a positive upward pressure on property prices.

The converse is also true. As the 'mortgage drought' became widespread from 2008 onwards, property prices responded by falling. The negative effect on prices was a result of:

- Reluctance to lend
- No money to lend
- Panic hoarding of cash to support bank balance sheets
- Very strict lending criteria
- High deposit requirements
- High arrangement fees
- Relatively high interest rates in relation to the London Interbank Offered Rate (LIBOR) and Bank of England base rate
- Low property valuations for mortgage purposes – i.e. erring on the side of caution.

If the property market were a human body, the blood supplying the oxygen for life would be the mortgage market. Without cheap, available and reliable finance, the whole system collapses. This is essentially what happened: many mortgage brokers and estate agents went into administration, were taken over or left the industry for good.

However, in recent years, the number of products and banks in the market have expanded, and property prices continued their relentless rise because:

Banks make profits by lending, not hoarding cash.

It was almost inevitable that after the worst shock to the global economic system since the Wall Street Crash of 1929, it wouldn't be business as usual as far as the banks were concerned. In the UK, high-street names such as Lloyds TSB, Royal Bank of Scotland, NatWest, Bradford & Bingley, Northern Rock, Halifax and Bank of Scotland among others now had the British government as a major shareholder or outright owner. Who would have guessed that a year or so earlier?

As the Credit Crunch phase of the crisis moved into global recession, banks saw the business priority as one of repairing balance sheets, not lending: although publicly open for business, in reality many had no appetite for it. Even so-called 'gold-plated' applications for finance had holes picked in the information provided by clients, as banks went through the motions.

However, banks are under constant pressure from shareholders to increase earnings per share and profits. In the case of state-owned banks in the UK, they also need strong profits to pay back those government loans. For the other banks that didn't seek or require UK state funding, their shareholders look to the board to increase value.

Banks make profits by lending money at a margin. This means that if it costs 2% to borrow money in the market, the bank adds a margin of 2% to cover its operating costs and profit, leaving the borrower paying a rate of 4%.

Here lies one of the problems that led to the Credit Crunch. Some banks were lending at a loss – isn't it incredible that a bank couldn't do the sums?

Of course, it wasn't as simple as that. One of the issues at the time was the banks' aggressive growth aspirations which were a truly global phenomenon. Market share became the philosophy of many, while risk-adjusted lending and margins were lost in the euphoria of stealing another 5% of a national mortgage market. For example, one well-known bank in the UK lost 0.5% on many mortgages it approved as the quest for market share led to loss-leading rates. Others continued to lend at sensible margins, and continue to do so today, with no government bailout.

Post-2007, banks across the globe have been readjusting to the new world order. Lower LTVs and higher fees are required for many mortgage products, and the scope and diversity of options for buyers has been reduced. Some banks have withdrawn popular products, while others have left the marketplace completely.

Following the economic crisis lending did increase again, albeit at a slow pace. But in the medium term competition will return, as banks are the quintessential business – and all businesses strive to make profits. In this scenario, buy-to-let investors should take advantage of the altered landscape in lending: there is money out there, and a specialist mortgage broker will help you find it.

This part of the chapter looks at the relationship between supply and demand for property, which ultimately determines its price in normal market conditions. The key component of demand is the availability and cost of mortgage finance. There is a strong argument supported by economic history that when finance is more widely available, demand increases – as do property prices.

The opposite is also true, which would suggest that in this picture, property looks an even more attractive investment as prices are subdued, competition for properties is limited and, as a result, vendors are more open to negotiating on price.

Many agents and property investors have only known the market to move in one way – and that's up.

To have been involved as an agent or investor in the UK 1989–1990 house price crash, you are probably no younger than fifty-something (similarly, the post-Credit Crunch recession, no younger than 35–37).

This is new territory for many in the industry, but what this illustration shows is that these opportunities don't present themselves often – and that when they do, the astute investor grasps them. (I emphasise 'opportunity' because, even in a property price correction, some properties are still overpriced and are certainly not bargains.)

As Warren Buffett says: 'Look at market fluctuations as your friend rather than your enemy; profit from folly rather than participate in it.'

Inflation and cash buyers

Mortgage buyers have the benefit of seeing their debt eroded due to inflation, while in some cases they may be able to increase rents. People with cash in the bank only see their savings eroding in real terms.

For example, while inflation is 11%, £200,000 in a bank account earning 4% interest (before tax) is a large loss in terms of purchasing power. Many people with this level of savings (and with more or less) are hedging inflation by buying property, and at auction.

Here's a real-life example that we purchased for a client.

Case Study
Distressed Assets: Liverpool L20 – August 2024

One of my mentees purchased post-auction a two-bedroom, end-of-terrace house: price before costs, £60,000 (costs are stamp duty, legal fees and auction fees, approx. 6%).

The property was in excellent condition, EPC C, tenanted with a rent per calendar month (pcm) of £900 or £10,800. The gross yield was 18%.

All things being equal and given that, historically, inflation has been a driver of property prices, this isn't a bad hedge.

Lesson

We didn't get the property we wanted, but this property was on our potential 'unsold list', which we would target for a post-auction offer. It's always useful to have options, and this was an alternative I never imagined would come to fruition as I thought it would be snapped up, given its location, condition and rental income.

There was a story behind the property: someone unfamiliar with planning regulations in the local area bought and converted it to an Airbnb-style let without permission. They applied retrospectively for planning, which was declined. I guess psychologically it was a huge blow, and as a consequence the property was sold quickly at auction.

Our post-auction offer was below the reserve and guide prices – undoubtedly another outstanding deal.

Important note: risk at auction

The property had been tenanted for some years. I spoke with the tenants at length and quickly learned that they were excellent tenants, very credible. I say this because in the Special Conditions of Sale relating to this property, Para 27.1 states:

> 'Should the property be tenanted, the Buyer will reimburse the Seller any Arrears of Rent owed by the said tenant due at the date of completion.'

This is a judgement call, and why I do the viewings and analysis with my mentees. I looked the tenant in the eye and asked the question, 'Is the rent up to date?' To date, I've not got it wrong. Their rent was up to date.

Additionally, most landlords wouldn't allow a tenant to be in arrears for long. Most will take action after the tenant has missed two payments (shortly to be three) and issue a Section 8 notice on Ground 8, 'at least two [three] months of arrears, where rent is payable monthly'.[7]

In my view, the risk of unpaid rent in this case was very low.

You will find gross yields on total costs in the 10% to 14% range in some cities in the UK, such as Liverpool, Bradford, Sunderland and other mainly Midlands and northern towns and cities. These are not the yields you'll find when purchasing 'on-market' properties, but those (genuinely) 'off-market' and at auction.

Also in October 2022, we bought at auction a property for a client which has a gross yield of 23%. We made an offer prior to auction and eventually settled on a price. (I will return to this example later in Chapter 11.)

---

7 'A Section 8 [of the Housing Act 1988] notice is available where you have granted an assured or assured shorthold tenancy and one or more of the grounds for possession apply. In practice, most landlords only use this notice where the tenant is in at least two months' of rent arrears and the fixed term of the tenancy has still got some time to run.' National Residential Landlords Association (NRLA) (2024) 'Section 8 notice: Grounds-based possession'. Available at: www.nrla.org.uk/resources/ending-your-tenancy/what-is-grounds-based-possession-section-8, accessed 5 January 2026. As a consequence of the Renters' Rights Act 2025, the ground for eviction of two months in arrears will be extended to three.

Repossessions

When buying in a falling or stagnant market, the key is to obtain value – if you aren't going to get growth in the immediate future, a margin needs to be built in at the front end.

You need a motivated seller, but it doesn't have to be a private individual: it could be a bank, company or developer. Depending on the particular market in which you are dealing, it may be worth targeting repossessed stock. The lender who has repossessed property after a loan default might not necessarily be holding out for a high price, just happy to recoup their outstanding loan.

Repossessions are usually easy to spot. Auction houses often refer to the seller as the 'mortgagee in possession'; while estate agents might be willing to give you the background to the sale, or it may be mentioned in the particulars. Even if this isn't the case, a frequent giveaway is white-and-red tape over the toilets and sinks in the property, as this shows that water has been drained from the system.

It's worth noting that in itself, a repossessed property is no guarantee of value. There could be any number of reasons why this might have happened, so it pays to do correct due diligence.

Banks have a duty to achieve the best possible price for these properties: legally, they must act in a transparent way to dispose of them. This can even include advertising that offers have been received at a certain level and requesting further bids, setting a deadline.

That said, in my experience, lenders and agents aren't always transparent and correct procedure isn't always followed. Some agents make banks think that a low offer is the best that can be expected so they can sell the property quickly and easily – sometimes off-market to a friend or colleague. (It happens, and it would be naive to think that it doesn't.)

The process that a bank follows tends to be this:

1. The property is marketed through a local or national agent (many banks use particular agents, so it's worth trying to find out which ones use which agents).
2. It will be marketed at a level near to, or at, the Royal Institution of Chartered Surveyors (RICS) valuation level.
3. The property is then gradually reduced in price until it sells.
4. If it doesn't sell, it probably will be sent to auction after a few months or so – or in some cases, straight to auction.

At the depth of the 2008–2009 crisis, no one wanted to buy these properties. But gradually investors cottoned on, and sale prices increased back up towards the mainstream market. However, if repossessions rise again and when the market is slow, supply will doubtless increase, presenting a further opportunity.

Lesson

The best route to buying repossessed property is through auction. Although at Distressed Assets we have been successful with buying through estate agents, it is a laborious process, also open to last-minute gazumping and corruption. We rarely buy or source properties through estate agents.

You might have the best bid, be a cash buyer and have a proven track record but not get the property. Sadly, that's what happens in some cases, but clearly not all. Corruption is as alive and kicking in the property world, as it always has been, but now it's done differently. I acknowledge that the vast majority of estate agents are completely honest and do a great job – but like any industry involving money, there are bad apples.

A property auction today is the closest platform you'll get to a free and open market: it can be manipulated with pre-auction offers, but this is rare. I have only encountered one dodgy deal, and we took legal action to unravel it and secured the property.

In general, auctions are a fantastic place to buy below-market value properties such as bank repossessed property and other 'problem properties'.

Auctions: the wholesale market

Auctions are a good way to find excellent-value properties, as the market is likely to be smaller. The reason that a property has come to the auction in the first place –because it needs to sell quickly, or has some issues with it – could play into your hands when looking for value.

This book reveals the mystery of the auction process and shows how anyone is capable of finding that bargain property. It's only risky if you don't know what you're doing.

Buying through receivers or administrators

When a bank repossesses a portfolio of properties from an investor or company, or takes possession of a development used as security for a loan, it usually appoints an administrator to ensure that:

- Rent is collected
- New tenants are found, if appropriate
- Any repairs are made
- Administrators never offer any legal guarantees on purchase, and documentation may be missing.

Receivers can be more straightforward to deal with: they're paid on sale of the property, so are more motivated to do the deal. Again, you might not have much information at your disposal and may need to take a view on whether there is sufficient information to proceed.

Both administrators and receivers have a strict legal framework within which they must act, so they aren't going to let a property go for bargain-basement prices. That would leave them exposed to recourse from the bank or individual who lost the property.

However, we have secured some excellent investments from these sources in the past (Chapter 13 looks at this in more detail).

Case Study
Distressed Assets: Sefton Park, Liverpool L8 – 2012

A developer went into receivership and the receiver, based in Manchester, was looking for a quick cash sale. The property was freehold in the Sefton Park area, had a large plot of land and three, two-bedroom, large, modern apartments recently renovated to a high standard.

We put a case together, provided proof of funds and proceeded to purchase the entire lot for £180,000, after initial lower offers were rejected. It remains in our portfolio, and we have tenants who have called it home for many years.

A combination of a post-Credit Crunch market and a development in receivership meant for a strong story in enabling this remarkable purchase. If this property were sold today, it would sell as an unbroken, freehold block with land for considerably more.

Property market cycles

There are bargains to be had in all market conditions, but the most lucrative is during a period of contraction or recession. These periods in the property market cycle don't come around often, with the last being after the Credit Crunch of 2008; but when they do, it's worth looking for opportunities.

I remember back in the post-Credit Crunch market, standing in a well-known London auction house with literally just a few others. That was the level of despondency prevalent at the time. Were there opportunities? Yes, many – some of which I discuss in this book.

Key points

- Property prices are determined by supply and demand.
- Many factors influence demand: the economy, availability and cost of mortgage finance, demographics and sentiment.
- Property prices move in cycles. Falling property prices should be seen as an opportunity.
- Inflation is an important economic indicator: its level impacts the level of interest rates, which in turn impact the property market.
- Inflation erodes the purchasing power of money, but also debt.
- When sterling is weak, UK property becomes more attractive for overseas investors.
- In the short run, the supply of property is fixed – both for sale and rent.
- Property supply in the rental market is fixed: as economists say, 'inelastic'. This supports strong rental returns for investors.
- As property prices fall, the returns from property rise in terms of rent. The astute investor targets high rental properties as prices fall.
- Rising interest rates should be viewed as an opportunity, not a threat.
- Repossessed property at auction presents an opportunity. Empty property has to be sold, and it needs a buyer.
- There are bargains in all market conditions at auction.
- The property market reflects the economy. Keep one eye on the economy and you'll understand where the property market is heading in the next year or two. Then, make a plan and be ready to take those opportunities.

Chapter 2
Euphoria, Panic and Distressed Assets: Market Psychology

'Bull markets are born of pessimism, grow on scepticism, mature on optimism and die on euphoria.'

Sir John Templeton, British investor[8]

In a book that discusses property markets and in particular auctions, it would be remiss not to look at participants' behaviour: the buyers and sellers of property, banks, estate agents et al.

The famous economist John Maynard Keynes wrote in 1936, in his seminal book, *The General Theory of Employment, Interest and Money*:

> Even apart from the instability due to speculation, there is the instability due to the characteristic of human nature that a large proportion of our positive activities depend on spontaneous optimism rather than mathematical expectations, whether moral or hedonistic or economic. Most, probably, of our decisions to do something positive, the full consequences of which will be drawn out over many days to come, can only be taken as the result of animal spirits – a spontaneous urge to action rather than inaction, and not as the outcome of a weighted average of quantitative benefits multiplied by quantitative probabilities.[9]

8 *The Economist* (2023) 'Investors are seized by optimism. Can the bull market last?' Available at https://www.economist.com/finance-and-economics/2023/07/25/investors-are-seized-by-optimism-can-the-bull-market-last, accessed 5 January 2026.

9 John Maynard Keynes (1936) *The General Theory of Employment, Interest and Money*, Palgrave Macmillan.

In other words, we make decisions based on 'animal spirits' or emotion, not after reasoned, analytical decision-making. The purpose of this book is to eliminate the urge to 'animal spirits'; instead, to make cold, hard, rational decisions based on thorough research and due diligence.

Figure 5 below illustrates this point succinctly. Throughout a market cycle, whether in stocks, commodities or property, investors and markets experience a variety of emotions.

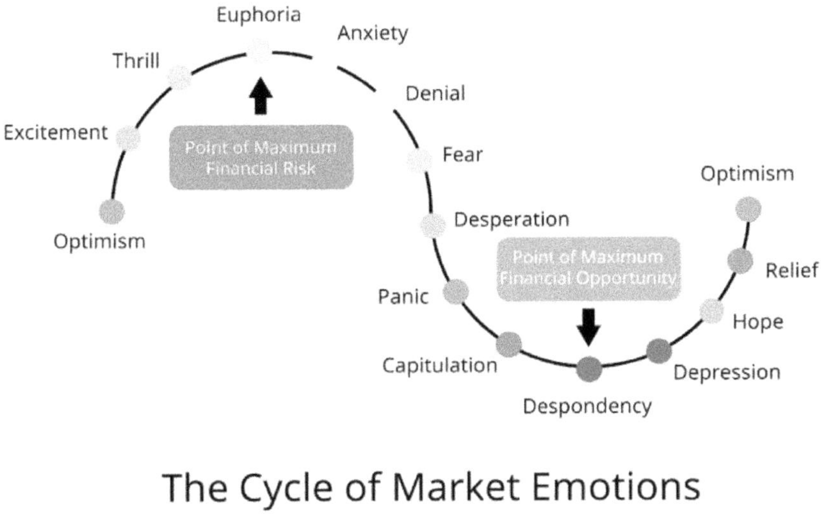

Figure 5: The cycle of market emotions

Source: Shutterstock (reproduced under licence)

A lesson from recent history

NASDAQ

One of the best examples of this behavioural phenomenon was the dot-com bubble of 1995 to 2000, which finally peaked on 10 March 2000. During the previous 12 months, the NASDAQ index of technology stocks more than doubled its value – and over the next 12 months was to lose it all again! The bubble had burst.

A bubble occurs when speculators see a rapid increase in prices and decide to buy in anticipation of further rises, rather than because the shares or properties are undervalued. This speculative nature of an asset bubble is characterised by the human emotions of excitement, thrill and euphoria – a feeling that you're the smartest thing in town and impregnable. The world is your oyster, and you're going to take it by storm.

It would be fair to say that, prior to the credit crisis, this was the position of many property investors – not just in the UK, but around the world. Property prices had been rising strongly due to strong economic growth, low interest rates, readily available finance and an insatiable appetite for property.

The property bubble

Whether you were investing in Liverpool, London or Leicester, it was a one-way street. Speculation and the anticipation of rising prices led to a boom in buy-to-let and jet-to-let (overseas property). At home and abroad, investors were attracted to the market for fear of missing out – and greedy in the hope of making a quick buck.

Euphoria is driven and reinforced by the media. Headlines of 20% annual house price inflation, stories of how people made a fortune in buy-to-let, parties and social gatherings where dot-com mania has now been replaced by property, property, property. The banks, not immune to a bit of hysteria themselves, relaxed lending criteria and increased the amount they would lend on a particular property: in some cases to 120% of its value, while others lent at a loss.

Estate agents joined the throng and competed against each other for market share, which translated into new instructions and sales. Competition between estate agents led to higher selling prices, as the confident seller wanted the maximum price. Similarly, property developers, understanding the market, raised their prices at the stroke of a pen – and all participants in the market were buoyant. Solicitors took on more staff to cope with conveyancing. Property companies sprung up from spare bedrooms, offering 'no money down deals'.

The education business took off too, with companies charging hopeful investors thousands of pounds for a weekend where they would learn 'the secret of how to become a millionaire'. Punters wanted to be the model in the glossy brochures, sunning themselves on their yacht. The fact that many had to use credit cards to purchase those secrets was of no concern, as the investment would pay itself back many times over. The fact that there are no secrets, and that anyone can do it from scratch, was irrelevant. This is the point of maximum financial risk.

This quote from the great Sir John Templeton describes that moment: 'The four most expensive words in the English language are, "This time it's different".'

Then collateralised debt obligations[10] brought the party to an abrupt end. Bang!

The Credit Crunch

It's easy, in the cold light of day, to retrofit events and say 'I told you so'. The reality is that very few people saw the Credit Crunch coming – not least the banks, who were buying and selling collateralised debt obligations as if they were AAA-rated investment grade. Moreover, although US interest rates rose from 1% to 5.35% between 2004 and 2006, the level of bad loans at the sub-prime level was an unknown.

As the economic news became worse, anxiety, denial and fear replaced euphoria at the private investor level, also in the City and in government.

The party was over, the bottles were empty and it was time for the hangover cure.

10 'A collateralized debt obligation (CDO) is a complex structured finance product that is backed by a pool of loans and other assets and sold to institutional investors. A CDO is a particular type of derivative because, as its name implies, its value is derived from another underlying asset. These assets become the collateral if the loan defaults.' C. Tardi (2025) 'Collateralized Debt Obligation (CDO): What it is, how it works'. Investopedia, 16 November. Available at: https://www.investopedia.com/terms/c/cdo.asp#:~:text=A%20collateralized%20debt%20obligation%20is,risk%20and%20freeing%20up%20capital, accessed 5 January 2026.

As stated earlier, it was the perfect time for investors to psychologically remove themselves from events, ignore 'animal spirits' and take a view on the opportunities that would present during unprecedented times. (Without doubt, this was my generation's Wall Street Crash which so paralysed economies from 1929 throughout most of the 1930s.)

The herd instinct

Markets move as herds. Individual emotion, behaviour and feelings are subsumed into the market. Going against the grain – which some do – is difficult, because if you get it wrong, you're the fool. And in the City, you're likely to lose your job.

Going back to the dot-com bubble, you had to have nerves of steel not to go with the tide of opinion, which, as it turns out, was highly speculative. Warren Buffett did just that, and stuck with his stakes in relatively unexciting stocks such as Coca-Cola and Gillette. He called it right: also during the height of the despondency, he was taking stakes in the likes of Goldman Sachs. Buffett's success emanates from his ability to isolate his thinking from the market – in other words, he controls his emotions.

This point of despondency creates a financial opportunity. For me, it was in the area of financially distressed assets and, in particular, property.

At the point of capitulation or despondency, investors sell assets – whether shares or properties. I know several people who held shares and watched them go down week by week, month by month, and finally sold at the bottom before the shares rallied. When stock markets crash, many amateur investors capitulate and sell, regretting every upward movement of the subsequent rally.

Distressed assets

The events of 2007–2008 created an opportunity for buying properties and other distressed assets at substantial discounts to market value (a topic we will return to later in Chapters 9–11 and 13). However, not everyone appreciated the timing. To be fair, they were so shell-shocked by events that the last thing on their mind was investing, or placing their funds anywhere other than under their mattresses.

Depression can lead to hope, and hope to relief. For many people, the events of the latter half of 2008 suggested the world was going to end as they knew it – forever. High-street banks were being rescued, there were emergency cuts in UK interest rates and politicians talking about recession for the first time, followed by an economic depression. Banks stopped lending, and businesses went bust.

However, Armageddon didn't descend and the world emerged, albeit slowly, from the brink – and with it, the emotions of the market changed to one of hope and relief. And so the cycle begins again!

Lesson

Many of us took a big hit in 2008–2009: in my case, from overseas property developing – where in a space of weeks you had no market, but all of the financial commitments. This was a salutary lesson for me personally, and for many others.

But in those bleak days, the opportunity for Distressed Assets was obvious, and we set about searching for and analysing opportunities across the UK.

We identified distressed property opportunities in London. As with most recessions, property developers face a shrinking market and cash flow issues. In some cases, we purchased properties for ourselves and clients at auction, also through receivers and through administrators.

Here is one example of many we did during that period.

Case Study
Distressed Assets: Noko Development, 3–6 Banister Road, Kensal Rise, London W10 4AR – 2009

After the Credit Crunch in 2009, the developer that built the scheme had gone into administration and several apartments were being disposed of by the bank via the administrators.

The process was laborious and took several months, but it was a worthwhile exercise, as the apartments were purchased for an excellent price of around £265,000, including parking (around 20% below true value). They were already tenanted at a good yield of around 6.5% in the fashionable area of Kensal Rise.

Because the market was weak at the time, the bank sold at a good level and the investor that purchased this made at least £65,000 in 12 months in a weak market.

Currently, these properties sell for around £450,000–£500,000.

Market psychology

Market psychology, reinforced by the media, presents many opportunities, as the example above and many others in this book prove. This quote from Warren Buffett is so true that you should have a poster made of it and place it in your office: 'Be fearful when others are greedy, and greedy when others are fearful.'

Fear and greed drive markets, and property is no different. Here is where you can have an edge, investing or buying opportunities through auctions.

Risk and auctions

I've lost count of the many times that I've told people what I essentially do. Although many focus on my military career, others on the lettings and property management we do, and others still on my sports and hobbies, when I say I buy property at auction and have done so for many years, you can see the fear flitting across their faces, as if I was a person from outer space pointing a ray gun at them, demanding to be taken to their leaders. Even highly experienced business people, not unknown for understanding risk, crunch their faces when they hear the word 'auction'!

This is why it's a great opportunity. The potential market is much smaller than the traditional estate agent route, and the bargains are much greater: the retail versus wholesale argument, as we've seen previously.

On a risk/reward basis, it's auctions all the way – which is why we now focus on auctions for all acquisitions, save for occasional off-market opportunities. There is no better, more transparent route than to buy at auction, having followed the due diligence tools you'll discover in this book.

The off-market illusion

Often, deals come my way that are off-market, genuine opportunities. They only come to me, not by email or to a WhatsApp group, because by definition those properties are not off-market – they're just being sold to a different market.

'Off-market' is being increasingly used by some estate agents as another marketing tool, giving the impression that the property deal is somehow exclusive to you – it's not. These deals exist for various reasons, but undertake your due diligence and ensure that they're good for you, not just for the sourcing agent. Remember my definition of off-market.

In February 2024, a client sent me an off-market opportunity they had been emailed by an out-of-town sourcing agent. I know the road well: we had recently acquired an excellent property there pre-auction for £60,000 and in good condition.

The 'bargain property' that the client sent to me was on the market at £75,000, and required a lot of work – that's a classic off-market illusion. It's not an investment property, just a sourcing fee!

As an astute investor you'll seek out distressed assets, and there are many definitions of what constitutes these. I will offer a simple one here:

'A problem property which must be sold quickly.'

This book points you in the right direction to find these properties, and gives you a few tools to analyse them. There are extremely decent short and long-term profits to be had if you get it right, while you could lose your shirt if you get it wrong. Research and a good team of advisors pay off handsomely.

Distressed Assets off-market strategies

This is a book about property auctions, but for completeness it's worth highlighting other strategies we use to secure outstanding distressed property deals before they get to auction. This could be the subject of a book in its own right, although currently we only cover these strategies and others in detail in our property investor workshops (for further information, see the end of the book).

Remember, we're looking for properties that have issues we can solve – that's where the value is found, not in the 'perfect property'.

Debt-for-asset swaps

Many people took a financial hit resulting from the double whammy of Covid-19 lockdowns and rising interest rates. Indeed, some who reside overseas didn't have the furlough arrangements that many in the UK enjoyed, and their income reduced significantly as costs rose substantially. Many went into debt, and this continues today.

A debt-for-asset swap is where you come to an arrangement with a property owner that you will pay their debts as well as a sum of money for any investment properties they may have. It's a win-win situation, as many debtors require cash quickly – bailiffs are knocking on their door. They neither have the time, nor in many cases the inclination, to wait. Even with an unconditional auction sale, the cash doesn't arrive instantly; but after 28 days – and even longer, given the pre-auction marketing process – there is also no guarantee the property will sell.

We use this strategy and simply transfer the cash, exchanging it for a TR1 (a legal document transferring ownership of a property with the Land Registry). The transaction only takes a few minutes. In this instance, another legal contract is needed to deal with the debt and any future liabilities arising, such as council tax or other claims.

It's worth emphasising that this strategy isn't for the novice property investor: only undertake it with professional legal advice. Furthermore, you'll still need to do your normal due diligence as per a standard property transaction.

Case Study
Distressed Assets: Liverpool L13 – June 2023

We purchased a ground-floor apartment originally sold for £60,000 in 2018: there were ground rent, service charges and other debts on the apartment. We paid the debts and for a consideration of £4,900, bought the property. Its market rent is almost £7,000 per annum. The gross yield is 47%, taking into account the debt plus consideration.

The numbers are spectacular, but there were issues with the property that required considerable effort. It was put up for auction in 2022 but withdrawn likely for lack of interest, given the issues. The existing tenant was also a major factor.

Lesson

Seek properties with problems you can resolve, as the uplift in capital value can be stunning. If it were easy, the owners would do it themselves – but they might have limited time, no patience for it, have decided to cut their losses, or the sitting tenant isn't paying the rent and is troublesome.

In all of these situations, if the deal is acceptable to both buyer and seller, go for it.

Case Study
Distressed Assets: Liverpool CH44 – September 2023

A ground floor two-bedroom apartment with garden originally sold for £62,000 in 2016. There were ground rent and service charge debts on the property, and it required about £5,000 worth of works to get it into lettable condition. At a total debt-for-asset swap of £17,500 plus £5,000 works, the yield is 32%.

In this case, the owner just wanted out and was selling their entire portfolio. They were open to a cash offer before placing the property in auction.

Property call options

This is a strategy I've developed: those familiar with financial markets will recognise the term. This is my definition:

A property call option is a right to buy – but not an obligation to do so – for a fixed price at some date in the future.

Distressed Assets has a property call option contract which both parties to the transaction sign, and a consideration is paid. At the end of the option, the property is either purchased or not.

The advantage for the seller is a guaranteed sale at the end of the call option contract. The advantage for the investor is a cracking deal – but only if they've valued the property correctly, and undertaken legal and property due diligence before entering the contract.

Case Study
Distressed Assets: Liverpool L20 – January 2024

Two one-bedroom apartments had been on the open market for a long time. Sales had fallen through for a variety of reasons but crucially, none were due to any issues with the properties. The leaseholder was keen on a quick sale, but not yet willing to go to an unconditional auction: they favoured conditional auction instead, which wasn't working.

We offered to buy the properties for a fixed price using a property call option contract, as they were in excellent condition, having been recently refurbished. The agreement was that we were committed to buy, and contractually neither party could walk away at the expiration date (Figure 6).

The collective purchase price a few years ago was £110,000. We took a six-month call option at £45,000, having assessed the value at £135,000 by the income capitalisation model of valuation (discussed in Chapter 4).

I'm not suggesting that we could sell these properties overnight for that price – it's simply what we would have to pay for a stream of income at, say, 10% gross return. The value at a 10% net return is £108,000. In either case, that's a significant uplift from £45,000.

COMPLETION STATEMENT

Property : **Bootle, Merseyside, L20 4LA**

Completion date : **26 January 2024**

Sale Price			**£22,500**
Less			
Deposit	£2,250.00		
		Balance due from buyer :-	£20,250
Add			
Buyer's legal fees			£1,194.00
SDLT			£0.00
Bankruptcy Search x 3			£9
Bank transfer fee			£45.00
Land registry fee			£20.00
Recorded delivery			£10.00
Less deposit paid on account		£300.00	
	Total due from client:-		**£978.00**
Amount due from client:			**£21,228.00**

Figure 6: Completion statement

Lesson

It's worth having a look at Chapter 6, as the key to successful investment in distressed assets is the Intelligence Cycle. You need to have lots of tentacles out, picking up information from every possible source – electronic, human and professional contacts.

If you don't have the time or inclination, outsource it to a reputable sourcing agent like Distressed Assets.

Types of properties

The types of properties you should seek might be:

- Bank repossessions
- An inheritance
- A probate sale
- A non-mortgageable property
- Leasehold flats – no management company
- A title defect or other legal issue
- A possible structural problem
- Bad tenants
- Criminality – e.g. a former brothel or cannabis farm
- Where the seller needs money quickly
- The property company enters receivership

– and the best place to buy them is at auction. (More on the mechanism of this in Chapter 11.)

Case Study
Distressed Assets: Liverpool L9 – January 2025

There are many reasons why sellers want a quick sale, and aren't willing or even able to sell through traditional channels. In general, cash flow reasons are often cited, but some people don't want the hassle of protracted, private treaty through an estate agent with no guarantee of a sale.

This was one such deal, in a good rental area of Liverpool. It was an unbroken, freehold block of two apartments tenanted at £1,150 pcm, or £13,800 per annum. The tenants had no arrears, and the block was in a good condition. We acquired it for a client at £80,000, with a gross yield of 17%. In my view, the rent could be easily raised to £14,280 per annum or even £15,000, pushing the yield to 18% or 18.8%.

We had a similar situation only a couple of months earlier in November 2024, acquiring a four-bedroom House in Multiple Occupation (HMO) where the rooms let for £450 pcm, or £21,600 per annum. The purchase price was £60,000, making a gross yield of 36%.

Both of these acquisitions were for the same client, and indeed they attended our very first Distressed Assets Property Investment and Sourcing Workshop in November 2023 (for details, see the end of this book). In the space of a few months, they have a gross income of £34,000 on an outlay of £140,000, which is 24%. Both properties could be traded or flipped for a good profit, but the client wishes to build a portfolio of below market-value properties producing an income. Given the in-built equity, they have options to leverage the properties and continue the journey.

Key points

- Bubbles in all markets are the result of 'animal spirits'.
- History tells us that the best time to buy is when sentiment is negative or weak.
- Target distressed assets for the best value, and at auction.
- Auctions are only risky if you don't know what you are doing and haven't done thorough due diligence.
- Be a leader, not a follower. Ignore the noise of the media and make your own decisions.
- Investors should look for opportunities at the point of maximum financial opportunity.
- By following a well-worn procedure and doing thorough due diligence, you can buy properties in any market conditions and be successful.

Chapter 3
Creating a Property Auction Investment Strategy

Strategy without tactics is the slowest route to victory.
Tactics without strategy is the noise before defeat.
Sun Tzu, *The Art of War*

I have been involved in strategy most of my life. As a youngster I played international-level sport, representing my country in the European Championships in Spain. But it didn't just happen. I had a plan and worked my way up from city to county and region, then national.

I'm a huge fan of defining a strategy right at the start of an endeavour, then developing the tactics – not the other way round. As a point, this was as valid 2,500 years ago in the time of Sun Tzu, as it is today. Buying property at auction, property investment and business are no different:

As Henry Mintzberg said: 'Strategy is not the consequence of planning, but the opposite: its starting point.'[11]

Where do you start?

Whatever you're planning in terms of investment, defining a strategy to achieve it has to be the first task. For the time being, you need to forget about anything but necessary detail and concentrate on the bigger picture. How many times have you heard the expression, 'Big hand, big picture'?

11 H. Mintzberg (2013) *Rise and Fall of Strategic Planning*, Free Press.

The starting point is setting yourself specific investment objectives: after all, if you don't have goals, how are you going to achieve them?

However, a strategy isn't something that must be set in stone, and you should be willing to adapt and change it if necessary, because sometimes the market or other circumstances force change on you. You may have experienced success with off-plan investing in a rising market, but this strategy is unlikely to work in a falling market and recession – so flexibility is key. Strategy is a plan to achieve your long-term goals.

Investing in buy-to-let property over the long term can be a profitable exercise for those who buy and manage their properties carefully. Property values tend to rise in line with economic growth, so unless the economy remains flat or in decline forever, it's a fair bet that a property you buy today will be worth (in real terms, and adjusted for inflation) more than you paid for it 20 years earlier.

This chapter will help you formulate a buy-to-let strategy in line with your investor profile and defined goals.

Your investor profile

To a large extent, your buy-to-let auction strategy will reflect your investor profile:

- Attitude to risk
- Age
- Dependents
- Wealth
- Security
- Personal characteristics
- Experience.

Your goals, ambition and desires will be largely influenced by your investor profile. We are all different, with different circumstances and needs, so no single strategy is suitable for all types of investor. Some of us will be one of the following.

The Entrepreneur Investor

The Entrepreneur Investor is focused, hasn't much time, wants the information presented succinctly and makes a quick decision based on numbers. They don't tend to be interested in too much detail – only the potential profit, risk and any spin-off opportunities which may arise.

The Analyst Investor

The Analyst wants detailed information and scrutinises every last detail, producing their own spreadsheets and charts. They are likely to deal in facts, not hyperbole. For them, the numbers determine whether an investment is a starter or not – once they've completed their analysis, they make a decision.

The Laid-back Investor

With a relaxed attitude to property investment, the Laid-back Investor is often hard-working and highly career and family-oriented. They tend to believe that once a property investment is made, it will look after itself – and that a good job is the best way to make money, with property providing a supplemental fund.

The Impulsive Investor

The Impulsive Investor follows the latest hotspots and may have properties scattered around the country or globe. They would consider looking at beach villas in Iceland, if that were the latest trend. This type of investor can be classified as a crowd follower and lacks any detailed strategy or idea of their intended goals.

The Information Junkie Investor

The Information Junkie cannot get enough intel. They spend most of the day on property websites and forums, listen to others who have been successful and turn up at all the property industry events. They will probably want to see every possible detail before making a decision, which means they often miss opportunities. They're confident in their own ability that they will invest successfully, after covering all the bases.

There are more types, and indeed you might be a mix of the above. The key is to sit down and really think through how your own personality, temperament and tolerance to risk fit in with a property investment strategy, and where relevant, bring on board a partner or family.

For example, the Laid-back Investor might want a hands-off investment that looks after itself while they're concentrating on other things. In this case, self-managed houses in multiple occupation (HMOs) and student properties would not be a good option.

Which type are you? Or to get the accurate answer, which one does your wife, husband, partner, colleague or friend think you are? You may be surprised by the answer.

Psychometric tests

It's not unusual to focus on what we're good at – and sometimes bury our heads in the sand when we have to deal with issues or tasks that challenge us, or we find boring and tedious.

We all have strengths as well as weaknesses: this is why in many cases the team approach works, balancing those strengths and weaknesses across a number of team members, the whole being greater than the sum of its parts.

The military, business and other sectors use psychometric tests to assess the suitability or otherwise of people for various roles and jobs. In property investing, you can use them to help you formulate a strategy that's most suited to your own personality type.

Crucially, what may work for one person might not work for another, so it's important to define yourself before deciding on a property investment strategy.

Questions to ask yourself

- Would I feel comfortable investing in a property that I couldn't visit inside 30 minutes by car?
- Would a large development project and its associated risks keep me up at night?
- Do I want a hands-off approach, or to be in the thick of it?
- Do I really know what I am doing – or should I learn more, or even ask for help?

There are many questions – this is just a sample – but the answers to a large extent depend on your personality type. Do you recognise yourself in any of the investor types in Chapter 3?

If we delete the word 'test' and insert the word 'suitability', we can see how defining yourself in terms of personality traits will assist you – and anyone assisting you, such as a mentor – to devise and shape a property investment strategy that you feel at ease with, and won't keep you awake at night.

Attendees on our property investment and sourcing workshops complete a simple psychometric test, while those on our mentorship programme have a more in-depth version. But in both cases, almost everyone is positive about the result: there aren't many (if any at all) who say: 'That's not me.'

What drives you as a buy-to-let investor?

This is the first question you need to ask yourself. The obvious and expected answer would be money – but what you really need to decide is whether your priority is short-term cash flow or long-term growth.

Are you:

- Looking to supplement your income after covering your property-related outgoings, or is it future equity that interests you more?
- A budding developer looking to make a quick profit?
- Looking to property to provide you with a pension in later life?

You might decide that your strategy is to find a happy medium: where your property provides respectable cash flow, while still offering the potential of good capital growth. Whatever the driver behind your decision to invest in buy-to-let, you need to keep it firmly in mind while researching and making your investment choices, to ensure your decisions are tailored to meet your goals.

Setting goals

The process of goal setting allows you to have greater control over your future. Research has found that people who set goals are more likely to:

- Focus
- Have greater self-confidence and accomplish more
- Be more content
- Suffer less stress and anxiety.[12]

Consider what you want to achieve. This can be expressed as a mission statement and act as a long-term driver for all of your other goals. An example might be:

'To invest in property to supplement my income by £6,000 per month.'

SMART goals

This is a great way to assess what you want to achieve from five different angles. Make your goals:

- Specific
- Measurable
- Action-oriented and achievable
- Realistic and rewarding
- Time-bound.

12 E. Locke (1968) 'Toward a theory of task motivation and incentives'. *Organizational Behavior and Human Performance* 3(2): 157–189.

Specific

You want the goal to be specific and quantifiable: for example:

'To achieve £6,000 per month additional income from buy-to-let property.'

It's also important that you write down your goals.

Measurable

Identify how you will measure each goal. In the example above, the first measurable point is when you actually have £6,000 per month additional income from property. For example, you might decide to stage your goals into £2,000 phases of additional income: Phase 1 – £2,000, Phase 2 – £4,000 and Phase 3 – £6,000.

Action-oriented and achievable

Describe your goals using action verbs. What will you do to achieve your goal? Set goals that are challenging, but not unrealistically high. Once you're there, set your sights higher, if this fits with your revised goals, and continue onwards and upwards.

Realistic and rewarding

Write down the reasons why the successful outcome of your efforts is so important to you, and create a strong mental picture of what that looks like – visualise it.

Ensure your goals are realistic, and imagine how it will feel when you've accomplished them. There will be times when you hit hurdles, find it difficult and want to give up and stick to the day job – well, don't! You've come this far, after all. Reread your reasons for the goal in the first place, recharge your batteries, discuss your goals with a friend or partner to make them even more real, then get back on track.

Time-bound

Set deadlines for each goal. You can be fairly flexible with deadlines and they can be modified as required, but deadlines that set time limits help to keep you on track.

Going back to the example above, you now have:

'To achieve £6,000 in additional income from property investment in six years, so I can work fewer hours, have more leisure time and pursue other interests.'

From this simple statement you can now make your plan with the three phases of £2,000, £4,000 and £6,000 as measurable targets within specific time frames. This set of sub-goals will keep you aligned and give you cause for celebration and assurance when you hit each of them. For example: £2,000 within two years, £4,000 within four years and £6,000 within six years.

When setting your goals, ask yourself:

- What skills do I need to achieve my goal?
- What information do I need?
- Who can assist me?
- What resources do I need?
- What challenges can hinder my success?
- Am I making any assumptions and if so, what are they?
- Is there a better way of doing it?
- Has the situation changed since I formulated my plan?

Decide on your strengths

Renovation or refurbishment projects to flip

If you're good with planning and detail and getting your hands dirty, why not contemplate a project renovating or refurbishing a property for profit? There are many projects like this in property auctions (see Chapter 10).

Buy-to-let and hold

If you are not the hands-on type, or your work or personal situation preclude the above, you might wish to consider a standard 'two-up two-down', freehold terraced house (with two bedrooms upstairs and two reception rooms downstairs), with a rental guarantee insurance product.

If you find it easier making decisions with other people, get a business partner on board to discuss options. Make sure it's someone who has different strengths and complements your skills.

If the thought of investing more than 50 miles from your home gives you sleepless nights because you're naturally more conservative in your approach, don't do it. Concentrate on your own part of the country, where the distance to your buy-to-let property isn't too great and you can physically see it. Alternatively, you might wish to engage company services to source the property for you, renovate it if necessary, then manage the tenancy on your behalf.

Work to your strengths, not your weaknesses. You know yourself better than anyone else, so this shouldn't be difficult. Do what you feel comfortable doing, and it will work for you.

Define your market

Once you've defined yourself, your strengths, weaknesses and goals, you're now ready to look at where to invest.

To define your market, use all the information you've collected about various areas to formulate an investment strategy that you are comfortable with and fulfils your long-term goals. To continue the example above, here's one example of a strategy:

> To invest in buy-to-let property via auction, with a significant discount to market value, to produce a monthly income of £6,000 within six years.

Alternatively:

> To renovate a large house, add value through additional bedrooms and bathrooms or convert it into a HMO or flats, and sell for a profit of at least 20% after costs.

The above examples are very different approaches to property investment and reflect investors' different strengths, as well as the relative stages, in the property market cycle. However, the mission statement allows you to narrow down your market significantly to match your goals. You can then collect information about the options you have, to make a more detailed assessment of where to invest.

Define your point of focus: become an expert

Using the first example above as the starting point:

> 'I will now focus all my energies, research and time into looking for property in an area I have identified, which has potential for my goal of income generation.
>
> I will become an expert in the Liverpool, Manchester, Leeds, Swansea, Glasgow or Belfast property markets and those auctions which serve my target area. If necessary, I will engage company services that specialise in my chosen market.'

I know this might appear a bit too simple, but after considerable research and taking time to decide what you want from your investment property, you should at least have narrowed down your choice. Now you can completely forget about properties with low yields (as income is the mission) and in areas you've discounted.

It's by focusing all of your time and energies in mastering a particular subject that you get the best perspective on it. Know your market inside out and be the specialist, because it's by specialising that you gain an edge over everyone else looking to do the same thing as you.

As Tony Robbins says: 'Where focus goes, energy flows.'

Identify, prioritise and implement strategy: take action!

For some people, this is the most difficult phase because they have to do something: it requires action. They conduct the research, analyse themselves, set realistic goals, formulate a strategy, get focused – and then go no further.

What a waste of time and effort.

I'm not underestimating how difficult it is for a novice investor to take the first step, but when you embark on a journey and the end is in sight, you have to give it a determined push. Having taken action, the strategy is implemented and you're now on your way. You can sit back, relax and wait for the income to hit the bank account. Just don't rest on your laurels!

Monitor performance and review strategy

Whatever you invest in, it's important to continually monitor your performance, especially the opportunity cost of your strategy. As Winston Churchill put it: 'However beautiful the strategy, you should occasionally look at the results.'

This is particularly important as market conditions change:

- If interest rates rise, what happens to my income?
- Should I fix my interest rate to secure a minimum income per month?
- Is my rent too low, as rental prices rise or vice versa?
- Is it a good time to sell, as property prices are at an all-time high?
- Could I achieve a better yield in an alternative investment or property?

This review is important, because by continually reviewing the performance of your portfolio against your goals, you can make the necessary adjustments to remain on target.

Strategy is where it all starts

Once you've defined your strategy, everything else will flow from there. By following the system outlined in this chapter, you'll gain a level of confidence and faith in your ability to formulate a plan.

Once your plan is in place, you can confidently seize the opportunities that property investment has to offer in all market conditions.

This chapter is more important than many in this book, although at first glance you might not think so.

Over the years, I've seen property investors running round like headless chickens, falling for the latest craze: some who bought hotel rooms, parking spaces, properties separated by about 300 miles and other projects. Their strategy was a shotgun approach to target shooting, where in reality you have to be a sniper taking a 1,000m shot.

At auction, you have to know exactly what you are looking for, within well-defined parameters.

Example

- Within an 8-mile radius of Manchester M14 postcode
- Freehold house
- Ceiling price less than £190,000
- No major works (or requires renovation)
- Let or vacant possession.

It doesn't have to be more complicated than that. In just five bullet points you have the basis of a strategy: as you've ruled out other cities and towns, apartments, leasehold and set a starting price.

As Michael Porter, American economist and founder of strategic management says: 'The essence of strategy is choosing what not to do.'[13]

13 M. Porter (1998) *Competitive Strategy*, Simon & Schuster.

Key points

- Strategy is where it all starts. Operating without one is like flying an aircraft in clouds without radar.
- Your investor profile determines which property auction strategy is suitable for your personality.
- You have to set goals – without them, you won't progress or know when you've achieved your target.
- Targets can move as circumstances change. Review your strategy – once a year is about right.
- Define your market; don't take a scattergun approach to property investment.
- Become an expert in both type of property and location.
- Be a doer, not a talker.
- Don't be afraid or shy to seek advice.

Chapter 4
Calculating Market Value and Maximum Bid

We are all valuers. How many times have you said to a partner or friend: 'That house selling on my road/in my area really isn't worth as much as that! Mine's much better; we have a new kitchen, a second bathroom and a garage – they don't.'

This is the basis of valuation. Look for properties which are similar in terms of location, type, age and bedrooms, then adjust the valuation based on differences such as a second bathroom, garage and new kitchen. A direct comparable is a substitute, although in the real world there will always be differences, even minor ones.

Before we decide what our maximum bid is going to be at auction, we need to work out the property's market value, then decide on an acceptable discount for the risk:

> Valuation of any asset relies on the well-established economic principle of substitution. This states that the buyer of an item would not pay more for it than the cost of acquiring a satisfactory substitute. Therefore, a person assessing the price to pay for a particular item will normally look to the price achieved for similar items in the market (the comparable evidence) and make a bid accordingly.

Royal Institution of Chartered Surveyors (RICS)[14]

---

14 Royal Institution of Chartered Surveyors (RICS) (2023) Comparable Evidence in Real Estate Valuation, 1st edition, April. Available at https://www.rics.org/profession-standards/rics-standards-and-guidance/sector-standards/valuation-standards/comparable-evidence-in-real-estate-valuation, accessed 5 January 2026.

As outlined in the RICS guidance note, 1st edition: *Comparable Evidence in Real Estate Valuation*, comparable data used by valuers should be:

- Comprehensive – there should be several comparables, rather than a single transaction or event
- Very similar or, if possible, identical to the item being valued
- Recent – i.e. representative of the market on the date of valuation
- The result of an arm's-length transaction in the market
- Verifiable
- Consistent with local market practice
- The result of underlying demand – i.e. comparable transactions will have taken place, with enough potential bidders to create an active market.[15]

An auction investor must be able to estimate a property's value before bidding, so as to decide whether it's a good investment or not and to set their maximum bid. Although they could ask for help from estate agents or surveyors, property valuation is a skill that all serious auction investors should acquire – one that's extremely useful in all market conditions, but particularly so in uncertain economic times.

This isn't rocket science, as most of us do the comparable method every time we go shopping: we're always placing a value on a product or service by comparing alternatives. Property valuations are no different, although there are different approaches to valuation, as we will see.

How to set your maximum price

Example

Let's say you have an auction property in mind, and the guide price is £100,000. After looking at comparables, you estimate the current market value to be £150,000. As an auction investor, you don't want to purchase a property at full market value, but for less. In this case,

15 RICS, *Comparable Evidence in Real Estate Valuation*, 1st edition.

the property may have other features such as a strong rental yield, so you might be willing to compromise slightly on price – but would still require a minimum 20% discount to invest.

By applying this process, your maximum bid will be not more than £120,000.

Market value

The International Valuation Standards Council defines market value as:

> The estimated amount for which a property should exchange on the date of valuation between a willing buyer and a willing seller in an arm's-length transaction after proper marketing, wherein the parties had each acted knowledgably, prudently and without compulsion.[16]

As mentioned previously, in more simple terms:

Market value is the price that someone is willing to pay for a particular property, given all of the circumstances and variables surrounding it at that specific time.

These include the condition of the property, state of the economy, recent transactions in the area and a host of other considerations.

An agent or surveyor will select some recently sold properties from the local area. These are known as market comparables ('comps') and form the basis of your potential investment property's market value.

The average person might feel that their own lack of experience and knowledge makes valuation a task best left to the professionals. But in most cases, unlike with commercial property, most of the information

16 RICS (2025) 'International Valuation Standards', 31 January Available at: https://www.rics.org/profession-standards/rics-standards-and-guidance/sector-standards/valuation-standards/red-book/international-valuation-standards, accessed 5 January 2026.

and market evidence required to complete a valuation is available to the public on the internet. One of the main sources of data is HM Land Registry, where all sales are recorded and registered.[17]

The key to valuation lies in selecting appropriate market evidence, interpreting it and applying the results in the most effective way.

Discounts to market value and below market-value Warning!

How often do you see properties marketed at a 'discount to market value' or 'below market-value?' These are property marketeer buzzwords, and in many cases the reality is pretty different from the hype. Often, you'll see these words in a sentence with 'no money down', which alerts you to the fact that it's a load of nonsense.

Over the years, I have been sent emails and texts offering me bargains on a patch I know as well as the best of them. There aren't many people who understand prices and rental values better than me in the areas in which I've specialised for decades. I can assure you, many of these 'deals' are not that great – and some are more expensive than buying through an estate agent.

New-build property has always led on the discount factor, but who decides the market value? Of course, the people selling them.

As always, do your own research. Become a valuer, seek out the bargains and don't be distracted by the marketing noise.

For me, that's the attraction of property auctions: they're raw and no hype (in most cases). Sound research leads to genuine, below-market value investments at wholesale prices.

---

17 These details are available at the Land Registry website: www.gov.uk/government/organisations/land-registry.

Selecting comparables

The most important stage in conducting your valuation is finding and selecting your market evidence. A perfect comparable would be an exact match to your property in terms of size, location and condition, as well as being a recent transaction on the open market. Often, the number of comparables to base a valuation on is debated: most UK surveyors look for three similar comparables, which is also a reasonable measure for an investor.

In your research, do be aware of some of the most common similarities to look out for, and measure the following.

Accommodation and features

The properties you select must be as similar as possible to the property you're valuing. For example, you can't accurately compare a two-bedroom, terraced house with a two-bedroom, new-build apartment – it would be like trying to compare apples with oranges.

Also consider to what extent there are similarities in:

- Size – square feet or square metres
- Number of rooms and layout
- Additional features – e.g. garage, garden, loft conversion or conservatory

– and match yours where possible. If the property you consider the best match to your potential purchase has a feature such as a conservatory which your property doesn't have, adjust the valuation – say by £8,000–£25,000, depending on quality and size.

Condition

A property's general condition can have significant impact on its value, as can any improvements such as a loft extension or additional bathroom. Be detailed and diligent in your research and choice, and don't take a property or its apparent condition at face value.

For example, terraced properties on the same street may seem identical from the outside, but the reality may be completely different. The first property could be in disrepair, the bathrooms and kitchen might be dated, perhaps the windows are single glazed and the property heated by a plug-in electric fire. Meanwhile, the second property might have a modern kitchen and bathroom suite, uPVC double glazing, central heating and a conservatory.

Naturally, the second property is going to achieve a higher market value than the first.

Time and market pricing

The property market is not static but dynamic and ever-evolving, even in so-called 'flat' phases. Just because a property achieved a particular selling price 12 months ago, doesn't mean there's reason to believe it will achieve the same price if sold today.

As a result, the most reliable comparables are from the most recent transactions.

In a bullish market where property prices are rapidly increasing, a transaction that took place four weeks ago may no longer be relevant. Alternatively, in a falling market, a transaction that took place six months ago might not be relevant either.

As ever, it's a judgement call – the more times you make it, the better you get.

Location

Location is a prime consideration when valuing a property. Desirable attributes include being close to a:

- Quality state or private school
- Nursery
- Park
- Beach
- Conservation area or national park

- Transport links
- Metro or underground station, train station or tram stop
- Smart village-type road, with small shops, restaurants and delicatessens.

Equally, being located on a main road, in a less desirable area or above a busy parade of shops can make a location less appealing, and so less valuable. Selecting comparables correctly is fundamental to success and an accurate valuation. There is more than one key variable to consider.

Sources for comparables

There are numerous sources for comparable evidence on the internet (some of the better ones are mentioned in Chapter 6).

Sale prices

In the absence of any relevant sold price data, look at the asking prices of comparable properties: this is OK, if you adjust for the market. In rapidly rising markets, some asking prices are exceeded; while in slow or falling markets, you can expect a lower price on completion. Here, there is a danger of overcomplicating what is essentially a straightforward exercise: just pick three comparables from the sold data, and if that's not available or is significantly out of date, look at the sales data instead.

Case Study
Distressed Assets: Liverpool L9 – 2022

I looked at a property in the L9 area of Liverpool to decide on the maximum bid at auction, and found sold data relating to three properties within about 500m. The sold prices were nine months, one year and two years old. I also looked at current sales data and rental figures.

Given the market's upward movement since the properties were sold, the current market conditions and recent sales data, I assessed that the target property's market value was in the region of £120,000.

I wanted a 25% discount, so set the maximum bid at £90,000. We bought it for less, and had the extra benefit of the property being under-rented.

Net yield (income)

Income capitalisation

Some investors don't even look at what the market value is, or should be. It's a highly subjective concept, and one person's idea of market value can differ from another's by a considerable margin. Indeed, many surveyors and estate agents often disagree on the price or value of a property – so what chance is there for the rest of us?

It's not uncommon for an investor to say they want a net yield of a certain figure.

Example

Here, let's call it 6%. A property at auction has a guide price of £100,000, with an existing rental income of £850 pcm, which is £10,200 per annum (10.2%). That is the gross yield, so to get the net figure we would have to deduct operating costs such as:

- Insurance
- Letting or management fees
- Provision for repairs
- Gas safety certificate (if applicable).

For illustrative purposes, the costs and provisions reduce gross yield to 8% net at the £100,000 guide price. According to this income capitalisation approach to market value, our maximum bid would be:

$$£8,000 \div 6\% = £133,000$$

Clearly, this is based on the purchase price, and doesn't include all of the fees (to include auction, legal and stamp duty: for example here, £7,000). Based on the total funds committed in cash, we would readjust the maximum bid to:

(£8,000 ÷ 6%) – £7,000 (fees) = £126,000

Our maximum bid of £126,000 is in effect a purchase price of £133,000, taking into account fees and stamp duty.

Tip

Some auction buyers, notably investors not too familiar with tactics, fix their maximum bids at obvious prices with a '0' at the end or a '5'.

Try to mix it up a bit: £126,000 would be a good bid, as the next highest is generally £127,000. Some bidders would have dropped out at £125,000.

Value based on size: pounds per square foot (£ per sq. ft)

Sometimes new builds – apartments particularly – are valued in pounds per square foot, which is also a useful comparator for other properties. Price per square foot is calculated by taking the sales price and dividing it by the square footage.

For example, a two-bedroom house with a square footage of 800 sq. ft ($74m^2$), which is marketed at £150,000. In this case:

£150,000 ÷ 800 sq. ft: £150,000 ÷ 800 = £188

In this case, the price per square foot is calculated as £188 (or £2,027 per m^2).

Online automated valuation tools

Most of us who own property, or are looking to buy, have come across online valuation calculators. You input a postcode, and a few variables such as the number of bedrooms, living rooms and condition, and it computes a value. It's all scientific and based on algorithms, sold data, comparables and so on.

I never use them. Read into that what you may.

What happens if you get the valuation wrong?

Warning!

When you get property valuations wrong, they can plague you for a long time.

We secured a repossessed property at auction for a client which was located in Bingley, West Yorkshire in February 2009, and had previously sold to the first owner as a new-build apartment in 2007 at £183,995. We purchased it for £74,000, a staggering 'discount' to the original price of 60%.

In reality, we achieved an excellent result for a delighted client in a prestigious development. It wasn't a 60% discount to market value, as the sales price was massively inflated and at a time that investors were piling into these projects with little (if any) due diligence, supported by the banks.

These properties don't sell for £183,995, 16 years later. Our investor's apartment is now worth about £140,000, so it more or less doubled in the period with good, positive cash flow.

As you will have seen from Chapter 2, this was the start of the Credit Crunch or financial crisis. The original buyer was caught up in the frenzy of the time, which many of us remember well.

Ignore the noise, do your own thing – but make sure it's based on research.

Common sense

The most important factor in any valuation is common sense – as mentioned previously, it's not rocket science. Most of us can look at a property and, using the tools on the internet and common sense, arrive at the market value and what we would be happy to pay for it.

Never lose sight of the fact that your common sense is your greatest asset. Deploying it wisely will reap dividends.

In reality, I use a hybrid model of all three traditional methods of valuation. They all tell you different things, but point towards what the maximum bid should be at auction. Many investors are looking for bargains, while others income – but the overall aim is value. There aren't much better methods to achieve value than buying at auction, but you need to be able to work out what value actually means.

Key points

- There is no reason why an investor can't value a property or estimate rent to a high degree of accuracy.
- Valuation is not rocket science – it's something that you can (and must) do.
- Valuation is just an opinion.
- Market value is the price someone is willing to pay for a property that isn't necessarily the same as the asking or guide price.
- Deploy common sense – it's your best asset.

Chapter 5
Property is a Numbers Game

When you invest in buy-to-let or commercial property, you're investing in a business. If it's your first investment, you are a start-up business; if it's your second or two hundredth, you're expanding it.

It's important to approach both the acquisition process and the development or management afterwards with a business mindset. Many times, investors get this wrong – it's a numbers game.

Essential factors

As a first-time, buy-to-let auction investor, you must consider:

- Why you're investing in buy-to-let property
- Your exit strategy or realisation of your investment
- Instructing an A-team of professional advisors:
  - solicitor
  - accountant
  - property sourcing agent
  - mortgage broker
  - insurance broker
  - lettings and property management agent
  - construction and building sector professionals (more on this in Chapter 10)
- Where to invest
- What type of property you should buy
- How you will raise the deposit
- If you should self-manage or instruct a letting agent.

The list above is not exhaustive. If you're intending to renovate a property, you need to add building and surveying professionals and possibly an architect, depending on the project's complexity (more on this in Chapter 10).

Be sure to approach property investing as you would any other business: you have customers, costs, revenue, assets, suppliers, debtors (hopefully, not too many!), short-term creditors, possibly staff and premises, marketing and accounts.

As owning property is the same as owning a business, so you need to use business techniques to ensure that you:

- Remain in business and don't go bust – cash flow is king
- Make a profit
- Expand the business
- Add value to the business, giving you the potential at some stage in the future to sell it
- Mitigate risk through insurance, planning and advisors.

A word of caution

The historical evidence suggests that investing in property is one of the most effective methods of acquiring and retaining long-term wealth. A quick glance at the *Sunday Times* Rich List, regardless of whether the economy is booming or in recession, illustrates this point. Many people on the list have substantial property holdings as well as their mainstream businesses – and indeed hold their wealth from these businesses in the form of property.

Property investment isn't a 'get-rich-quick' scheme, but over time it does reward those who are patient. Those who aren't, buy at the top of the market and sell at the bottom; whereas those who are, are those to whom the impatient sell!

Crunching the numbers

All successful businesses have both eyes on the numbers. This chapter introduces you to essential investor concepts to help you make fully informed and profitable decisions.

Opportunity cost: a guide to making the right decisions

Opportunity cost is an extremely important concept to understand. Numerous definitions are to be found in the many learned texts on economic theory – usually in their first few pages, as this isn't just the cornerstone of economics – but also form the basis of all investing in property and more. It underpins everything.

As long as you adhere to its principles, you will be a successful property investor. This is my definition:

Opportunity cost is the true cost of what you have given up to get something else.

In other words, the 'foregone alternative'. Governments around the globe have to make these decisions continually and formalise their decision-making processes through annual budget statements. The austerity measures introduced by many countries during the second decade of the 21st century following the credit crisis are a classic example of opportunity cost in action. In the UK, for example, cuts in military expenditure, the police and other departments were made, while the budget for overseas aid was increased. This conscious decision by government to forego some things to increase others is opportunity cost in action.

In our lives, if we're fortunate enough to have £150 to spend on a birthday treat, we have a myriad of ways in which to spend it. Choosing a meal out rather than, say, a couple of tickets for the theatre or football means the opportunity cost of that decision is foregoing those options.

Investors are faced with similar choices from a huge and complex array of alternative products: cash, government or corporate bonds, collective investment vehicles such as investment trusts or unit trusts, individual shares, foreign exchange, commodities such as gold, silver, copper and oil, antiques, art, wine, films, crypto, Bitcoin and so on – the list is almost endless.

As a property investor, opportunity cost should direct you to the best property deals where there is underlying value: such as purchasing for a real discount, buying an under-rented property, or one where you can add value by increasing the number of bedrooms, a loft conversion or extension.

If you compare alternatives, including other ways to buy such as at auction, you should naturally focus on where to obtain value.

All properties are not equal. That is the point of opportunity cost and why it's important to invest in assets that offer significant value – not just at point of acquisition, but over the medium-to-long term.

An investor has to make choices based on experience, common sense and advice. Property is as good as – or even better than – all of the examples given above. And one of the reasons is gearing.

Gearing magnifies your returns

Put simply, gearing is using a mortgage or other loan to buy a property. In the USA, the term is 'leverage' and in non-business-speak, 'borrowing'.

The reason that gearing or borrowing makes investing in property so attractive is that you can have both control and ownership of an asset for a small proportion of its overall cost. Additionally, if you purchase the asset (property) below its true market value, the return on your own cash invested can be substantial. Chapter 7 deals with raising finance in more detail; here, let's illustrate the point.

Example

Investor A invests in a buy-to-let property acquired for £100,000, and they pay cash. Five years later, they sell the property for a 30% capital gain. The capital return (excluding rental income and costs) is 30% or £30,000.

Investor B buys the property next door, also for £100,000. Instead, they take out a buy-to-let mortgage for 75% of the value of the property. The mortgage provider secures the £75,000 loan on the property, while Investor B pays the other 25% as a deposit. In technical terms, they have 75% gearing because the bank has loaned them 75% of the purchase price.

Five years later, Investor B sells the property for a 30% capital gain. The return (on cash invested, excluding rental income and costs) is now 120% or £30,000.

If we take this a stage further, Investor A could have invested in four of these properties with the capital they had, rather than investing all of the cash in one property. If they had done that, the capital gain would have been £120,000 rather than £30,000, and the return on cash 120%.

Before we continue looking any further at gearing, it would be useful to introduce the concept of return on investment (ROI). Up until now we have referred to 'cash invested'.

Return on investment

ROI is the total profit expressed as a percentage of the amount of cash initially invested.

This concept will help us with a more in-depth analysis of gearing, its advantages and disadvantages. Here's another example to illustrate one of the key advantages of gearing: that it magnifies returns. Both cases exclude costs and tax.

Example

Investor C invests in five properties at £100,000, with mortgages arranged at 50% loan-to-value (LTV). They invest £250,000 cash, and the bank lends them £250,000. At the end of seven years, they sell the properties for a capital gain of 50% or £250,000. Their gross ROI is:

£250,000 ÷ £250,000 x 100 = 100%.

Investor D invests in the same properties, but at 75% LTV. Their cash invested, or deposit, is £125,000 and gross ROI is:

£250,000 ÷ £125,000 x 100 = 200%

In this example, excluding rental income and costs, Investor D achieves double the ROI as Investor C through a greater level of gearing.

Clearly, this example is illustrative as, in the real world, Investor C's income will be greater than Investor D's, all being equal – but it's the impact on capital that this shows.

Gearing also magnifies your losses

In the UK since the Credit Crunch, we have experienced very low interest rates for the past 14 years. People have been accustomed to gearing to maximise their exposure to rising property prices, until 2022 and the economic shock of inflation when interest rates started to rise, as well as mortgage rates.

As the great Warren Buffett said: 'Only when the tide goes out do you discover who's been swimming naked.'

In the examples above, if property prices had fallen by 25% over the period and both sets of buyers need to sell (you don't want to be a forced seller), the maths would look very different:

Investor C's portfolio would now be worth £375,000, while they owe the bank £250,000. They would walk away with £125,000 of their original investment or 50% of it.

Investor D's portfolio would now be worth the same, while they owe the bank £375,000. They would walk away with nothing, after losing £125,000.

The example is extreme and is here to illustrate the point that gearing can also magnify losses – it's not a one-way street. However, if a buy-to-let investor has a plan and treats their investments as a business, only in extreme circumstances will they have to sell at a loss or be forced to sell due to cash flow reasons (a topic which will be discussed in greater detail later in this chapter).

As Winston Churchill said: 'He who fails to plan is planning to fail.'

Cash flow: the king of all investment concepts

In simple terms, cash flow refers to the movement of cash in and out of a business over a period of time. For example, if you receive £40,000 per annum in rent but your outlay is £50,000 cash for mortgages and other expenses, you are in negative cash flow: not a great place to be, which over time can result in catastrophic business failure.

When businesses and property investors are highly geared, a small rise in interest rates or unforeseen cost can put them out of business. It's essential for property investors to conduct a sensitivity analysis or stress-test the effect of a rise in interest rates on their cash flow. This is critical and can forewarn you of any difficulties to come.

Alternatively, if you're receiving £50,000 per annum in rent and your cash outlay is £30,000, you are in positive cash flow. It's firmly here we want to be as buy-to-let property investors.

Sensitivity analysis or stress-testing

As mentioned above, you don't want to be the buy-to-let investor who has to sell at auction quickly because you are overgeared, or overleveraged, as interest rates shoot up. It's extremely important at the beginning to have a feel for the wider economic environment in which you are participating:

- Am I in a rising interest rate environment, or one that's falling or flat?
- Should I fix my buy-to-let mortgage for two, three, five or 10 years?
- Would I get a better rate releasing equity from my home?
- What if I can't keep up payments?
- Are rents rising or falling?
- Is the property market rising or falling?
- What is my break-even point?

Example

Let's look at two scenarios (Tables 1 and 2).

Table 1: Property purchased at auction and refinanced for £200,000 at 50% LTV

	Interest rate					
	5%	**6%**	**7%**	**8%**	**9%**	**12%**
Mortgage at 50% LTV (£100,000), interest-only	£5,000	£6,000	£7,000	£8,000	£9,000	£12,000
Net rent before servicing debt	£12,000	£12,000	£12,000	£12,000	£12,000	£12,000
Cash flow	**£7,000**	**£6,000**	**£5,000**	**£4,000**	**£3,000**	**0**

Here, break-even would be at 12% interest rates.

Table 2: The same example, but at 75% LTV

	Interest rate				
	5%	6%	7%	8%	9%
Mortgage at 75% LTV (£150,000)	£7,500	£9,000	£10,500	£12,000	£13,500
Net rent before servicing debt	£12,000	£12,000	£12,000	£12,000	£12,000
Cash flow	**£4,500**	**£3,000**	**£1,500**	**0**	**–£1,500**

Here, break-even would be at 8% interest rates.

Hopefully, these examples will make you stop and think about gearing in a rising interest environment. For a very long time we have only experienced falling and low rates. It's always worth having a plan B: reviewing your portfolio and cash flow to identify if and when you might have a problem – it's simply good practice.

The Credit Crunch and gearing

A lesson from recent history

One of the major contributory factors to the Credit Crunch was the high gearing of many sub-prime mortgagees in the USA. As interest rates began to rise in 2004, many could not keep up payments, defaulted and had their properties repossessed. These defaults made many of the investment-grade packaged debt obligations sold by banks to banks and other institutions toxic.

In essence, although there is a lot more to it, this was the heart of the Credit Crunch. Since then, gearing or leverage has almost become a bad word.

Well, here is a defence of it.

Why people borrow

Businesses and individuals borrow money for a multitude of reasons. For businesses, it might be to purchase stock, expand the labour force or reduce costs by consolidating debts at a lower interest rate and better terms. They borrow to reduce costs or expand operations.

Individuals borrow money for many different reasons: property purchase, new car, holidays, weddings, divorces, school and university fees and so on. This reliance on credit, sometimes at extortionate rates, was also a contributory factor in the crisis. Since then many people, businesses and governments have been encouraged to 'deleverage': the process by which debts are paid back. At the individual consumer level, borrowing money at high levels of interest (30% plus) for consumer durables and lifestyle is not a good idea.

Don't live entirely on credit

Living on the 'never-never' is a generational thing. In previous generations' day, saving and sacrifice were the route to acquiring cars and holidays. Prudence and living within your means were the watchwords: it was the same philosophy among friends, colleagues and extended family. Post-war Britain taught people the value of everything – they appreciated even the small luxuries among the rationing and rebuilding.

It's difficult to put your finger on when that philosophy changed, but it has. My generation (and certainly today's) don't see the need to wait until tomorrow to get something you can have today. Mass consumerism, spurred on by media advertising pressure, social media such as Twitter and Facebook, banks' willingness to lend, the abundance of credit and an insatiable desire to consume have all contributed in part to the financial crisis which began in 2007.

This hangover from the tsunami of credit will take many years to work its way through the system, but don't think it won't return in the future – it will. Collective memory in the City, Wall Street, banks and beyond will fade, and those who lived through these times will retire and be replaced by others wanting to make a name for themselves, seeking more innovative ways in which to make money, encouraged by government policies – as they have one eye on the tax revenue such schemes can generate.

History has a habit of repeating itself: which is why property in all market conditions is a sound investment.

Borrowing money from a bank to buy an asset that provides return in the form of capital growth and income is a good idea: even more so when you can buy at auction a property substantially below its worth in the open market. Borrowing to your comfort level to invest in assets for your long-term future is sensible, but be sure to treat it like a business, and use the tools set out in this book.

You don't want to be a distressed seller – the way to avoid this is to concentrate on cash flow.

Warning!

As this book recommends throughout, take professional advice from a mortgage broker or financial advisor as to the merits of gearing in your own particular and unique circumstances.

Be across rental income

One of the key problems associated with the Credit Crunch, and the subsequent property market recession, was that many investors were lured into the market with the prospects of huge capital gains: they either didn't understand or bother about rental income.

As with all booms, it's difficult to see where the bust was coming from – and certainly, no one out there saw the sheer scale and depth of the financial crisis in terms of property prices, as measured by income or affordability.

One of the main lessons of the Credit Crunch is ignoring rental income and net yield at your peril. Cash flow is king, but particularly so in difficult market conditions.

Having looked at the key investor concepts of opportunity cost, gearing and cash flow, let's introduce a few more. There are many investment ratios you should consider when buying property and measuring success, comparing options or otherwise.

The most basic of the calculations is the best and what many seasoned investors look to maximise and use as a measurement tool when comparing properties in their portfolio.

Yield

Yield is the ratio of rent to purchase price. Many investors use the total purchase price, which includes costs including auctioneer's fees, legal fees and stamp duty. There is little point in expressing a positive yield if costs exceed rent, so the most useful and meaningful calculation is:

(Rental Income – Operating Costs) as a % of (Purchase Price + Costs) = Net Yield

Some people refer to this net income figure as cash flow. (There is a worked example below.)

Acquisition and operating costs

Acquisition costs are associated with investing in buy-to-let property. Some costs to consider are:

- Auction fees and any Special Conditions of Sale fees
- Legal fees for conveyancing
- Survey or valuation fees
- Mortgage or bridging brokers and arrangement fees
- Stamp duty
- Property company fees (for professional services).

Your operating cost statement details all the costs involved in running your property business. Generally, it's calculated on an annual basis, but it can be monthly.

The costs of owning and operating a buy-to-let property, regardless of geographical location, are:

- Mortgage or other finance repayments
- Insurance – contents, buildings and public liability
- Maintenance – repairs, fixtures and fittings, white goods
- Service charges (where applicable)
- Letting agency fees
- Marketing for holiday homes – including brochures, website and membership fees for third-party advertisers
- Personal expenses in connection with ownership and letting, such as travel
- Ground rent (where applicable).

All of these expenses need to be factored into your operating cost statement and cash flow.

Example

A three-bedroom house purchased at auction for £126,000 with a rent of £14,700: an excellent buy. Let's work out the after costs income, net income or cash flow (depending on the terminology you use). For illustration purposes, this is a useful layout for you to copy.

Annual Statement

Total rental income		**£14,700**
Operating expenses:		
Insurance	(£400)	
Letting fees	(£1,176)	
Maintenance	(£800)	
Gas certificate	(£85)	
Total operating costs	**(£2,461)**	
Net operating income		**£12,239**
Debt service (mortgage) 6% interest-only at 50% LTV	(£3,780)	
Before tax cash flow		**£8,459**

If the total costs of purchase were £6,000, then the net yield before tax would be:

$$(£8,459 \div £132,000) \times 100 = 6.4\%$$

Contingency fund

Before we leave the subject of operating costs, it's key to emphasise the importance of building a contingency fund that you can call on when needed. You never know if and when you might need this money – but say for example, the unfortunate day comes that a path needs to be dug up due to a problem with the drains, you'll be grateful that you've set aside funds that are immediately available.

Apart from adding cash from another source for contingency, you could channel any revenue which you had earmarked for voids (i.e. when the property is empty and not producing income), maintenance or repairs that isn't spent in year to the fund.

Rent reviews: increasing income

It's good practice and sound financial management to review whether the rent you're charging your tenants is at the market rate. This is a good way to increase income when, in all likelihood, your costs are rising – and a judgement call if you have good tenants who pay well and keep the property in excellent condition.

On many occasions, doing nothing can be the best approach. But it has financial risks (opportunity cost) for you if rents are rising in the market, as well as your costs.

Many of the properties we target at auction are under-rented – some, considerably so.

In a recent auction, a property was let at £400 pcm (£4,800 per annum). The guide price reflected this, but the market rent should have been £575 to £595 pcm (£6,900 to £7,140). At the higher figure, the difference is £2,340 – an increase of almost 50%.

The tenants have lived in the property for many years and, when I viewed it, said they understood the rent would be increased.

This is an extreme case of an under-rented property and I don't know the story behind it; but as ever, it presented an excellent opportunity.

Reduce costs: speak with your letting agent

Many lettings and property management companies are open to discussion about fees, particularly with a good client and someone who has a number of properties under management. (We certainly do, and offer our portfolio landlords rates commensurate with their confidence in us to manage their properties efficiently and profitably.)

Increasing rents and reducing costs can only help cash flow. It should be something you consider annually.

Make your cash work harder

Successful investors in all asset classes understand the principle of making your cash work hard for you. As property investors, our cash works very hard from day one, as most people leverage their investments by using a mortgage as part payment.

Property has that innate quality: you pay a small percentage of the price, but have full control over the asset. Moreover, as mentioned previously, you can invest substantially below market value by acquiring property at auction or through administrators, receivers or banks. At the outset, your cash is working to full capacity.

Return on equity: time erodes the efficiency of cash

An irony is that the more successful an investment, the less efficient it becomes in the return an investor receives over time. Let's look at the concept of return on equity (ROE).

ROE is a measure of financial performance calculated by dividing net income by a property's equity:

ROE = Net income as a % of the equity in a property

For example, Investor E buys a property for cash in year 1 at £200,000, and their equity is £200,000. If the net rent is £12,000 per annum, the return on that equity is 6%:

£12,000 (net income) as a % of total equity (£200,000) = 6%

Over the next seven years, property prices rise by 60% and net rents rise by 25%.

The ROE is now:

£15,000 ÷ £320,000 = 4.7%

Over a seven-year period this property's value has increased substantially, but the return in terms of income is much reduced. Many people wouldn't lose sleep in such a situation, but this might make you think of alternative uses which could increase that 4.7% back to 6% or even greater, depending on the market at the time.

It's food for thought.

Portfolio building

One of the greatest risks in buy-to-let is investing in only one property – this really is putting all your eggs in one basket. If that property is unoccupied for any period, your business effectively loses 100% revenue. Conversely, if you have five properties, your revenue is only reduced by 20% – or in the case of 10, by 10% and so on.

There are three fundamental questions to ask yourself when building a property portfolio from scratch:

What's my tolerance to risk? Where 1 is 'least risky' and 10 is 'very risky' on a sliding scale.

How am I going to raise the necessary funds to invest?

What's the end state – why am I investing?

Asset management

Many property investors benefit from active asset management, particularly those who have a portfolio of properties, hectic schedules and live overseas. Clients vary in terms of wealth, profession and geographical location, but the one thing they have in common is wanting their assets to grow in value and be professionally managed.

Asset management is the process by which a property investment is researched, acquired, let and managed, where ROI is maximised through active and ongoing management. This is fundamental to increasing returns and maximising your portfolio performance – as well as reducing costs. In practice, it can involve:

- Advice on where to invest
- Advice on what property type and why
- Whether new mortgage products are available, which can reduce costs
- Updates on insurance requirements and costs
- Ensuring that buy-to-let property investment is legally compliant
- Regular rent reviews

- Advice on adding value
- Advice on when to sell and reinvest
- Tax advice where appropriate
- Regular communication between the asset manager and investor to ensure ongoing goals and targets for the portfolio are agreed.

Many buy-to-let investors ignore this aspect of the investment process. Once they've purchased a property and have it let, they think that's it. For some, this works and over time they make solid returns; but through a considered management process they would make even greater ones.

This is an area in which I have extensive experience and would vouch that portfolios that are actively managed outperform those that aren't. To a large extent it's common sense, as most things in property are – but rent reviews, cost reviews and disposals where necessary to fund acquisitions (following the principle of opportunity cost) all increase returns to the investor.

Key points

- When you invest in buy-to-let property, you're investing in a business.
- You must have a strategy and understand why you're investing.
- How will you exit or realise the investment?
- Instruct your A-team of professional advisors.
- Take expert advice on raising finance from an experienced mortgage broker.
- Cash flow is king.
- Be patient, and invest for the long term.
- Opportunity cost reminds us of the need to have cash working as hard as possible for us.
- Gearing magnifies both returns and losses.
- Revaluation and remortgage can help build a profitable portfolio for the long-term.
- Distressed assets are a strong investment with built-in equity from the outset.

- Control your operating costs and monitor cash flow.
- Asset management is key for maintaining and raising the value of a property portfolio.
- Remember that property investment is a numbers game.

Chapter 6
Research and Risk

Time and energy spent researching are seldom wasted. The military have a saying for it: 'Time spent in recce (reconnaissance) is time never wasted.' It's as true in the army as it is in property investment or business.

Having formulated a strategy based on your investor profile, attitude to risk and goals, researching the market in general and locality in detail, the next step is to turn the concept into a plan. As the American investor Peter Lynch famously said: 'Investing without research is like playing stud poker and never looking at the cards.'[18]

The Intelligence Cycle

The Intelligence Cycle is a structured process used to gather information, convert it into relevant intelligence and pass it to those who require it – the decision makers. The US Central Intelligence Agency (CIA) uses the following process, which is mirrored by other agencies across the world:

- Planning and direction – needs and requirements
- Collection
- Processing
- Analysis and production
- Dissemination.[19]

---

18 P. Lynch (1989) *One Up on Wall Street: How to Use What You Already Know to Make Money in the Market*, Simon & Schuster.

19 Central Intelligence Agency (CIA) (n.d.) 'The Intelligence Cycle'. Available at: https://www.cia.gov/spy-kids/static/59d238b4b5f69e0497325e49f0769acf/Briefing-intelligence-cycle.pdf, accessed 5 January 2026.

To be a successful buyer at auction, you have to become an intelligence analyst or detective. Sherlock Holmes would have been a great success on the auction circuit with his meticulous eye for detail and skill at obtaining the facts, then analysing them and producing a plan!

To bid successfully or choose not to bid at all, you need to get as much information about the property or properties as humanly possible. Having decided on your needs and requirements, then collect information using all of the sources available – the internet, on the ground, legal pack, speaking with people and so on. Having done that for all the properties of interest, process the information and discard the properties which are obvious non-starters for one reason or another. Don't be put off if that's most of them, as we're in the business of looking for bargains.

Having successfully filtered your options, analyse them using the tools in this book. If you're looking to buy just one property but have shortlisted three, you'll need to rank them and take a view: for example, if they are lots 4, 70 and 110 in the auction, you have to be sure it's 110 and not the others you want.

In this case, you now have intelligence on the properties, not just a lot of loose, raw data and facts which are meaningless – particularly if you're trying to rank the options. You also have a structure.

Decision point

This is where a level of skill is required. You've ranked the options as lots 110, 70 and 4, but unfortunately, they will be sold in numerical order. What if you get to 110 and it's one of those lots which takes on a life of its own: that is, an unfathomable bidding frenzy? It's incredible (and not entirely predictable) that a lot can attract a following, smashing any maximum bid that you've carefully analysed as good value in the heat of the moment. There is no way of predicting this.

Again here, you have to take a view. Carefully analyse your maximum bids, and lower them for the second and third-rated properties. If lot 4 sells at reserve, then all things being equal, buy it. It's a good property and stacks up; otherwise it wouldn't have been on your final list.

It's better to buy your third-rated property cheaply, than your first-rated property at your maximum bid.

In a recent auction, we were successful acquiring a property at 37% below where we had set our maximum bid. Wherever that had ranked before the day started, it was top of the list at the end.

This is the fascinating thing about auctions. On another day, that may well have been very different – it all depends on who is participating, and why.

Collecting the information

The key stage in the Intelligence Cycle is collecting raw data to process and analyse. Cast your net wide, and use all the available resources (some of which are detailed below). Also, keep in mind some of the pillars of successful property investment which have stood the test of time, such as:

- Location
- Demand
- Supply
- Operating costs
- Price paid.

In both good times and bad, quality decisions always prevail.

Location

As clichéd as 'location, location, location' may sound, successful buy-to-let investment is about choosing the right one.

We often have investors coming to us after they have bought in auction, requesting lettings and property management services – and we're always happy to help. Many are first-time auction bidders and, to be frank, have bought stock that wouldn't make our list of options. Whether advised by others or going it alone, some can make big mistakes.

Some of the properties require works that weren't foreseen by the investor, while others had 'tenants from hell'. I could see why a landlord wanting a quiet life would get rid at an auction. These issues are all solvable with contractors and lawyers.

But you can't fix location!

There is no substitute for local knowledge. Anyone buying out of area, be it Bolton, Barnsley or Basildon, should visit the area and foster contacts who can give an unabridged, warts-and-all opinion of your property ideas and location.

I talk about 'war zones' and the need to avoid them. Even though I've lived in Liverpool from birth and know Merseyside and Wirral like the back of my hand, I still drive out to areas to run a detailed recce of the locality. Success or failure in buy-to-let can be a difference of just 500m. Get the location right, and the rest falls into place.

Buying just based on a postcode isn't a great idea, as roads and streets vary. At Distressed Assets, we often receive emails and calls to the office asking if one particular postcode is better than another for investment purposes – but it just doesn't work like that.

Forget postcodes. Unless you want to buy particularly expensive properties, towns and cities all have their Alderley Edge, Blundellsands and Knightsbridge.

In a recent auction where we weren't able to view the properties internally, I drove round the options which I'd shortlisted from desk research. The postcodes were fine – until I saw a couple of things in one street which were a red flag. All the other criteria favoured buying the properties, but gut feeling and decades of experience told me that a few of them were best avoided.

Remember to keep your chosen strategy in mind at all times, and don't allow yourself to be influenced by other factors when choosing your location. Regardless of whether a location is filled with detached, four-bedroom houses and close to a well-regarded school, if your strategy is to achieve high rental yields and immediate cash flow, it won't necessarily be suitable compared with a neighbouring location of predominantly 'two-up two-down' houses.

These properties are the engine room of buy-to-let and can produce excellent cash flow and long-term capital growth. Just as importantly, freehold gives you control – as those investors who have leasehold properties with management companies and ever-increasing service charges understand only too well.

The ripple effect: up-and-coming areas

When property prices and rents become expensive relative to incomes in a particular area, new buyers and tenants move to the next cheaper postcode or district, but remain close enough to take advantage of the attractions of their preferred, more expensive first choice.

The attraction might be proximity to family, transport, work or leisure, but eventually prices will go up in the new area as well, due to the ripple effect. As properties become more expensive to buy and rent, there is new demand to seek properties further out from the earlier centre of activity, causing them to rise. Look out for:

- Cities, towns and districts undergoing large-scale regeneration
- Investment by large multinationals creating employment
- New transport links
- The building of a new sports arena or stadium. (For example, during the financial crisis we sourced excellent properties for investors near the new Olympic stadium in Stratford, London.)

In Liverpool, one of the biggest areas of regeneration outside the city centre has involved football stadia. At the time of writing, Liverpool FC has redeveloped its ground and works are continuing, while Everton FC is building a new ground in the dock area. These have multiplier effects, as described in Chapter 1.

Some years ago, Anfield, Liverpool FC's ground, was surrounded by derelict properties, before the club had a change of plan. We managed to buy a freehold block of three apartments at auction which, at the time, was on a road of predominantly derelicts, certainly with no view. However, they were tenanted. There was little interest, even from local property investors.

Today, with the derelict properties demolished, the property is on a new, tree-lined boulevard with views of the new stadium stand and a wonderful aspect (Figure 7).

This is the sort of local knowledge you should seek in whichever part of the country you invest, if it's not your home town.

Figure 7: The road today

Source: Shutterstock (reproduced under licence)

When I lived in London, where the ripple effect is most pronounced, rapid changes in perception of where to live were enormous. Then, Notting Hill, Battersea, Clapham and other areas weren't held in the regard they are today. Similarly, prior to the major redevelopment of Liverpool city centre, who would have wanted to live there? Now it's a thriving, bustling hub of economic and social activity – not just for locals but for the many tens of thousands who visit the city by air, rail, road or cruise ship.

Property prices and rents

Researching historic property prices within an area will help you assess how its market performs in terms of capital growth, as well spotting bargains.

The internet is the best source of information for this type of research. As well as property marketing websites such as Rightmove, Zoopla and OnTheMarket, which help you gauge capital and rental prices for the area, you can look at reliable house price indices published by companies such as Nationwide and Halifax, among others.

Indices explained

House price indices have been published in the UK since 1973. Originally published by mortgage providers, the government soon began to produce its own. The various indices provide average house prices throughout the UK, compiled from different sources.

There are five main indices referred to daily in newspapers and by economists, provided by:

- Nationwide
- Halifax
- UK House Price Index (HPI)
- Rightmove
- Hometrack.

The main confusion surrounding these indices, which leads to much market and economic speculation, is that no two are exactly the same; in some cases, the average house prices stated in them vary considerably. The reason is the way in which they are compiled and where the data is sourced from. Prices are measured at different stages of the buying cycle, and the values taken from different sources.

How each of the main five indices are calculated is outlined below.

Nationwide and Halifax – The Nationwide and Halifax indices are both based on the values of their own mortgage approvals for the previous month, and are seasonally adjusted.[20]

UK House Price Index – The HPI uses house sales data from HM Land Registry, Registers of Scotland and Land and Property Services Northern Ireland, and is calculated by the Office for National Statistics. The time lag between sale completions and registration means the index is dated, but it does provide actual sales data and hard facts, rather than softer interpretations of house price movements based on asking prices, for example.

Rightmove – Rightmove's house price index is compiled from property asking prices listed on its website by UK estate agents over the previous month. It's often criticised for not reflecting what people are actually paying for properties, only being concerned with the frequently inflated asking prices at the beginning of the process. The index is not seasonally adjusted.

Hometrack – Hometrack's index uses a repeat sales methodology. It uses pairs of price points for properties that have sold more than once, to compare price change on a like-for-like basis over time.

Auction-specific research

The house price data and market analysis provided by the indices we've looked at are useful, whether you're buying a property by private treaty (i.e. through an estate agent or direct to the vendor) or through an auction. But they will not find you an auction property.

20 'Seasonally adjusted' is recognition that annual house price data are influenced by seasonal trends. It takes into account expected fluctuations throughout the year, and adjusts the data to reflect this.

Where to find auction properties

Interestingly, auction properties are advertised on the main portals, but that isn't where to go to find them.

First, subscribe to the email newsletters or text message services from the auction houses in your area of interest. You should receive alerts about forthcoming auctions and can then look at their websites for further information.

Second, note that many auctions are national, so you might find a property in Carlisle being sold at auction in London.

Initially, you may just see particulars without photos, but as the lot is populated with information, eventually prior to auction you will be able to download the legal pack. There is enough information on auction houses' websites to make an informed decision.

Time is ticking

When the lot is uploaded to the website, it's usually available to buy. Many auction investors base their entire strategy on making pre-auction offers in the hope – and to be fair, the probability – that some sellers will say 'Yes'. This is why you see many lots on the website with 'Sold Prior To Auction' very early in the auction process, weeks before the live auction.

Tip

If you see a lot that interests you, don't think you have plenty of time before the auction to view and do the analysis shown in this book. Another hopeful investor may beat you to it. Act, and don't delay!

Targeting the auction bargain

Targeting a bargain at auction is different to the more traditional route of buying through an estate agent. Bargains will drive you to an area; while with an estate agent, many buy-to-let investors have a favourite area, generally one in which they feel they are experts.

At Distressed Assets we do have favourite areas, even roads where we've developed and retained freeholds and properties. But you have to go where the bargain is located – it won't come to you.

However, there are certain postcodes where we don't buy: whether the numbers stack up or not, we won't touch them. It's these postcodes where those who don't know the area can be in for an expensive shock.

Research is not just about data sets, internet searches and legal packs. This is undoubtedly very important, but so is researching beyond the paperwork and putting a few miles in on the ground. As mentioned previously, there is no substitute for visiting the area, even if you have to get on a train or plane and stay overnight.

Local areas are very different during the week than at weekends. They're also different during the day than at night. Before buying a property at auction, you have to know that difference. In some cases investors, particularly those from out of town or who reside in another country, employ local buying agents or property sourcing agents to do this for them. This isn't a bad idea, but not all property sourcing agents are equal – you have to be careful sorting the wheat from the chaff.

There aren't many of these with extensive experience of auctions. Pointing would-be investors at properties on Zoopla, as some do, is not the same as purchasing via auction. I will return to this later in the chapter.

Essential Information Group

If you want a resource to find an abundance of valuable data about property auctions, lots, forthcoming and past auctions, the Essential Information Group site is for you (www.eigpropertyauctions.co.uk). It will save you time trawling the different auction house websites, as it consolidates all the available information in one place, including auction packs.

You can analyse historical sold prices when doing market value analysis, and it will flag up whether the property you're interested in has been to auction before. If so, you have to ask yourself: why?

Further, one of the most useful features of the site is that it allows you to search for properties that match your strategy, such as freehold houses within a certain radius of a postcode, and can alert you via email as lots become available.

If your strategy is to look for unsold lots, there is also a search facility for that.

Internet search

The internet has revolutionised research, whether in the property market or any other area of interest, from the most obscure subjects to the most popular. It's a resource without equal.

As we've seen, property investment is about research and due diligence. Get that right, and with a fair wind you'll do very well over the medium-to-long term. If buy–renovate–sell is your strategy, research and buying at the right price is critical because, if you get it wrong, you haven't the benefit of time for it to work itself out in your favour, should property prices be falling and building costs and interest rates rising.

Websites and portals come and go. These are the ones that will add value to your research.

Property auction-specific: Essential Information Group – fee payable.

Property investment in general:

- Hometrack – fee payable for value-added service (www.hometrack.com)
- Property Market Intel – fee payable (www.propertymarketintel.com)
- PropertyData – fee payable (www.propertydata.co.uk).

There are many others on the internet, free portals such as Rightmove (www.rightmove.co.uk) and Zoopla (www.zoopla.co.uk). But if you want to research property like a professional, a subscription to one or two of the above will give you an edge on the amateurs – and the cost will repay itself many times over.

Ask for a free trial: test them all, then choose the one that meets your requirements.

Human intelligence

Human intelligence (HUMINT) is gathered by means of interpersonal human contact as opposed to the internet and portals. It's a military term applied here to property investment.

Sources of HUMINT for the property investor are:

- Estate agents
- Letting agents
- Tenants and neighbours
- Buying and sourcing agents
- Surveyors and builders.

Estate agents

Many estate agents know their markets very well. If you aren't living in the area where you're intending to invest, a visit to one or two agents would be helpful in gauging demand and prices.

If you're looking at buy–renovate–sell, this is extremely important as the agent is likely to provide you with an exit. They also advise on a realistic price and what you need to do during renovation, without going overboard and not recuperating your outlay.

I often view properties available for auction and know immediately if they have been renovated by an investor from out of town. Generally, some treat the properties like their own homes and go completely over the top, installing high-end, more expensive fixtures and fittings than they should.

We purchased a small block of flats from a London-based investor who apparently ran out of money and needed to take it to auction to recoup some of it. Even worse, the block doesn't have planning permission or building regulations certification, but has a high specification. We will resolve the issues moving forward.

Letting agents and property managers

Once you've decided on a lot or lots, you need to research further into the levels of demand and supply of rental properties. You also want to study rental prices, both to ensure that the numbers stack up and the potential investment will be a good one.

The best way to conduct this part of your research is to talk to a letting agent. Here are a few useful questions you can structure into the conversation during your phone call or visit with each agent:

- How much rent would you expect to achieve on this property?
- Would this be furnished or unfurnished?
- How long would you expect it to take for tenants to be sourced and the property rented?
- Can I expect long void periods between tenancies?
- What fixed period can I expect the tenants to occupy the property? What's the norm: six months, 12 months or longer?
- Has demand always been high?
- Has demand increased or decreased?
- Does this type of property have a high turnover of tenants?
- How have rents changed over the last year or so?
- Do you imagine rents will increase in the area over the coming year?
- What's your opinion of the area in general?
- Are there any factors you are aware of that could have a positive or negative impact on the property market and rental values in this area which I don't know about?
- Do I require a selective licence – i.e. a licence from the local authority to legally let the property?
- Can you provide a rental guarantee? (A rental guarantee is an insurance-based product whose policy pays if a tenant defaults on their rent. It's paid for a specific period and can include eviction in the terms.)

- What are your fees?
- What are your tie-ins (i.e. how much notice to give the agent to 'resign'), should I wish to dispense with your services?

Lettings agents know their market and will be happy to help, especially if they think you might become a new client.

We have a lettings and property management business in Liverpool called Tuna Fish Property (www.tunafishproperty.co.uk) which covers Merseyside and Wirral. Initially, we managed just our own properties and blocks, but soon took over those we developed and sold to investors, as some felt they were being ripped off by some agents with huge fees – not just for letting, but also repairs.

The tipping point was an email from an investor client who lived overseas, asking whether it was normal to charge £300 to put an electric panel radiator back on a wall after it had been accidently knocked and fallen off. It just required a couple of screws.

That was 13 years ago. We decided to set up our own lettings and property management company, which has gone from strength to strength, leading with low fees, value and customer service. It has grown and we now manage from large, expensive houses in the likes of L17 and L18 to smaller properties right across the region. We also manage blocks, most of which we own, but we also manage for other freeholders and right to manage (RTM) companies.

As a developer, I didn't want to get involved with property management, but my hand was forced when we found the fees and repairs charged by some high-street agents to be excessive, so we started our own.

When instructing a letting agent, ensure you read the contract small print carefully – in particular, any tie-ins. In terms of fees, use your gut instinct as to what is fair and research well, as you'll see a huge disparity in fees between agents doing exactly the same job (although ironically, some charging lower fees might be doing it much better).

Don't be taken in by prestige offices in swish locations, glossy brochures or new branded cars. Remember, you are paying for this!

Tenants and neighbours

When viewing a property, I go out of my way to build a rapport with the tenants – albeit for just a few minutes – as it's incredible what you can find out. I'm a people person as it is, so it's not forced or awkward: with many of them I'm genuinely interested in what they do for a living, what football team they support and what they think of the property, are there any issues and so on.

This information about the property is invaluable: it cuts through the agent's marketing spin. You learn about the leaking roof, boilers breaking down, damp, fuse boards tripping and any antisocial behaviour in the road or street. It's amazing just how forthcoming many tenants can be on this: they're appreciative that you're taking such an interest. They might be your future tenants, and they know it.

For various reasons, such as vacant possession or the landlord not telling the occupiers they are selling, there are no tenants to glean inside information from – so the next best thing is to gently knock on neighbours' doors. (I appreciate this is not for the faint-hearted, but in all of the years I've been doing this I've not had anyone answer who was nasty or annoyed. Being 6'2" and a former soldier may help(!), but most people you come across are decent enough and actually quite happy to help.)

Warning!

I don't recommend this approach as suitable for everyone. You must be aware and conscious of your own personal security at all times, as you don't know the personal circumstances of those whose doors you may be knocking on, or who they might be expecting.

To reiterate: research is extremely important and the key to success. It's very important to undertake online due diligence, but also not to forget that there is no substitute for gaining vital information from people on the ground.

Both forms of information or intelligence combine to give a full picture of the property you intend to bid on, and as such should mitigate most of the risk as well as giving you an edge.

Buying and sourcing agents

Good, experienced and ethical property sourcing agents can save you time, bypass your limited knowledge of an area and source you a great deal, beating the competition.

Sourcing agent checklist

1. Don't pay a fee upfront – not a penny. If they're good, they will have the confidence that their property stacks up and you will complete on it.

2. You must have a contract. If you're unsure, have a solicitor look at it. The contract must state that payment will be in full on the day you complete on the property. Also, it must not be an exclusive contract: you cannot be tied to just one sourcing agent.

3. No property, no completion, no fee – do not agree to pay expenses. If they can't pay their own, move on.

4. Ask what experience they have to be a property sourcing agent. Ask to see solicitors' completion statements to prove what they are saying is true. How many properties have they bought for themselves, and how many for clients?

This is the crux of the matter, as many make claims on websites. Get them to prove it – if they can't, your due diligence has been successful. Conversely, if they can, you can move to the next stage.

5. Ask what areas they recommend, and why:

- How do they source their deals?
- Are they open market or off-market?
- Are they taking a fee from the seller?

This is also crucial, because if they are being paid by both buyer and seller, this is conflict of interest.

6. Be careful of any tie-ins with contractors or lettings and property management companies. Do your own research; don't just take the word of the property sourcer who may have a vested interest.

Property auction sourcing agents: use specialists

You don't want anyone without an extensive track record of property auctions sourcing property for you. It's normal property sourcing but 10 times more complicated, and the risks are much greater, as is the reward.

I only know personally one or two people who source properties at auction for clients and they are highly experienced, knowledgeable and live and breathe property auctions, just like myself.

It's a specialist field: you need an expert who has done it for a minimum of 10 years in all market conditions, for both themselves and clients. This is crucial. They must have experience of risking their own money. Those of us who have done so treat clients' money as if it's our own. We follow exactly the same due diligence – arguably even more stringently.

In our case, I have a pack already prepared for clients of sample properties, mainly bought by us but also a few clients, detailing:

- What we have bought and why
- Solicitors' completion statements.

Anyone walking the walk will have no problem in supplying you with this information. If they cannot or will not, move on.

Surveyors and builders

There is more about surveyors and builders in Chapter 10, but it goes without saying that they bring both local knowledge and technical expertise to the team. As with all professions and trades, go with a recommendation if you can.

Handling risk

> The central principle of investment is to go contrary to the general opinion, on the grounds that if everyone agreed about its merits, the investment is inevitably too dear and therefore unattractive.
>
> John Maynard Keynes, economist[21]

One of the great benefits of buying property at auction is that many people think it's 'very risky', so the number of competitors for the same properties is less than it should be. It's not risky if you follow the principles in this book.

During the analysis phase, when doing your own written investment appraisal, be sure to include a heading for risk. A written appraisal is good practice: it structures your analysis in a logical format and helps you make a decision based on all of the facts. It's also useful when comparing options.

Risk management

Risk management is something we do every day, whether we're crossing the road and avoiding cars, or going to the GP when we're not feeling well. We take steps to avoid being hit by a car or suffering a heart attack through managing risk and, in the latter case, by seeking professional help (Figure 8).

21 J. Stepek (2019) The Sceptical Investor: How contrarians bet against the market and win – and you can too, Harriman House.

Figure 8: Risk management

Source: Shutterstock (reproduced under licence)

Property is no different. We can manage some of the risk ourselves, and some of it has to be outsourced to professionals – our A-team (see Chapters 5 and 10).

During the due diligence phase you will:

- Identify risks
- Assess their probability of having a negative impact
- Put measures in place to mitigate and control them.

This can be through professional advice, insurance or some other measure. One risk that is difficult to control is market risk – particularly when it's catastrophic and global.

Market risk

In 2007, I developed property in Cyprus with others on a substantial level, running into tens of millions of pounds. We also land banked and had a programme of building for the next eight to 10 years. The investment story was good, with EU accession and gas and oil exploration offshore. There was a business-friendly environment where local banks, some backed by holding companies in Greece, were liberal with loans for developing and buying property.

Everything went well. Then bang, the Credit Crunch!

For those who remember the time, no one could have foreseen the severity and consequences of the collapse of Lehman Brothers and other financial institutions. The Credit Crunch was of historical proportions, and indeed that type of market risk was impossible to predict.

The fallout was global, not confined to just the UK and Cyprus. As mentioned previously, this was my generation's Wall Street Crash.

Market risk is less of a concern with auction properties already built and producing income, if you take a medium-to-long-term view. Indeed, any property investing should be viewed over many years, not just one or two. In the real examples illustrated in this book, the discount to market value achievable at auction is your hedge against market risk.

When prices face a shock, the one investment you don't want to be holding is off-plan – and that's speaking from experience.

Clearly, this isn't the case with a buy–renovate–sell strategy or land development, and as such you need to ensure that the exit – that is, the sell – is feasible at a profit.

Essential questions

You will need answers to these questions.

The property:

- Why is this property in the auction?
- Has it been in the auction before – the auction merry-go-round?
- Does the property fit my strategy?
- Is the property structurally sound?
- Are there any issues such as damp, a leaking roof?
- When can I view it?

Legal:

- Are there any issues with the title or notices on the Office Copy Entry (OCE)? (The OCE confirms ownership, title, charges, and restrictions on the property.)
- Are there any restrictive covenants that could stop my plans for the property?
- Are there any searches and if so, are there any issues?
- In the absence of searches, do I have insurance?
- Is the property in an area prone to flooding?
- If leasehold, what are the terms of the lease and are there any 'showstoppers' (i.e. anything in the lease that's a red flag and I shouldn't proceed)?
- Is there a management company?
- Is the freeholder absent?
- Does the property have planning permission?
- Does the property have building regulations certification?

Financial:

- How am I paying the deposit and fees?
- What are the auction fees and other fees stated in the Special Conditions of Sale?
- How will I pay the completion monies in 28 days or less?
- Are there any tenant arrears – if so, am I responsible for them?
- What happens to my bridging loan or mortgage product if interest rates rise sharply?

Auction:

- What is my maximum bid, and why?
- Do I understand the online or room bidding process and registration?

You'll have many more than this, but it's important to get into the habit of asking yourself pertinent questions. In the military, to get to a position where you can make quick operational decisions as a commander, you start by analysing situations on paper. At almost every turn, you ask the question: 'What if?'

This isn't a bad way to approach property and business decisions: always question what you are doing and if something were to go wrong, how you would deal with it.

Example: What if interest rates go up after I've taken out a mortgage on the auction property?

Answer: I've fixed my mortgage for five years, at an interest rate where my monthly cash flow is good.

Or:

I'm not overleveraged at 50% loan-to-value, and have run a sensitivity analysis or stress-tested increases against my cash flow. I'm well positioned to ride out any rate increases.

Success at the auction: what next?

Compliance risk

Once you complete, it's important to double-check that you have all of the compliance documentation and that it's genuine.

Ensure you have:

- A compliant gas certificate
- An Electrical Installation Condition Report (EICR)
- Confirmation that the tenancy agreements are accurate
- Confirmation whether a deposit has been lodged – this will need to be transferred to your deposit scheme

It's also best practice to:

- Visit the tenants immediately to introduce yourself
- Give them contact numbers, in case of emergency
- Ask if there are any property issues that need addressing
- Check the smoke detectors are in the correct place and working – the tenant should sign to say that you have done this.

Moreover, if your new acquisition is in a selective licensing area – note that some local authorities require you to purchase a licence to legally let your property – you will need to apply for one. Costs vary, and schemes generally last five years before you have to pay again. (It's effectively a tax, although councils and government would disagree.)

Key points

- The Intelligence Cycle provides a structure and process to follow while researching. Decide on your plan, collect information, process it, analyse it and then act (dissemination) on it.
- Subscribe to an information source that the professionals use – level the playing field.
- Use HUMINT – speak with estate and lettings agents, tenants and neighbours as you collect your information. It shouldn't all be about what you can find on the internet or via property portals.
- Use a property sourcing agent, if you find that this will work best for you. Ensure you do due diligence on them: ask to see proof and evidence of their claims.
- Thorough research reduces risk: don't go anywhere near an auction unless you have done it to an excellent standard.
- Have a risk management plan: identify, assess, control and review. Write it down so you can refer back to it.

Chapter 7
Raising Finance

You can't buy an auction property without the financial means to do it. For many people this is a stumbling block, as raising finance against the clock has many pitfalls and the stakes are high.

Under no circumstances should you enter a bid in an auction without knowing where the completion monies are coming from: it's not 'entrepreneurial' or 'brave', it's foolish – and could cost you more than just the deposit, which itself is a lot of money.

Among the other steps you must take, you need to raise finance as part of your plan.

Most books and articles about raising finance to buy property begin by recommending a good mortgage broker as a place to start. On my list they're second – not because they're second best or less important than anyone else, but because you need to know which entity is buying it before you attempt to raise finance. That's the real starting point for everyone.

Before you do anything else, talk with an accountant about the most efficient way for you to purchase the property – whether that's in one name, two names, a limited company or other entity, as this will have tax and liability implications.

Get it right at the start of your investment journey, rather than trying to fix it at a later stage.

The different types of finance

Cash

This reflects the liquidity of cash: whenever you wish to use it, it's just a case of transferring money from bank to bank. No valuations, surveys or fees (unless charged by your bank); the funds are simply there on time and in the right amount.

There are many people sitting on a lot of cash, and not necessarily older people. One of the issues presently in the UK is relatively high inflation. As mentioned previously, for many years we've been accustomed to low inflation and low interest rates, but that has changed for now. I have seen an increase in the number of new, cash-rich clients wanting to buy property as a hedge against inflation (see the example in Chapter 1).

Plan B

There may come a point when a cash buyer wants to take some funds out of the property to invest further, or for other reasons. When a property is purchased, it's imperative to do enough due diligence to ensure the property is mortgageable (for more on this, see Chapter 8).

Bridging finance

If you've ever been to a live auction, you will have seen advertising banners and staff from bridging companies working with the auction house. Bridging and auctions have been associated with each other for a long time.

As the name suggests, bridging is designed to connect the purchase with an eventual exit over a short period of time. This could be:

- An immediate flip
- An added-value flip – a refurbishment or 'problem property' fixed
- A long-term, traditional mortgage.

Either way, a bridging loan is a short-term solution and shouldn't be considered the final destination. Generally, bridging companies lend on most residential and commercial property, if the project is feasible from a risk perspective.

Bridging finance lenders set rates based on:

- The applicant's financial status
- Personal circumstances
- The amount borrowed by each person

Eligibility criteria and conditions apply, and each application is looked at on an individual basis. But beware – the rates are relatively expensive.

Bridging finance is only a means to an end, and an expensive solution to a short-term problem. It shouldn't be considered an alternative to funding a property purchase through a more competitive mortgage.

Lending rates can change, particularly in an era of rising interest rates. Loan-to-values (LTVs) change too dependent on risk, as do fees and terms and conditions.

The best route for up-to-date, professional and authorised advice is to talk with your mortgage broker, as there will be a multitude of questions to ask:

- What are the arrangement fees and interest costs?
- Are there any immediate or initial fees?
- Are there any leaving or exit fees?
- What are the minimum and maximum periods of the loan?
- What are the legal fees and valuation fees?
- Are there any hidden costs?
- How much can I borrow?
- What is the LTV?
- Are there any minimum loan sizes?
- How fast can I expect to obtain funds?
- Does the lender have restrictions on the type of property or condition?
- What is the cash amount I can expect?

Be sure to investigate the options and criteria thoroughly, because you don't want to lose your deposit – possibly more – if you fail to complete.

Tip

In terms of planning, the key question is: 'What will I receive, net of all costs?'

This determines the size of any deposit you may have to contribute.

Private finance: high net worth individuals

At Distressed Assets, we have considerable experience dealing with high net worth individuals and investment companies willing to lend on acquisitions and developments. To a large extent, the relationship is based on trust but backed by legal charges deposited at the Land Registry and mortgages on properties.

Rates of return are agreed and exit written into the agreement. This is a much more secure, speedy and reliable form of quick financing, particularly if the auction property is the first phase of developing a project which may last a number of years.

Friends and family

This is identical in terms of documentation and outcome to private finance, but allows friends and family to fund your purchase. This can be a route for many to get onto the property investment ladder, but provides legal reassurances should things not go to plan.

The legal documentation and the way it is set up are critical to make this work legally and efficiently, ensuring everyone remains on good terms.

Crowdfunding

This is a relatively new concept and, as it says on the tin, a group of investors come together on an internet platform to help fund your project. There are companies out there regulated by the Financial

Conduct Authority which have a similar business model.

Here are some pros and cons of crowdfunding (Table 3).

Table 3: Advantages and disadvantages of crowdfunding

Advantages	Disadvantages
• Crowdfunding can be a fast way to raise finance with no upfront fees • Pitching a project through the online platform can be a valuable form of marketing • Sharing your idea, you can often get feedback and expert guidance on how to improve it • Your investors can become your most loyal customers through the financing process and may be keen to continue the relationship with a new project • It's an alternative finance option if you have struggled to get bank loans or traditional funding	• It won't necessarily be an easier process to go through, compared with more traditional ways of raising finance – not all projects that apply to crowdfunding platforms get onto them • When you are on your chosen platform, you need to do a lot of work to build up interest before the project launches • If you don't reach your funding target, any finance which has been pledged is usually returned to the investors, so you'll receive nothing

Equity release

Some of our clients release equity from their homes or other assets to invest in property auctions. Usually, the interest rates are more favourable than most other forms of borrowing.

Commercial or portfolio finance

Buy-to-let investors with a number of properties, or those wishing to purchase multiple properties, can access commercial finance. There are many advantages to using commercial finance, not least that you only deal with one or two lenders – but the market is very tight.

Many mortgage brokers have good relationships with banks, and specific private commercial finance specialists can advise on the most appropriate one to approach, given the investor's needs. For example, some banks devolve lending to local areas and, within specific financial limits, decisions can be made locally without the need for extensive underwriting.

Mortgages

A mortgage is a loan to finance a property purchase, with the property acting as security. A mortgage can be secured for up to 40 years (dependent on buyer age), with most lenders requiring the borrower to be under 70 at the time of application.

Should the mortgage terms not be met by the borrower (mortgagor), the lender (mortgagee) has a right to challenge for ownership of the property through the courts – in other words, apply to repossess it.

As we've seen, many of these properties are sold at auction. Generally, there are two options with mortgages:

- Repay both the capital and interest – repayment mortgage
- Repay only the interest – interest-only mortgage. It's a good idea to organise another investment to repay the capital on this loan at the end of the term.

Interest cover ratio

Most buy-to-let mortgages are regulated by the Bank of England's Prudential Regulation Authority. Usually, the amount you can borrow is determined in part by the rental cover. In most cases, monthly rent from the property *should be at least 125% of the mortgage payment*, but note that in some cases the interest cover ratio will be higher, at 145%.

Example

Investor A wants to borrow £100,000 at 6% per annum on an interest-only basis, which requires monthly payment of £500 to the lender. The rent from the property should be at least:

£500 x 125% = £625

or

£500 x 145% = £725

Some mortgage companies also expect successful applicants to have a minimum income of at least £25,000 per annum – in some cases, you will need to provide income and expenditure details.

Mortgage broker

There are many options when looking to secure a mortgage. You can approach lenders directly, but that only gives you a narrow range of options that this particular lender is offering at that point in time. You can look through the press or on price comparison websites for the best deal, although in many cases the small print, terms or arrangement fees may not be suitable for you.

Tip

When you need professional advice on any aspect of property or business, always look for an expert in that field – whether architects, surveyors, solicitors, accountants or tax advisors.

You could read books or articles on the subject, but no amount of reading or research can give you the practical, hands-on experience that these people have gained. When searching for a mortgage, talk to a mortgage broker.

It's a truism that some people are better at some things than others, and it's no different with mortgage brokers. Personally, I became so frustrated with many aspects of the mortgage market post-Credit Crunch that I started my own financial services company to have a greater, more in-depth relationship with lenders.

In many cases, you can waste time and money approaching lenders who don't want to lend. Some products, particularly commercial finance on larger transactions, are negotiable – which can save the borrower huge sums in interest payments and fees. You don't need to start a financial services company to obtain a mortgage, but shopping around and looking for a recommendation is a sensible alternative.

A good mortgage broker knows exactly what products are available in the market, at any given time, and has access to computer systems that quickly narrow them down according to criteria such as LTV, type of deal or interest rate. Mortgage brokers also often have access to exclusive deals with better rates or lower fees than high-street offers, saving you significant amounts of money.

Once the broker has understood what you're looking to achieve, they should be able to suggest the best mortgage for your needs. Additionally, they will monitor and process your application from start to finish, freeing up your time to deal with other aspects of your life. Good brokers liaise with underwriters and solicitors, ensuring your application is on track, as well as dealing with any issues or questions, that may come up, swiftly and efficiently. Their role is your personal guide through the mortgage maze.

Mortgage broker checklist

Here are some simple questions to ask to help you find the right mortgage advisor:

- Is your company regulated?
- Is your company independent or tied to a lender?
- Can you search the entire UK mortgage market?
- Is your company independent for protection products?
- Is a fee payable and if so, when?
- Do I have to pay you a fee if my application is unsuccessful?
- Will you apply for a Decision in Principle (DIP) while I search for a buy-to-let property?
- Will you deal with the entire process and liaise with the lender?
- Will you give me regular updates?

These are not exhaustive but give you a feel for the kind of questions you should ask.

Different features and types of buy-to-let mortgage

The first decision to make is whether you want an interest-only or repayment buy-to-let mortgage.

Interest-only mortgages

As mentioned earlier, an interest-only mortgage is based on borrowing a capital sum and repaying the interest over a set period. Taking up the previous example again, if Investor A borrows £100,000 at an annual interest rate of 6%, the total payable in interest to the lender per annum would be £6,000, or £500 per month. If the term were over 25 years, the loan of £100,000 would still be owed to the lender at the end of the period.

The advantage of interest-only mortgages is that they help cash flow, as payments to the lender are less each month than a repayment product. The disadvantage is that the mortgage isn't paid down during the term, so a repayment vehicle should be used such as a stock market-related product, self-invested personal pension (SIPP), individual savings account (ISA), workplace pension or other property assets which can be sold to repay capital. In the latter case, an investor might have several buy-to-let properties with the aim of selling a percentage of their portfolio to have debt-free property holdings at the end of the mortgage term. The final option to pay off the debt is to sell the mortgaged property.

Capital repayment mortgages

With a capital repayment mortgage (also known as a capital and interest mortgage), the borrower pays off part of the capital plus interest on the outstanding amount every month. The mortgage is fully repaid at the end of the term.

Standard variable rate

The standard variable rate (SVR) isn't a product as such, but the rate on which many lenders base their deals; also the rate that you automatically get after your fixed or tracker rate is finished.

After a fixed-rate deal of say 2.99% over two years, the mortgage rate (and monthly payments) would jump to the lender's SVR, which could be 6%, a huge increase in this case. Borrowers need to be aware of this, as the shock of mortgage payments doubling overnight can have a big financial impact.

A good mortgage broker keeps in regular contact with clients as their needs and circumstances change. Additionally, they know when their current deal comes to an end and can suggest other suitable deals, perhaps with a different lender. This process is known as remortgaging.

Fixed-rate mortgage

A fixed rate does what it says on the tin: an interest rate that is fixed for a set period – usually between one and five years, but could be much longer.

The advantages of this type of mortgage are that it helps borrowers to budget and protects them against rising interest rates. The disadvantages are that when interest rates fall, the borrower doesn't benefit from lower payments. The interest rate is usually less competitive due to its cautionary nature, and at the end of the fixed period, payment could increase dramatically (as we saw in the SVR example earlier).

Tracker rate

A tracker mortgage tracks the Bank of England base (or in some cases LIBOR) rate by a margin. For example, if the Bank of England base rate is 3% and the margin is 2%, the rate that a borrower pays is 3% + 2% = 5%. As the base rate rises, the interest rate on the mortgage automatically tracks the rise.

The same is true for falling rates. In the example above, if the Bank of England's Monetary Policy Committee were to vote to raise the base rate by say 0.25%, the borrower could expect their rate to rise to 3.25% + 2% = 5.25%. The rise in the base rate is automatically passed on to the borrower.

Here, the advantage and disadvantage of this type of mortgage product is plain to see. In a rising interest rate environment, expect to pay more; as rates fall, you pay less.

Discounted rate

A discounted-rate mortgage is basically a SVR mortgage with a discount off the headline rate for the first few years. The advantages and disadvantages are similar to those of a tracker mortgage. However, moving from the discount to the full SVR can be a shock: again, this is an issue your mortgage broker should be advising you on towards the end of your current deal.

Capped rate

With a capped rate, the interest rate is prevented from going above a certain level. The advantage of this type of mortgage is that interest payments don't spiral out of control; the disadvantage is that normally they don't have as competitive a rate as other deals, so initially proving relatively expensive.

Offset mortgage

A buy-to-let offset mortgage works like any other buy-to-let mortgage, but it also allows you to offset any savings against the loan, so that you only pay interest on the balance.

For example, if you have a £200,000 buy-to-let mortgage and savings of £100,000, you would pay interest on the £100,000 offset debt only. It's important to note that while your savings are offset against your mortgage, they don't earn interest.

There are other types of mortgage product in the market and, as stated earlier, these change almost on a weekly basis. The best port of call is your trusty mortgage broker, who can give you the latest deals and discuss your requirements.

Mortgage checklist

Here are a few questions to ask yourself (and your mortgage broker) about the suitability of any mortgage product:

- Do I fully understand the difference between interest-only and repayment mortgages, and the impact on my cash flow and balance of debt?
- Am I happy that the mortgage fits my risk profile?

- Would I prefer to see a reducing balance on the mortgage over time, or be content with the cash flow and tax benefits of interest-only?
- Do I have a repayment vehicle in place such as a SIPP, savings or even an inheritance?
- Are there any extended tie-ins with a lender once the initial deal finishes?
- Have any fees been added to the mortgage, such as arrangement, booking or valuation fees?
- Do I understand exactly why I want to remortgage?
- Is my income and expenditure likely to change in the next few years?
- Am I likely to have access to a windfall in the next few years, and would I look at paying a lump sum to reduce my mortgage?

It's important to determine your objectives, whether they're consolidating debt, raising capital to purchase further investments, or getting a more competitive rate and/or cheaper monthly payments.

The mortgage process

In an inflationary and rising interest rate environment, the mortgage process can be problematic and varies from lender to lender. A good mortgage broker can help, as they apply to many different lenders for their clients, while experience tells them where the path of least resistance lies. In other words, they know which lenders want to lend, and which ones are merely keeping up appearances while effectively being closed for business.

There is no point applying for a mortgage with a lender who is looking for any excuse not to lend. This wastes everyone's time and energy, and it adds an unwanted search on your credit file (a subject we'll return to later in this chapter).

Initial enquiry

If you decide to apply for a mortgage via a mortgage broker, you will receive a 'terms of business' letter that details exactly:

- The level of service you can expect
- Whether a fee is applicable
- Who you can complain to, if necessary.

The mortgage broker then conducts a fact find consisting of these questions, which helps them provide you with the best advice:

- Date of birth
- Current residential status
- Single, married/civil partnered or cohabiting
- How long you have been at your current address
- Any dependents
- If you are on the electoral roll
- Employment status
- How long you have been with your current employer
- Employer's details: job title, gross salary and any bonuses or commissions
- Any second income – if so, how regular is that income, and should it be taken into account?
- Any foreseeable changes to your circumstances – e.g. marriage or civil partnership, redundancy, new job
- The affordability test – can you afford to pay all your monthly outgoings: mortgage, council tax, gas, electricity and water?
- If you have ever had a mortgage application refused
- Any savings plan, ISA or endowments – provide full details
- Any loans, hire purchase agreements, credit cards or store cards – provide full details
- Any overseas investments where you have foreign mortgages
- Insurance – life assurance, critical illness cover, buildings and contents insurance. (These might need to be reassessed as circumstances change – i.e. your mortgage amount has increased but your life cover hasn't, possibly making you underinsured)

- Any assets such as cars, jewellery or property – so a full picture of your financial position can be ascertained.

You will need to gather documents together to support your application, which may include:

- Passport
- Driving licence
- Utility bills
- Latest three months' bank statements
- Last three months' salary statements
- Latest P60 or three years of accounts, if self-employed
- Copies of loan or credit card agreements.

Decision in Principle

Once the mortgage advisor has done the fact find and assessed your needs around risk, affordability and available deposit, they can obtain a DIP.

This is by no means a guarantee of a mortgage; rather, indication that the lender is willing to lend, given the information supplied.

Application

At this stage, the lender looks in more detail at the application. Further details might be required from the potential borrower, which are assessed by a team of underwriters to determine suitability and risk against the lender's criteria.

Essentially, almost all lenders require the level of information produced in the fact find above.

Valuation

If the application is successful, the next stage is instruction of a valuation. If you haven't already done so at this point, you should also instruct a solicitor.

The valuation is far more important than it used to be. In previous times, some valuers would overvalue property; now, the converse is sometimes true. This is another advantage of buying at auction and securing real discounts to market value.

One of the great advantages of buying property at auction for what is in some cases substantially below-market value, is that the LTVs and other numbers stack up – even in a rising interest rate environment.

'Cheap money', which we have been used to for such a long time, is now gone. For how long, we don't know. Will it ever return? We don't know – so it becomes imperative, just from a mortgage viewpoint, never mind value, to acquire properties which have immediate equity; or once a problem is fixed or the property is renovated, rises in value.

As we've seen previously, it's even better to identify properties that are under-rented.

Case Study
Distressed Assets: Liverpool L9 – December 2022

This was a three-bedroom, terraced property in excellent condition and a good rental location. It was acquired for a client via auction in London.

The key factor with this property was that it was substantially under-rented. The rent at £450 pcm was what you would expect from a less-than-average, two-bedroom terrace. The market rent was £595–£650 – a substantial difference.

As it happens, some factors were in our favour and we bought it for £66,000: a gross yield of 11.4% at £625 pcm. The property was bought for cash, but eventually will be mortgaged. This is the standard you should be aiming for; substantially under-rented, below-market value and no renovation costs.

To seek excellent deals, look beyond local auction houses to wherever they're found. Over the years, we have bought for ourselves and clients in London, Liverpool, Manchester, Preston and Newcastle-based auctions – be sure to seek value.

Mortgage offer

The mortgage offer should come next, a copy of which will be sent through to your solicitor. The solicitor carries out all necessary searches on both the property being purchased and the applicant(s) for the mortgage. (A list of searches can be found in Chapter 8.)

Completion

At completion, the following happens:

- The mortgage is signed by all parties and is activated
- The buyer or borrower's solicitor prepares a completion statement which outlines how all monies have been disbursed
- The lettings and property management company (or yourself, if self-managed) collects the keys from the auction house or their agent, and/or makes contact with the tenants, if the property is occupied.

Credit ratings

A credit rating is an assessment of a person's reliability in meeting their financial obligations. It's an important factor in obtaining (or not, as the case may be) a mortgage. The file on which it is based details all loans, mortgages, hire purchase agreements and regularity of payments.

In general, regular payments per an agreement are good, while irregular and missed payments are bad. You can request your credit rating from any of the credit ratings firms in the UK, usually for a small fee: Experian (www.experian.co.uk) or Equifax (www.equifax.co.uk).

How to influence your credit rating

If your credit rating is poor, there are ways of improving it. Some points to consider:

- Ensure you are on the electoral roll
- Keep up payments and don't pay late or it may appear on your credit file. Missing a single payment can mean the difference between obtaining a mortgage and being refused
- Stability is good as far as your credit rating is concerned. Living at the same address for some time, owning not renting, being employed instead of self-employed are all factors which can impact your credit rating
- Pay off existing debts
- Repair any historical problems – if there is a default on your credit file, pay it. If you need to dispute it, contact the company that registered it and resolve it. The sooner you deal with these issues, the sooner your credit file will start to look healthy again
- Try and keep searches of your credit file to a minimum, as every time your file is accessed, a 'footprint' is left. If there are too many of these, it could harm your profile with a potential lender.

Key points

- A good mortgage broker will help you obtain the most appropriate mortgage product for your specific requirements.
- Understand the differences between interest-only and repayment mortgages.
- Analyse the different mortgage options according to how you see future movement in interest rates.
- Look at all options for raising a deposit for your buy-to-let investment, including releasing equity and borrowing from family and friends.
- Portfolio finance is available from mainstream banks and private banks.
- Send the documents requested by your mortgage broker or lender as quickly as possible.
- Protect your credit rating, and ensure you repair any historical issues.
- Keep searches of your credit file to a minimum.

Chapter 8
The Auction Legal Process

As we've seen, this book arms you with the tools and techniques to become successful at property auctions. Throughout, it has emphasised that taking professional advice where necessary is the sensible – and usually the most cost-effective – thing to do. Of all your advisors, none is more important than your legal representative.

There are no shortcuts to getting it right, and you should instruct a solicitor to examine the legal pack before bidding at auction.

In my case, I look at many properties before a major auction. There are auctions every month in my area of interest; more, if searched for across the country. It would be impractical, administratively cumbersome and expensive if I were to instruct a solicitor to check the legal pack of every property I look at – so I don't. I take a filtering approach (more on this in Chapter 11) and reject properties at various stages – including the legal stage – as I know what to look for after doing this for such a long time.

This chapter equips you with enough knowledge to filter out any properties where the legal pack raises a red flag. Eventually, you'll narrow down your target properties, before auction day, when you can instruct a solicitor to report on the pack. This chapter also gives you the pertinent questions to ask.

The auction legal pack

In Chapter 11 we'll look at the legal pack in the buying process, but it's such an important part of purchasing auction property that going into more depth here will pay dividends.

What can you expect to find? Many auctions just have the following documents:

- Contract of sale
- Royal Institution of Chartered Surveyors (RICS) *Common Auction Conditions*, 4th Edition (2018)
- Special Conditions of Sale
- Energy performance certificate (EPC) – note the EPC rating if buying to let, as you cannot let the property if not rated E or above. From 2028, all lets will need to be C or above. EPCs are valid for 10 years, so it may be useful to note when the current EPC expires.

Official copies of the title register and title plan. Others provide more information, to include:

- Search information – including local authority searches, drainage and water search and any other searches applicable to the location (see below)
- The property information form (TA6)
- The fittings and contents form (TA10)
- If the property is leasehold, an official copy of the lease and the leasehold information form (Leasehold Property Enquiry – LPE1) which provides detailed information about ground rent, insurance and service charges for prospective buyers[22]
- Where applicable, documentation relating to planning permissions and building controls
- For commercial properties, relevant Commercial Property Standard Enquiries forms.

Note that, if no searches are included, your solicitor can obtain 'no-search' indemnity insurance which is usually at nominal cost. However, this is often restricted to environmental matters only and offers limited protection. As much as realistically possible, you should inspect, survey, investigate and enquire about the property fully before bidding.

22 The Law Society (2023) 'Leasehold forms: LPE1 leasehold property enquiries form'. Available at: www.lawsociety.org.uk/topics/property/leasehold-forms, accessed 5 January 2026.

As stated elsewhere, the thinner the legal pack, the more due diligence you need to do – particularly with leasehold properties. Most of the terms above are defined below, but before that we'll expand on two key documents: RICS' *Common Auction Conditions* and Special Conditions of Sale.

Common Auction Conditions, 4th edition

If property auctions were a sport, the *Common Auction Conditions* would be the rules of the game. It provides a framework for how auctions are conducted throughout the UK: 'The *Common Auction Conditions* are designed for real estate auctions, to set a consistent practice across the industry.'

The document also sets out what it defines as a prudent buyer:

A prudent buyer will, before bidding for a lot at an auction:

- Take professional advice from a conveyancer and, in appropriate cases, a chartered surveyor and an accountant
- Read the conditions
- Inspect the lot
- Carry out usual searches and make usual enquiries
- Check the content of all available leases and other documents relating to the lot
- Check that what is said about the lot in the catalogue is accurate
- Have finance available for the deposit and the purchase price
- Check whether VAT registration and election is advisable.[23]

The conditions assume that the buyer has acted prudently. If you choose to buy a lot without these normal precautions, you do so at your own risk.

The prudent buyer criteria are reproduced here as they succinctly define the process you should follow. There are some things such as searches which you may find are difficult to do before exchange of contract – but

23 RICS (2018) *Common Auction Conditions*, 4th Edition, 'Important Notice', p. 1.

you should complete them during the 28 days between exchange and completion if possible, or take out ‘no-search’ insurance (which your solicitor should be able to arrange, see above and caveat in Chapter 8).

The *Common Auction Conditions* is your reference guide for property auctions. Be sure to download it and keep it as a handy reference source as you become a property auction expert.

Bouncing the bidding off the wall

Before we move on, I would just like to highlight a paragraph in the RICS 4th Edition which can answer a common auction question:

> A3.5. Where there is a reserve PRICE the SELLER may bid [or ask the auctioneer to bid] up to the reserve PRICE but may not make a bid equal to or exceeding the reserve PRICE. YOU accept that it is possible that all bids up to the reserve PRICE are bids by or on behalf of the SELLER.

When the auctioneer looks at the wall, ceiling or point, they’re bidding the price to the reserve, not a competitor.

Rent arrears

It isn’t common knowledge, even to some people who’ve been around property auctions for a while, that you might have to pay rent arrears on a property from before you owned it:

> G11. Arrears
>
> Part 1 – Current Rent
>
> G11.1 ‘Current rent’ means, in respect of each of the TENANCIES subject to which the LOT is sold, the instalment of rent and other sums payable by the tenant on the most recent rent payment date on or within four months preceding COMPLETION.

> G11.2 If on COMPLETION there are any ARREARS of current rent the BUYER must pay them, whether or not details of those ARREARS are given in the SPECIAL CONDITIONS.

In addition to the above, you must examine the Special Conditions of Sale for any further arrears which are due from the buyer.

Special Conditions of Sale

Every lot will have Special Conditions of Sale attached to it, and it's the most important document in the entire legal pack. It sets out:

- The address of the property and details of the seller's solicitors
- Land Registry title number
- Seller's name
- Any variation to the *Common Auction Conditions* – such as varying the time in which completion must take place after a Notice to Complete, from say 10 days to five, and any costs payable to the seller's solicitors. It's not uncommon to pay £300 plus VAT
- Any other costs which the buyer must pay – e.g. searches obtained by the seller and their legal fees (or a contribution towards them)
- Whether the property is tenanted or sold into vacant possession
- Any information pertinent to the sale of this specific property.

Tip

This is the key document in the legal pack. Before you take advice from your solicitor, read and digest its contents as there may be special conditions on this particular lot which are a 'showstopper' and you can move on without incurring costs.

The law

The law relating to property buying within England and Wales is very much geared towards the seller. No doubt you'll have heard the term caveat emptor ('let the buyer beware') which is pertinent in the purchase of property.

The buyer has the responsibility for checking the property and legal ownership. The seller is not required to disclose anything, but what they do disclose must be correct. For this reason, any purchase must be undertaken carefully, asking as many of the right questions as possible. It's a matter of making the right enquiries, doing the right searches and being informed of any missing information or liabilities.

That's the theory – but the reality at auction is that, in many cases, that information is scant. Yes, the seller has to be truthful, but they can leave out some of the most critical information, such as service charges, if it makes the purchase unappealing.

Warning!

A common trick with leasehold properties is not to include the lease in the auction pack. Why would some law firms do that? It doesn't take Sherlock Holmes to work out that there is a big issue.

Under no circumstances buy a leasehold property at auction without having a qualified solicitor or conveyancer reading and reporting back on the lease.

At the very least, you should check the term (length) of the lease, rent increase provisions and the clauses on disposals and forfeiture which set out under what circumstances you can sell or transfer or the lease can be brought to an end by the freeholder. In some leases these clauses can be onerous, so take care to check them carefully.

Further, investigate and ensure there is a management company in place, find out how long it has been overseeing the building and what the service charges are per annum. Then, investigate the rate at which the service charges increase year-on-year; also, what next year's budget will be if you're close to the end of the year when bidding.

There are many issues with leasehold flats in particular – not least cladding – don't be the fool on whom someone else offloads their poor investment!

Understanding the legal process

Although, traditionally, solicitors have dominated the marketplace in providing legal services, this has begun to change over the last 30 years. Law firms now recruit staff with a mixture of qualifications and experience in the property field: this can include solicitors, legal executives and licensed conveyancers, all of whom hold recognised legal qualifications and are regulated by independent bodies.

Where 'solicitors' are referred to within the context of this chapter, the title could equally be 'legal executives' and/or 'licensed conveyancers'.

Choosing your legal representative

It's essential to do your homework before appointing your legal representative, in much the same way as you would when choosing any other service or product. Don't just go with the first entry you see on the internet when running a search.

When choosing your solicitor, consider the following:

- **Recommendation** – This should be the strongest factor when choosing any service provider and is particularly valuable here. If someone you know and trust is prepared to recommend a service they've used themselves, it's likely to be good quality.
- **Availability** – When buying any property, it's always important to access your legal representative easily. With some larger firms it can be difficult to get hold of your solicitor, so it might be worth considering a smaller firm.
- **Fees** – While these are an important factor, basing your decision entirely on cost isn't advisable. If the quote is very low, it could be that quality of service might not be good. Always ensure you get a full, written quote on initial enquiry to enable you to budget and compare with any other quotes.

- **Capacity** – turnaround times are crucial for auction purchases, so make sure the firm has enough staff and time available to get the work done and everything in place before the completion deadline. Small is good, but not too small in case of unavailability due to illness, holidays, etc.

My wife is a lawyer: she has consistently said over the years to go with the right person, not necessarily the firm's name – and that it doesn't matter where they're located. She is right, and this is also true of any other advisor such as a mortgage broker.

Above all else, as mentioned previously, go with a recommendation if you can. We use a law firm many miles away and have found them to be exceptional. It isn't the first law firm we've used over the years, but the first where we can reach a partner or junior with a phone call when we need to do so.

Location is no longer a factor when instructing solicitors and mortgage brokers: it's all about quality of service.

Acting for lenders

When purchasing a property with a mortgage, bear in mind that the lender also requires a solicitor. This is often dealt with by your own lawyer, although lenders may insist on separate representation – which can lengthen timescale and increase cost.

Your solicitor is required to represent the lender's interests and comply with their terms and conditions. What may be acceptable to you, in relation to a property, might not be acceptable to your mortgage lender. As mentioned previously, during your due diligence on the property you want to bid on, make sure that it is mortgageable.

If the lender is unwilling to accept the title to the property, they can withdraw the mortgage offer. Wherever possible, it's advisable to have the mortgage offer (or at least an agreement in principle) in place before bidding if you are reliant on lender finance.

If, for example, the lender is unhappy with some aspect of the title to the property, or insists on specialist surveys before releasing funds, you might not have the mortgage money in time for completion (or worst-case scenario, not at all) – but you will still be contractually bound to buy the property on that date, regardless.

If your interests and that of your lender conflict during the transaction, your solicitor might be obliged to stop representing one or both of you.

You may be a cash buyer (many of our clients are), or you might use bridging, private or crowdfunding to purchase your auction property. But you may wish to mortgage the property and leverage it over the long term.

As mentioned previously, bridging is not designed or intended to be anything other than a stopgap.

It's worth re-emphasising here: *you must ensure the property you buy is mortgageable*. You must be able to get traditional buy-to-let finance, otherwise you'll hit a buffer. If you want to exit further down the line, resale will be difficult because you'll be limiting the market to cash buyers only.

The issue is having finance in place to meet the 28 days-or-less completion deadline – in most cases, traditional mortgage finance cannot cope with that time frame. But you may wish to use it later, which is the key point.

The main issues which can prevent you from mortgaging the property are:

- No planning permission
- No building regulations
- No freeholder (absentee)

- No management company
- No defined access
- No right of way
- A defective lease – when the terms of a lease are considered unfair by a leaseholder, the lease may be deemed defective
- Land Registry charges
- Environmental matters – particularly flooding and contamination
- Non-standard construction.

Interestingly, some of these 'problems' are also opportunities for the astute auction buyer. We have bought and fixed most of them and, at the same time, added significant value – so straight away there lies a mortgage strategy.

Buy with alternative finance, fix the problems, then mortgage at a higher value and release cash for the next deal. However, this is clearly not without risk, and may better suit the Entrepreneurial Investor discussed in Chapter 3.

Money laundering and identity fraud

To safeguard against identify fraud and money laundering, the legal profession has strict conditions to ensure that it properly identifies clients and the sources of funding they are using to purchase a property. You will be asked to provide proof of identity and evidence of where and how you are raising the cash. You also may be required to provide banking evidence.

If funds are being raised via a third party, the solicitor will need to identify them too and determine the basis on which the money is being lent to you.

How to speed up the conveyancing process

Have two forms of up-to-date photo ID ready to send to your solicitor. If you don't meet your solicitor face to face, the ID documents will need to be certified, which you can easily do at a post office for a small fee.

Have proof of your source of funds ready to send to your solicitor as soon as you instruct them. Solicitors are obliged to carry out ID and anti-money laundering checks as part of their regulatory requirements, so having these documents ready will help speed up these initial steps.

Searches

Many auction packs do not contain searches. There is a trend (certainly with the properties we target) for minimal information to be available. As you will have noted throughout this book, that suits our purpose, as it deters some buyers and reduces the competition.

Your solicitor will run searches for you after exchange of contract and before completion; but you're more likely to receive the results after you have completed.

When dealing with any property purchase, your solicitor should identify the searches relevant to the particular area where the property is situated and recommend to you the relevant ones to be carried out. If you're buying a property with the aid of a mortgage, these searches need to be carried out as a condition to lending. The searches obtain information from various official bodies, including local authorities, Environment Agency, water suppliers and Coal Authority.

There are various methods of instigating and obtaining search results: your solicitor can advise you on the most appropriate route, as the method you use can make quite a difference to the speed, efficiency and accuracy of the results. The aim of these searches is to indicate any factors which may directly affect the property.

Local authority

This search is dealt with by the local authority and provides the following information:

- Whether the road outside the property is maintained by the local council – if not, the property owner may need to contribute to maintenance and repair
- If there are any plans to change road layout
- If any planning permission or building regulation approvals have been granted at the property – and if so, if they are completed
- If the property is listed
- If the property is subject to any enforcement notices or local land charges.

Environmental

This search is done by the Environment Agency to establish whether the property is built on, or near to, contaminated land. It also states whether the property has been subject to any other adverse environmental factors: for example flooding, which may affect use of the property and insurance.

Chancel

This search checks historical records to determine whether the property is in an area with potential liability for contribution to parish church repair. Usually, your solicitor can obtain an insurance policy against this liability, if required, for a fee.

Water and drainage

This search confirms:

- Whether the property drains to a public sewer and mains water services
- The location of the drains to the property
- Whether there are any drains within the boundary of the property
- Whether the authority has given consent to build over any drains.

Other searches

Depending on where the property is situated, there might be other relevant searches including:

- Mining
- Waterways
- Railways
- Commons registration.

Title deeds and types of ownership

Within England and Wales, there are three different legal titles and two main types of property ownership. Most land is registered at HM Land Registry, but occasionally the property is unregistered.

Freehold

This means that ownership of a property is purchased outright, and doesn't come to an end unless or until you sell it.

Leasehold

Following purchase, the buyer has the right to occupy the property for a given length of time. This can be significant: typical leasehold properties are granted for 99, 125, 250 or even 999 years (the latter is, to all intents and purposes, equivalent to freehold). The leasehold property can be bought or sold by the owner during the term of the lease, although sometimes there are restrictions on this in the lease.

Various grades of registered title can exist within the freehold and leasehold categories.

Absolute title

An absolute title is the best title that the Land Registry issues, which the buyer can obtain. This means your ownership is guaranteed by the state.

Qualified title

This occurs where documents of title are missing or not provided, resulting in the Land Registry being unable to grant absolute title.

An example of this is the 'Good Leasehold' title, which can be issued when the Land Registry considers everything to be in order in relation to the lease on the property, but has been unable to clarify details relating to the original freehold title from which the lease was granted.

Good leasehold is quite common in certain areas of the country. This issue is usually covered with defective title insurance, which protects both the buyer and mortgage lender against any financial loss which may occur as a result. This type of insurance is often used in property transactions.

Possessory title

The Land Registry gives this description to the title or ownership of a property where it isn't entirely satisfied as to the seller's ownership, due to a discrepancy. This can happen if, for example, the title deeds have been lost. The Land Registry is only satisfied that the person is lawfully in possession of the property, and so grants this level of title.

If the title is then registered for more than 12 years, the seller can apply to the Land Registry to upgrade it – which is usually a relatively straightforward process. However, if the title has been registered for less time, your solicitor will advise you as to the risks of proceeding with purchase of it. (Note that indemnity insurance may be possible in this situation.)

Joint ownership

If you're buying a property jointly, there are different ways to own it that you need to consider. The most appropriate way depends on your individual circumstances. This also can have an impact on your tax position, including capital gains, income and inheritance tax. The two main ways in which property is held are joint tenants and tenants in common.

Joint tenants

Here, the property is owned in joint names: neither owner is entitled to a distinct or separate proportion; each owns the whole property. The property passes automatically to the survivor on first death, despite any provisions that may be made in a will.

Tenants in common

The property is owned in joint names, where each owner holds a specific share in the equity of the property. On first death, their share passes in accordance with the terms of their will – or in the absence of a will, on their intestacy.

This can be useful if the purchasers are contributing unequal amounts to the purchase price. Solicitors may advise buyers to sign a Declaration of Trust which sets out the proportion of the shares in which the property is held.

Limited company

A growing number of investors are using limited companies to purchase and manage property portfolios. Get advice from an accountant as to whether this is suitable, given your own circumstances.

Indemnity insurance

This chapter has made reference to indemnity insurance, specifically for issues concerning a property's title. It's also available for other legal issues, protecting you against costs from enforcement action or a third party claiming rights over the property.

Normally, indemnity policies are advised when an issue is either too costly or time-consuming to resolve during the conveyancing process. They're relatively inexpensive and provide a good hedge against risk; in some cases a mortgage company will insist on one, if required.

However, it's worth bearing in mind that indemnity policies are only an option if certain conditions are met. For example, if you have an extension with no planning permission but someone has already approached the local authority to ask them about lack of consent, you wouldn't be able to meet the conditions for an indemnity policy – they usually require that no approach has been made to the authorities.

You can indemnify against a host of legal issues, including:

- Planning permission documentation
- Building regulations not being in place, or missing paperwork
- Breach of leasehold covenants
- Chancel repair liability
- Lost title deeds
- Absence of easement – access and services
- Absent landlord
- Environmental search failed
- Japanese knotweed
- Unknown third-party rights
- Insolvency Act – previous transaction
- Lack of party wall agreement.

This is just a short list for illustration; do consult your solicitor on what you require, based on the information available in the legal pack or conveyancing process.

Auction exchange of contracts

This is the time when the buyer commits to buying the property, and the seller commits to sell it to you: when the gavel falls in the auction room, or the pop-up window online states that you are the winning bidder.

The deposit (usually 10% of the purchase price) is paid to the auction house with its auction fee.

Reminder!

Insuring the property – don't forget this. Many new auction investors either don't know or forget that the property becomes the buyer's responsibility after the gavel has fallen and they carry the risk.

The RICS *Common Auction Conditions* 4th Edition state:

> G3.1. From the CONTRACT DATE the SELLER has no obligation to insure the LOT and the BUYER bears all risks of loss or damage unless
>
> (a) the LOT is sold subject to a TENANCY that requires the SELLER to insure the LOT or
>
> (b) the SPECIAL CONDITIONS require the SELLER to insure the LOT.

Completion date: 28 days or less

The completion date is the day that the property is legally transferred to the buyer: the time frame will be clearly stated in the Special Conditions of Sale. The buyer's solicitor arranges for the money to be available for this date and the buyer, in turn, need to pay their solicitor the balance due to complete the purchase.

The buyer also pays their solicitor's fees and disbursements, which may include stamp duty, registration and search fees, among other items.

On the day of completion, the buyer's solicitor sends the balance of the purchase money (i.e. the purchase price less deposit paid) to the seller's solicitors. This payment is made via the banking system. Once the money has been received, the seller's solicitors contact the auction house to confirm that they can release the keys to the property for the buyer or agent to collect.

Usually, there is a deadline in the contract (often, 2pm) by which time all monies need to have reached the solicitors. If this doesn't happen, penalties can occur – which can be quite hefty. It's essential that the buyer ensures all payments have cleared their solicitor's bank account in good time for the completion date.

Notice to Complete

This is covered in more detail in Chapter 11. Essentially, if you don't complete within the time frame stipulated in the Special Conditions of Sale, you will be issued a Notice to Complete: this gives a 10-day deadline to complete.

Fees and disbursements

Typical fees and disbursements are as follows:

- Solicitor's fees – charged by law firms, these may differ considerably. You should ask for a written quote prior to instructing.
- Search fees – several searches should be done after exchange of contract, if they haven't been included in the legal pack.
- Survey and/or valuation fees – these depend on the type of survey done. If you're mortgaging, the lender will charge a valuation fee.
- Stamp duty – for current rates and any exemptions or reliefs, visit www.gov.uk/stamp-duty-land-tax.
- Land Registry fees – these are payable (usually via your solicitor) to register the property in your name, following completion. Again, this is based on the purchase price of the property (for the current fees, see www.gov.uk/government/organisations/land-registry).

- Apportionment of ground rent and/or service charge – when buying a leasehold property, payments for service charges and ground rent are calculated to the day of completion. If the seller has already made advance payments, you might be required to refund these.
- Hidden costs – there may be other costs, so be sure to check the Special Conditions of Sale. These could include:
    - document engrossment fees – i.e. fees for a copy of a legal document for signature by the parties
    - deed of covenant
    - indemnity insurance
    - contribution towards seller's legal fees
    - landlord's fees or management fees for consent to the transfer, if buying a leasehold property
    - rent arrears.

This is why it's always advisable to have a contingency sum factored into your budget. The amount will depend on the type and cost of the property you're buying.

Process

As mentioned previously, on the completion date, as set out in the auction legal pack, the buyer's solicitors send the money to the seller's solicitors to complete the purchase and keys are released to the buyer, or contact is made with the sitting tenants. The buyer's solicitors register the buyer as the new owner at the Land Registry, and a copy of the deeds is sent to the buyer (and their mortgage company, if applicable).

Key points

- Instruct a solicitor early: one who understands and has experience of buying property at auction. They must have the capacity to turn this transaction round quickly.

- If feasible, instruct a law firm on a recommendation. Do not rely on a random internet search.
- The location of your solicitor or legal representative is irrelevant – it's all done online these days.
- Request a quote.
- Decide how you wish to purchase the property, but take the advice of an accountant first:
    - joint tenants
    - tenants in common (equal or unequal shares)
    - limited company or personal name
- You're committed to buy at exchange of contract – as the gavel falls in the room or virtually online – and pay a 10% deposit and the auctioneer's fees.
- You're committed to complete purchase on the property according to the time frame set out in the Special Conditions of Sale. It could be 28 days or less.
- If you don't complete on time, you may be issued a Notice to Complete, incurring an additional fee.

Chapter 9
Investment Opportunities at Property Auctions

There are so many investment opportunities at property auctions that the issue you face is one of choice. Where to start? This is why it's important to work out your strategy before the auction, as this naturally eliminates the vast majority of the lots, enabling you to focus on what's relevant and most profitable for you.

The type of property you should invest in will be determined by the goals you've set yourself. A mistake that some investors often make when embarking on buy-to-let is assuming that properties are all similar in the way they perform as an investment – that more or less any one will do.

I've had auction buyers seeking a lettings and property management company ring our office after they have bought – with little, if any, due diligence – only to find that they've 'won' a dreadful property in a poor location and condition. Selection shouldn't be made solely on price, but value – which means location, size, condition and rentability.

Price and value are two very different concepts, as Warren Buffett succinctly puts it: 'Price is what you pay; value is what you get. Whether we're talking about socks or stocks, I like buying quality merchandise when it is marked down.'[24]

Let's look at the distressed asset opportunities you will typically find for sale at auction. Buffett's 'quality merchandise when it is marked down' is not a bad thought to have in mind when you're trawling the auction catalogue.

---

24 Warren Buffett (2009) 'Letter to Berkshire Hathaway shareholders'. Berkshire Hathaway, 27 February. Available at: www.berkshirehathaway.com/letters/2008ltr.pdf, accessed 5 January 2026..

Problem properties and distressed assets

As mentioned previously, many properties are sold at auction with 'problems'. The more the better, as the competition puts them in the 'too difficult' bracket. This enables you to snap up a bargain, should you be able to resolve those issues. At Distressed Assets, we have spent many years buying properties which have had problems and gone on to resolve them, enhancing their value in the process.

Properties and land are offered by all sorts of sellers:

- Private individuals
- Investment companies
- Local authorities
- Housing associations
- Utility companies
- Police proceeds of crime units
- Probate sales
- Fixed charge receivers – who sell property on behalf of mortgage providers (e.g. banks) to recover the debt after borrowers default

– and others.

They may:

- Be derelict
- Have structural problems
- Have short leases
- Have no management company
- Be missing the freeholder
- Have restrictive covenants
- Have no planning permission
- Have no building regulations certificate

– and many other problems.

As we've seen, many lots are distressed assets which may be repossessions, bankruptcies or where a seller wants to sell quickly for cash for personal reasons, or to settle a debt.

I saw a lot of this in the period following the 2020 Covid-19 lockdowns in the UK, when many people were financially challenged and liquidated assets to help their families. There were some overseas investors whose countries didn't have the generous lockdown financial help provided in the UK, who had to sell properties here to settle debts in their home countries.

This first part of this chapter shows you some of the lots you can expect to find at auction, some of the problems they will have, and the remedies to enhance value. These aren't hypothetical, but real case studies stretching over 14 years since we switched to buying investment properties solely from auctions – such were the huge differences in value with private treaty estate agent sales and the level playing field of the auction where the transaction and players are much more transparent.

The second part of the chapter looks at the types of tenancies to consider and some to avoid.

Leasehold apartments

Studios

A studio apartment in the right location is relatively easy to let and manage. Performing best in busy inner-city areas, this type of property can provide steady rental yields. Typical studio apartment tenants are young professionals, students, temporary workers and people requiring a weekday base where commuting to work isn't feasible.

However, studio apartments can have a relatively higher turnover of tenants compared with other property types, as some people choose to rent them while saving for a larger property. When choosing this type of property, it's important to target a location with high rental demand, reducing your risk of voids. Something else to bear in mind is that studios can be more difficult to finance and sell, although in the latter case location, as ever, is the key to a successful sale.

In recent years, studios have been overdeveloped across UK cities, and excessive service charges have seen lots at recent auctions selling for 50% of the original selling price or less.

I know of one development where the service charge is £2,500 per annum on a studio apartment of 25m^2. The rental value is £450 pcm, so after letting fees it nets about £400. To move into profit, the apartment would have to be let for more than six months. If there is a mortgage on the property and any voids, the sums are very different.

However, there is a strategy you can use to buy at auction for a huge discount and achieve significant uplift in capital value and income – it's called right to manage (RTM) which we'll examine later in this chapter.

One and two-bedroom apartments

Larger apartments are popular with young professionals, sharers and couples, and tend to perform best in inner-city areas where employment, transport links and amenities are good. This property type can provide strong, secure cash flow and be less susceptible to void periods. However, when choosing a one or two-bedroom apartment, it's imperative to get the location right for an advantage over the competition, such as parking space, a nice terrace or good view.

It's clear that not all apartments are equal. Some are more difficult to let, such as above a takeaway, restaurant or bar. Our experience suggests that the higher the apartment is in the building, the greater the demand – as long as there is a lift. It's likely that the leaseholders will have paid more in terms of pounds per square foot and can charge more rent, as the desirability should be greater. Apartments lower in the building, maybe with an obstructed view and less natural light, can compete on price – which many successfully do.

There are always a price and market which satisfy particular demand.

In our lettings company, our strategy is to pitch the property – any property – above the prevailing market rate. We don't seek to follow the market, but to create it. In the vast majority of cases it works, and in some cases we have smashed the ceiling on rents in a particular locality – especially where the competition is weak or there is shortage of supply. This is less easy to achieve where supply is abundant, as it is in some cities where there are many apartments with similar features.

But you can offer incentives to tenants, reassure them that you will look after them and be responsive, and as many will be from overseas: you'll be the only person they know on arrival in the UK. Many will be mature students and after referencing, including right to rent (i.e. confirmation of immigration status), a large number will be prepared to pay 12 months' rent upfront – which is always a bonus for a property owner.

As with studio apartments, the level of service charge, efficiency and fairness of the block management company are critical factors whether to purchase a leasehold apartment. Additionally, you must look at the level of ground rent and how often it's uplifted in line with inflation.

Case Study
Distressed Assets: Leigham Court Road, Streatham Hill, London SW16 – March 2009

We had been to have a look at this property in SW16, which was a two-bedroom refurbishment of a dilapidated block of flats. The property looked good and there were many people viewing it. It was very rentable, given its condition and location.

We took the view that it would sell for far above what we were prepared to bid and thought we would take a look again after the auction. We checked to see if it had sold and, to our surprise, it hadn't.

We contacted the auctioneer and purchased the property on behalf of a client for £155,000 after the auction. The guide price was £165,000. The property wasn't connected to the gas, and it took a bit of effort before it could be rented – but it immediately yielded 8.5% and was easily worth in excess of £200,000 at the time.

Note

As the property wasn't connected to gas, this placed it in the 'problem property' category. Even this relatively small task was enough to put some people off, reducing the interest in the property. Properties in that development now sell for about £450,000.

Lesson

This was purchased when the UK was in the grip of the Credit Crunch. Actual buyers were a rare species. It is times when others aren't buying that real opportunities present themselves.

At auctions, there are opportunities in all market conditions. In rising markets, falling markets and stagnant markets, you will always find a bargain at auction. But combine weak sentiment and an auction, it's a property investor's dream.

Warning!

I have mentioned this elsewhere in the book, but it's worth repeating.

Do not bid on a leasehold apartment without a solicitor reading the lease and reporting to you formally in writing. One of the tricks of the trade is not to include the lease or service charge information (indeed, the entire LPE1 document, which details information about a leasehold property) in the legal pack.

Buying a property like this without checking is not just unwise, it's foolish.

Serviced accommodation and Airbnb

There has been a growing tendency in some cities for apartment owners to rent their properties using the serviced accommodation or Airbnb model. There isn't a problem with this, and many property owners make a decent living from it.

A word of caution

Prior to auction, make sure you get a copy of the lease and understand the specific 'rules' of your property which can exclude things such as running a business from it or temporary service accommodation lets.

The fact that others are doing it doesn't mean it's officially allowed. This may have implications for you if there is an issue such as a fire, or a new freeholder and/or management company enforces the lease. The latter may occur if there are complaints from leaseholders about noise or antisocial behaviour from stag or hen parties, for example.

To reiterate: make sure you do your intelligence-gathering homework before you bid, not after!

Legislation

At the time of writing, it is being suggested that short-let properties might need a specific licence to operate, as well as planning permission in the near future. Licences are already required in London and Northern Ireland, and have been introduced in Scotland.[25] (In my view, eventually a licence will be required throughout the UK.)

This is worth bearing in mind, if you're considering this route, and should be incorporated into your due diligence.

Blocks of flats: title splits

Our main strategy over the past decade has been to buy unbroken, freehold blocks of flats. Many have been sold by housing associations raising cash, or private investors looking to downsize their investments or retire completely.

The example in Figure 9 is typical of the stock we've bought from housing associations over the years. This property is freehold, and comprises two large apartments with separate entrances. The building is well maintained with excellent external render and a

25 Scottish Government (2025) https://www.mygov.scot/short-term-let-licences 9 October, accessed 5 January 2026.

fairly new roof, uPVC double glazing and gas central heating. This is 'bread-and-butter' buy-to-let at its very best.

Figure 9: Unbroken freehold flats

Clearly, one of the attractions of blocks of flats is ease of management and economies of scale. As the freeholder – and if you manage the block yourself – you have statutory obligations for health and safety, including maintaining and testing the fire alarm every six months and emergency lights every week. You must have a fire risk assessment done by a competent person, after you purchase the block, and act on their recommendations (engaging a third-party professional risk assessor is recommended). Most are graded according to urgency, and you will be given anything from 'immediately' to six months to rectify.

Another attractive point is that you can create long leasehold interests in the individual flats, and sell them. This way, you can pay back the original purchase price and retain apartments, or sell them for a profit. Prior to June 2022, the leasehold interests – i.e. the individual leaseholds created by selling individual flats, creating ground rent – which the leaseholder must pay to the freeholder every year.

In the old days, a block of say, 10 apartments with a ground rent of £250 per apartment (£2,500 per annum) could be retained for income (rising by the retail price index (RPI) and/or consumer price index (CPI) every 10 years, for example), or sold to a specialist investor for multiples of up to 26x earnings. In this example, the capital value of the ground rent would be £65,000, but in recent times that multiple of 26 has fallen.

Although creating ground rent is no longer an option, managing a building can still earn you income if you choose to do it yourself. It's a standard practice in service charge management to include a block management fee in the annual budget.

However, in most cases freeholders will not be a block manager. They may have their own company, like we do, or outsource it. As owners of many freeholds across Merseyside and Wirral, we know that block management is something where you really do have to dot the i's and cross the t's. We're talking about people's lives here, and you don't get a second chance to put something right.

About five years ago, I was sitting in Ewood Park, the Blackburn Rovers football ground, when my phone rang. It was my property manager, who said there was a fire in a block we owned – thankfully, no one was hurt. This was on a Saturday, and on Monday morning at 9 a.m. the fire investigation officer arrived at our office to inspect the fire documentation for the building. Everything was in order, as it should be.

However, many of the blocks we have purchased over the years have had inadequate fire safety provision – and indeed many blocks we're invited to manage are the same, particularly when residents self-manage.

I cannot overstate that this is not optional. It's mandatory and carries heavy penalties if you get it wrong.

Case Study
Distressed Assets: Bootle L20 – 2016

This was a freehold block of six apartments that we bought for £140,000 in 2016. It was purchased from a housing association, which means that it met certain minimum requirements.

We needed to do some renovation works, which we did ourselves to keep costs low but quality high, and sold three apartments to pay back the initial investment, retaining three. The freehold was retained, earning £1,500 per annum, increasing by CPI every 10 years.

Lesson

A small block of flats is an excellent investment, it gives you options. If you wish to sell any, you can raise cash while retaining apartments and the freehold. You also can increase the value of apartments relatively easily, as long as the building itself is in a good condition and well located. An additional source of income can be derived from block management, giving you control over costs and standards.

Mortgage buyers

A block of flats would be an ideal purchase for someone buying with finance. You could buy for cash, or raise the money through the means discussed in Chapter 7. If it's by bridging then, after completion and any works, obtain a mortgage and operate the building. When the term of the mortgage is finished, you have the option to sell apartments to the value of the debt, retaining others debt-free.

It's food for thought.

The lease plans are below (Figure 10) to give you an idea of the configuration.

Figure 10: Lease plans

Unbroken freeholds: the hidden value

Sometimes, the owner of an unbroken block of flats doesn't necessarily see the break-up value, if it's never crossed their mind. They may be content renting the block and earning a good living doing so – but a day may come when they either have to or want to sell.

In this case, the owner wanted to sell as they had other projects ongoing which were taking their time and energy. We made an offer before auction, and it was accepted.

Case Study
Distressed Assets: Liverpool L15 – 2016

Our pre-auction offer was accepted for a freehold property in the L15 area of Liverpool, which was configured into 12 apartments and a large plot of land to the rear (Figure 11). Our intention was to create long leaseholds and sell the individual apartments. There were works necessary to bring the apartments and block up to standard, but it didn't take long.

Payback was the sale of nine apartments, the profit being the retained freehold and ground rent income, management, plot of land and three apartments. It was a good deal, and timing played a part.

Figure 11: 12 apartments and land – L15

Leasehold versus freehold: the hidden cost of leasehold apartments

Ground rent

As we've seen previously, when you purchase an apartment you buy the leasehold interest, typically 99 to 999 years, with the freehold usually retained by the developer or sold to a specialist investor.

As a consequence, the owner of a leasehold property usually pays an annual ground rent to the freeholder (for leases prior to June 2022, see below), and in most cases an annual service charge to a management company. The amount payable is different for each development and often depends on the size of the property, its location and the extent of any communal facilities or services, such as a concierge, gym or pool. This is something which many investors fail to include in pre-purchase cash flow forecasts, but it can eat into revenue and profit considerably.

Leasehold Reform (Ground Rent) Act 2022

On 30 June 2022, the Leasehold Reform (Ground Rent) Act 2022 became law. The legislation entails that ground rent cannot be more than one peppercorn per year – which, in effect, means zero. Note that this only applies to new leases. The ban also applies to retirement homes and came into force from 1 April 2023.

The following are exceptions to the Act:

- Existing leases
- Leases granted pursuant to contracts exchanged before 30 June 2022
- Business leases
- Statutory lease extensions
- Community housing leases
- Home finance plan leases.

With any leases prior to 30 June 2022, a buyer will still have to pay the annual ground rent and any uplift stated in the lease. Most leases have a provision for ground rent to be uplifted by the rate of inflation every so many years: as mentioned previously, a typical time period might be every 10 years, uplifted by RPI/CPI.

A £250 annual ground rent, created with a lease in November 2015, is uplifted to £348 in 2025.

It's worth bearing this in mind when doing your pre-auction calculations. There is a useful calculator for this on the Bank of England website.[26]

26 Bank of England (2022) 'Inflation calculator'. Available at: www.bankofengland.co.uk/monetary-policy/inflation/inflation-calculator, accessed 5 January 2026.

Service charge

The lease will contain a provision to pay a service charge to a management company to insure and maintain the building, which may cover:

- Building insurance
- Liability insurance
- Lift insurance (where applicable)
- Management fees
- Fire alarm maintenance, including weekly testing (where appropriate)
- Cleaning of communal parts
- Provision for maintenance and repairs
- Accounting fees
- Legal fees (where applicable)
- Communal electricity and/or heating charges
- Refuse collection
- Internet provision
- Reserve or contingency fund for unbudgeted spending.

The list is not exhaustive, as there may be employees such as a concierge, or facilities such as a pool and gym – but this gives you an idea of what constitutes a typical service charge.

Some management companies invoice for the total amount at the start of the accounting period in line with the provisions of the lease, while others offer a monthly or quarterly standing order. You can make a significant uplift in two scenarios when buying a leasehold property (in both situations, we have considerable experience):

- High service charge and poor management
- No management company.

High service charge and poor management: what is right to manage?

The Commonhold and Leasehold Reform Act 2002 provides leaseholders with a right to acquire the landlord's management functions. In effect, this becomes self-management, although most right to manage (RTM) companies appoint a professional management company of their choice. The key word here is 'choice' – as there is no choice before an RTM action.

RTM is only available to leaseholders of flats, not houses. The process is relatively simple: the landlord's consent isn't required, neither is a court order. There is no need for leaseholders to prove poor or expensive management by their landlord. RTM is available whether the landlord's management has been good or bad.

RTM is exercised by serving a formal notice on the landlord. After a period of time, the management transfers to the RTM company which has been set up by the leaseholders. Once the RTM has been obtained, the landlord is entitled to membership of the RTM company.

Case Study

We block manage RTM properties and organise and lead such actions.

In essence, leaseholders need a leader within their block to organise sufficient numbers (50%) and begin an RTM claim against the landlord. This can be time-consuming and not without difficulty, so many leaseholders appoint agents like ourselves to manage the action.

Once the RTM is in place via an RTM company, a management company of choice can be appointed. The management company works for the leaseholders: together they look at ways to reduce the service charge, which in many cases has been inflated by insurance commission, excessive management fees, waste, accounting and other charges.

Reducing the service charge and improving the property's cash flow can lead to an increase in the price that someone is willing to pay for it.

Lesson

If you are time-poor, instruct a company to assist you with the RTM process and organising the other leaseholders, as it will pay off handsomely. Many investors have a fixed idea of what they want as a net cash return on their investment and decide the price they'll pay for a property based on that.

The lower the costs, the higher the net return and the higher the capital value of the property, all other things being equal.

No management company

Normally, properties which don't have a management company, or where the freeholder is missing, aren't mortgageable. Generally, they're only available to cash buyers or those with private funding. The guide price reflects the issue, but in my experience, these type of properties offer exceptional value.

Case Study
Distressed Assets: Bootle L20 – 2015

This wasn't strictly an auction purchase, but acquired through a fixed charge receiver, however, it represents a problem property with a missing freeholder and no management company.

We have acquired some excellent properties over the years from receivers and administrators (a sample of which is in Chapter 13).

This property, containing two flats, was purchased for £47,000 in 2015. We applied to the Duchy of Lancaster to purchase the freehold and did so at £1,500 plus their legal fees of £1,000 plus VAT. To put this into perspective, back then the value to us of the freehold, once the leasehold interests were created, was £13,000. Not a bad return on investment, for knowing how to fix this problem, and adding significant value to the flats.

The two flats were sold in 2016 for £111,000 and the freehold retained, generating £500 per annum in ground rent, with an RPI uplift every 10 years.

Lesson

These are the types of properties which should be high on your target list, whether at auction or through receivers and administrators. (In

Chapter 13, we'll look at examples where we acquired incredible properties from developers who had gone into receivership and the companies' assets were sold.)

It isn't just during challenging economic times that properties like this and others come to market – just a question of knowing where to look.

Small and medium-sized houses: 'two-up two-down'

The workhorse of buy-to-let is the small-to-medium-size house, in particular the 'two-up two-down' terraced house often associated with the Midlands and northern England, although they are found across the entire country.

This type of property usually offers strong potential for capital and rental growth. When situated in a good rental area – for example, close to a good school or other sought-after amenities – it attracts families and working couples. In most cases, this type of property has a lower turnover of tenants, with families especially wanting longer lets, and demand in general is consistently high.

In some parts of the country like Liverpool, there is a culture of renting. Families rent in neighbouring streets and roads and, once settled, look after the properties, make a comfortable home and many stay for years – even their entire lives, providing a property owner with long-term stability.

Of the many properties we have bought and sold over the years, we have always purchased where there is a problem. As I keep pointing out in this book, the bargains go hand in hand with the problems; all you have to do is resolve the issues or get assistance to help.

Case Study
Distressed Assets: Anfield, Liverpool L4 – 2020

We purchased this large, three-bedroom end terrace for £45,000. It's a couple of minutes' walk from Liverpool FC stadium and had its issues, chiefly being an illegal, former cannabis farm. The property would sell today for more than £100,000 and is currently being converted from a standard buy-to-let on an Assured Shorthold Tenancy to an Airbnb letting.

The market at Anfield for this type of quality accommodation is strong, and although it's aimed at those attending matches during the football season, there are also off-season opportunities with pop concerts, stadium tours and other tourist-type activities.

Lesson

Don't be put off by a few holes in the walls and ceilings of a property, or its history. Some people would never buy a property like this, which for the astute property investor is a good thing, as the competition disqualifies itself. Over the years, we have purchased many former cannabis farms – all have proven to be outstanding investments (Figure 12).

Figure 12: Former cannabis farm – outstanding opportunities

Large houses

Many investors assume that the larger the house, the better the investment in terms of rental income and capital growth. This isn't always the case, so it's important to weigh up all of the options before purchasing a bigger property.

Although you can expect to attract larger families and achieve a higher rent, if there is a low level of demand for these in the area, you're likely to find sourcing tenants for this kind of property a lot harder – resulting in longer void periods, and possibly a lower annual income than you would receive from a smaller, fully let property.

There are strategies for successfully investing in larger houses and attaining strong demand and high rental yields. Choosing a large property in a popular university town attracts students and sharers, although there are both advantages and disadvantages with this type of let (which will be discussed later in this chapter).

Like every other property in this book, buy a distressed large house and the possibilities are endless.

Case Study
Distressed Assets: Liverpool L21 – May 2023

A former cannabis farm in a very good location, this was an outstanding purchase pre-auction at £96,000. The property is almost 2,000 sq. ft with four bedrooms, two bathrooms, two living rooms and a large garden (Figures 13a and 13b).

It required £16,000 in work, which we undertook for the client, and based on £112,000 total cost as a large house, yields 11.7%.

The property has scope to be converted into two apartments, an HMO or used as serviced accommodation. The buyer has many options going forward.

Figures 13a and 13b: Former cannabis farm – a fantastic purchase yielding 11.7% with further development opportunities

Case Study
Distressed Assets: House in multiple occupation conversions

We have developed these types of properties in Liverpool and Wirral over the years and converted them into HMOs with the intention of selling them to investors. It has been a successful strategy, as the demand for these investments has been strong and shows no signs of abating.

If you wish to do this, you need to consider the rules and regulations concerning both room size and ratio of bathrooms and kitchens to occupants. You also have to ensure compliance with fire regulations, which means fire doors, correct hinges and frames, closures, smoke seals and a means to detect and alert occupants to a fire.

Finally, you need an HMO licence for these types of properties. These regulations are not suggestions, neither is the licence: they're mandatory and enforced. There are unlimited fines and a criminal record for non-compliance.

It's worth noting that in HMOs, it isn't sufficient to put stand-alone, battery-operated smoke detectors on every level of the property, as done with standard Assured Shorthold Tenancy arrangements in houses. HMOs are much more of a commercial arrangement, and commercial-type fire systems may be required.

The reference source in the UK for all matters relating to fire and residential housing is the Local Authorities Coordinators of Regulatory Services (LACORS) *Housing – Fire Safety: Guidance on fire safety provisions for certain types of existing housing.*[27] Be sure to get a copy.

Don't be put off by the regulations if you want to pursue this option at auction, whether to convert and let for yourself, or to convert then sell on, both will work if you understand what the requirements are, you adhere to them and you don't go with a builder you find on the internet, but one who is recommended.

As ever, seek three quotes, but make sure you compare apples with apples by providing a detailed Schedule of Works to be costed. HMO conversions aren't expensive, no matter what anyone tells you – unless, of course, you're going for top of the range with en suites in every room.

Before doing that, carefully consider the area in which your HMO will be located, and your target market. I have seen HMOs in areas where I wouldn't buy a standard property, but where out-of-town owners have spent considerable amounts of money without any thought for the type of tenant attracted to the area. The property could be five stars with bells and whistles, but if it's in the wrong area, you won't attract professional tenants – and more than likely, simply create a headache for yourself.

There are excellent courses organised by reputable landlord organisations such as the National Residential Landlords Association.[28]

27 LACORS (2008) Housing – *Fire Safety: Guidance on fire safety provisions for certain types of existing housing.* Available at: www.cieh.org/media/1244/guidance-on-fire-safety-provisions-for-certain-types-of-existing-housing.pdf, accessed 5 January 2026.

28 National Residential Landlords Association (n.d.) 'Training academy'. Available at: www.nrla.org.uk/training-academy, accessed 5 January 2026.

Liverpool City Council has an excellent web page which I'm sure will be replicated in the city or region of interest to you. It contains the key legislative information you need to know if considering converting a house to an HMO, such as:

- HMO licence conditions
- Guidance on the standards and management of HMO properties
- LACORS fire safety guidance
- Landlords' guide to fire risk assessment in residential properties.[29]

This will save you considerable time trying to search for the information on the internet.

It's relatively straightforward to convert a property into an HMO. Figures 14a and 14b illustrate a kitchen upgrade that also increases the number of cookers and out-of-sight additional fridges and freezers, to comply with regulations.

Figure 14a: Before renovation

29 Liverpool City Council (2018) 'HMO licence guidance', 1 October Available at: https://liverpool.gov.uk/business/licences-and-permits/landlord-licensing/houses-in-multiple-occupancy/hmo-licence-guidance/ accessed 5 January 2026.

Figure 14b: After renovation

Create a development template and stick to it

Whether you're converting a property into an HMO or taking on a much larger project, use a template. It makes life much simpler, particularly if you're doing back-to-back projects over a long period of time.

We use the same kitchen designer and a standard kitchen, appliances, flooring company and flooring and bathroom fittings throughout (Figure 15). No need to reinvent the wheel!

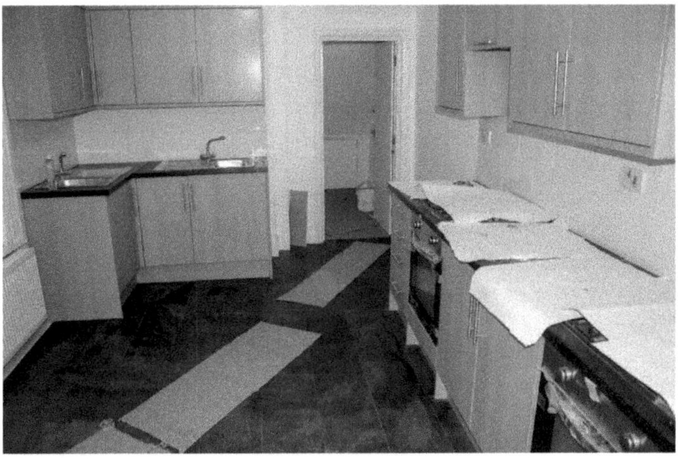

Figure 15: Kitchen in HMO

Commercial property

Commercial property is a specialist subject and beyond the scope of this book (there are many good sources of information available on the internet and in books).

At Distressed Assets, we have purchased commercial property, even accidently become shop owners after buying blocks for residential purposes. We also purchased a former bank in similar circumstances when buying residential, and obtained planning permission for flats. The bank was extremely interesting, with its reinforced heavy, submarine-like steel doors. What was more interesting is that, completely randomly, we discovered a secret basement. It was dry, clean and used to store documents – an Aladdin's cave. Even the auctioneer didn't know it existed!

Case Study
Distressed Assets: Liverpool L3 – 2009

I can offer some expertise in the commercial property world, as we purchased a five-storey office block in a prime Liverpool city centre location at a local auction during the height of the Credit Crunch.

It didn't sell at auction and we didn't bid, as I thought it wouldn't attract much interest, given the financial crisis. I was right. We negotiated with the Law of Property Act (LPA) receiver – the receiver appointed by the bank to sell the property – and acquired it for an excellent price (for more on LPA receivers, see Chapter 13).

It was a great purchase, as we took a floor for our business at the time and let the other floors. The income was excellent, and it came with underground parking. However, as an office block, it started to lose value as the tenants left one by one: some because they ceased trading, others because they were downsizing due to the recession.

Commercial property is very much at the mercy of the economy, but this also opens up opportunities for the astute auction buyer. I decided to develop the block into 25 apartments, five per floor, and sold them off-plan some years later (Figure 16).

I could write a book about this whole story, but for these purposes it illustrates that commercial property can be converted for other uses at a profit. There is always a plan B.

Figure 16: Plan B – 25 apartments in Liverpool L3

When buying blocks of flats with commercial property on the ground floor, there may be ways to enhance value through change of use. We've done it with planning permission for flats. You can either sell the commercial with planning or develop, then you have further options. Alternatively, if occupied and paying rent, you can keep the shops (as we have also done), adding a different strand to a diversified portfolio.

These change-of-use development opportunities at auction are growing: in difficult economic conditions, many shops are forced to close. Before buying specifically to develop, you should take advice from a planner on the probability of gaining planning permission for your intended use.

Figures 17 illustrate the progress when converting office to residential. It can be quite quick with a motivated team of contractors.

Figures 17: Change of use from office to residential

Ground rent portfolios

Ground rent portfolios are popular at auctions and, as the name suggests, provide an 'annual rent' to the owners that is paid by leaseholders. Terms vary according to the lease, but generally modern-day provisions allow for an uplift according to inflation. The leases we have created uplift the ground rent by CPI every 10 years.

Ground rents are very attractive, and there is a strong buyers' market in parts of London for this type of investment (as mentioned previously, prior to June 2022 these must be paid). No matter what happens, every year, you demand the ground rent in a prescribed form – and almost without fail, the money is paid. It's inflation-proof.

If it isn't paid, this is a breach of the lease and, after a few reminders, legal action can be taken. In the worst-case scenario – although extremely rare – a leaseholder can lose their property (it has happened, but it's rare). Additionally, what many leaseholders don't realise is that there is a provision in many leases to recover legal costs from the non-paying leaseholder. Suddenly that £250 debt, with reminder charges and legal fees, could stretch to more than £1,000.

This is one reason ground rent portfolios are popular. Indeed, many have additional management rights, which is a further source of income.

Other auction investment opportunities

Renovation and development opportunities are covered in Chapter 10, but there are myriad investments for sale at auction, from industrial sites and churches to car parks and garages – almost anything you can think of in the world of real estate. Some are opportunities, while others are only viable for specialists, those with considerable experience and deep pockets.

It's advisable to cut your teeth on bread-and-butter projects before looking to convert a warehouse into 200 luxury apartments with a cinema, restaurants, commercial units and a marina.

How to de-risk a property investment

Over the years, whether on operations in the army or in business afterwards, I've looked at how I can de-risk a situation – and property is no different. Put in place these three things, and you can go a good way to securing your investment and achieving peace of mind.

Buy well

By that, this means do due diligence or pay someone else to do it for you – but after you've done your due diligence on their track record. Ensure you're paying below-market value and the techniques in this book are there to assist you. You have to start with your strategy, and I commend Chapter 3 as a means to help. There is a well-known adage in property that you 'make your money when you buy, not when you sell'.

Buildings and liability insurance

Ensure that the building or house you own is fully insured for the correct rebuild valuation. The Building Cost Information Service (BCIS) online tool can help you.[30]

Additionally, check the amount you're covered for, including any liabilities. Above all, take advice from an insurance broker, don't just use comparison sites.

Rental and legal insurance

In uncertain economic times, this product is invaluable: we advise all our clients to take it out. Look carefully at the terms and conditions, but many policies will want the tenant referenced to the highest standards and offer rental cover for 12 to 18 months, depending on your provider. It also includes eviction cover.

Appoint a good managing agent

You need eyes and ears on the ground: someone who really knows what they're doing. The higher the fee doesn't necessarily mean the higher the level of competence or value. Don't pay more than 12% for management, no matter if they're giving away free chocolate bars to new clients.

Always go with an agent who is a member of the UK Association of Letting Agents, or Association of Residential Letting Agents.

Types of tenancy arrangements

There are different types of lets that you should consider when investing in buy-to-let, and each type carries its own level of risk and reward. As mentioned previously, you need to evaluate both the type of investor you are and the return you expect, while also considering the level of risk you're willing to take.

30 Building Cost Information Service (BCIS) (2025) 'Free calculator'. Available at: https://calculator.bcis.co.uk/calculator/calculator.aspx, accessed 5 January 2026.

Below is an outline of the most popular lets, and the advantages and disadvantages associated with them.

The Renters' Rights Act 2025 received Royal Assent on 27 October 2025 and applies in England. The principal reforms affecting tenancy arrangements will come into force on 1 May 2026. The Act introduces significant changes to the letting of residential property, possession procedures, and tenant rights. Landlords, investors and tenants should ensure they are familiar with the new requirements. Further details are set out in the Guide to the Renters' Rights Act (6 November 2025).[31]

At a glance highlights:

Key Legal Changes

Abolition of Section 21

- Section 21 "no-fault" eviction notices are abolished from 1 May 2026
- New tenancy structure
- Assured shorthold tenancies are replaced with assured periodic tenancies
- Fixed-term tenancies effectively end
- Tenancies operate on a rolling periodic basis from inception

Strengthened possession grounds. Landlords may still regain possession where legitimate grounds exist, including:

- Sale of the property
- Landlord or close family occupation
- Serious or persistent rent arrears
- Antisocial behaviour

Rent increase controls

- Rent increases limited to once per year
- Increases must follow a statutory notice process
- Tenants retain the right to challenge increases via tribunal

31 Guide to the Renters' Rights Act 6 November 2025. Available at: https://www.gov.uk/government/publications/guide-to-the-renters-rights-act/guide-to-the-renters-rights-act accessed 5 January 2026.

Enhanced tenant rights

- Tenants gain the right to request a pet (subject to reasonable refusal)
- Blanket bans on families with children or benefit recipients are prohibited
- Enforcement and penalties for non-compliance
- Landlord Registration & Property Portal

The Act introduces a mandatory national digital landlord database, commonly referred to as the Property Portal.

Key points:

- All landlords letting residential property in England will be required to register
- Registration will apply to both:
    - The landlord
    - Each individual rental property
- Letting or marketing a property without registration will be unlawful

Comment

There has been extensive media coverage of the Renters' Rights Act, some balanced, some less so. I would encourage landlords and investors to read the legislation in full and form their own informed view.

As a lettings and property management business operating in Liverpool, we have hands-on experience managing tenancies day to day. We are well versed in tenant relations, compliance, repairs, and risk management for both landlords and tenants. Issues such as repairs, damp, mould, and other hazards are dealt with promptly, and we operate strict tenant-referencing procedures. All tenants are underwritten with rent guarantee insurance, and if an applicant cannot meet insurer-approved referencing standards, they are not accepted.

In my view, the Renters' Rights Act should be seen as an opportunity rather than a threat. If it discourages some investors from buying at auction, that can work in favour of experienced property investors, leading to lower purchase prices and stronger rental yields for those who remain active in the market.

Standard buy-to-let

Assured Shorthold Tenancy agreements

Standard buy-to-let, usually granted as an Assured Shorthold Tenancy, is for a fixed period: typically between six and 12 months. After this fixed period has ended, the tenancy automatically becomes a rolling, statutory periodic tenancy where the landlord has the right to regain vacant possession under a Section 8 notice (Section 21 will be withdrawn),[32] or revise rents when the correct notice is given.

Standard buy-to-let is the most popular type of property investment in the UK for the private property investor. As with any form of investment, it's important as part of your risk management plan to assess both the advantages and disadvantages, then make an informed decision (Table 4).

32 HM Government (2023) 'Housing Act 1988', updated to 27 January 2025. Available at: www.legislation.gov.uk/ukpga/1988/50/contents, accessed 19 January 2025.

Table 4: Factors to consider with buy-to-let

Advantages	Disadvantages
• The tenant pays your investment costs • Tax planning can increase profits • Can buy below-market value at auction and so reduce the risk of negative equity • Can add value through development or renovation • If management is outsourced, this can be a hands-off investment • Get an insurance-backed rental guarantee which significantly reduces cash flow risk • It's a hedge against inflation • In uncertain economic times, there is no substitute for the security of bricks and mortar. This security has been centuries in the making	• A long-term investment and relatively illiquid, although can be sold quickly at auction if required • Significant time commitment, if self-managed • Bad tenants can be a headache and costly • Voids – the property may be empty, but you still have to pay the mortgage, council tax and service charges (if leasehold) • Increasing interest rates can eat into profits for those with mortgages • High service charges and possibly poor management with leasehold flats

Regulated Tenancy agreements

When you read the legal pack, if you see anything other than an Assured Shorthold Tenancy agreement, pause and take stock. The one tenancy arrangement that jumps out is the Regulated Tenancy agreement – which has both opportunities and pitfalls for property investors.

Regulated Tenancies go back to the Rent Act 1977, and apply to residential tenancies started before 15 January 1989. Regulated Tenancies provide tenants the right to live in the property for life. They usually pay a 'fair rent' set by an officer at the Valuation Office Agency. This rent is usually lower than the equivalent market rent and can only be raised every two years through application by the property owner to the Agency.

As with Assured Shorthold Tenancies, it's the owner's responsibility to maintain the structure and exterior of the property, but the internal condition of the home is the tenant's responsibility.

The auction investment strategy for this is patience. Usually, these properties where there is a sitting regulated tenant are offered at a discount, as rents are generally lower and the tenant is there for life, with possible succession rights. A regulated tenant is allowed to transfer the tenancy to a close relative, if they have lived in the property for two years before the death of the original tenant. In event of a succession, the new tenant must pay a market rent, not an artificially lower one.

This is an investment which technically may come to fruition when someone dies. This has a strange feel to it, but it is what it is, so either sell or let it at a market rent.

Assured Tenancy agreements

Assured Tenancies pre-date Assured Shorthold Tenancies and are likely to be from the period 15 January 1989 to 27 February 1997. As with Regulated Tenancies, there are some peculiarities, such as you can only evict with a Section 8 notice, and there may be the possibility of succession rights.

You will need to read any Assured Tenancy agreement in detail, and ask your solicitor to report on it prior to bidding. It's very important to know what type of tenancy the occupier has before committing, as this has implications for management of the property.

House in multiple occupation

We looked briefly at development of HMOs earlier in this chapter, but it's worth bearing in mind that this isn't just the name of a property, but also the tenancy arrangement:

> A house in multiple occupation (HMO) is a property rented out by at least three people who are not from one 'household' (for example a family) but share facilities like the bathroom and kitchen. It's sometimes called a 'house share'. If you want to rent out your property as a house in multiple occupation in England or Wales, you must contact your council to check if you need a licence.

> You must have a licence if you're renting out a large HMO in England or Wales. Your property is defined as a large HMO if all the following apply:
>
> - it is rented to 5 or more people who form more than 1 household
> - some or all tenants share toilet, bathroom or kitchen facilities
> - at least 1 tenant pays rent (or their employer pays it for them)
>
> Even if your property is smaller and rented to fewer people, you may still need a licence depending on the area. Check with your council.[33]

The HMO licence imposes tight management constraints, mainly relating to fire and electrical safety but also on the number of bathrooms, toilets and washbasins per head. As rules change and others aren't rigorously enforced, it's wise to understand exactly what the requirements are before, not after, you purchase your HMO or a property you may wish to convert to one. It's worth considering the factors in Table 5.

33 HM Government (n.d.) 'House in multiple occupation licence'. Available at: www.gov.uk/find-licences/house-in-multiple-occupation-licence, accessed 5 January 2025.

Table 5: Factors to consider with HMOs

Advantages	Disadvantages
• Can develop a large house and add value by creating an HMO • Higher yields than standard buy-to-let • Increasing demand due to demographics – you may be able to let your property to a company on a yearly or longer contract, such as Serco • Can be sold as an HMO or with planning permission to restore to a single dwelling • Voids are covered to a certain extent by other rooms, so spreading financial risk	• Requires a more hands-on approach from the landlord • Higher turnover of tenants • Obtaining finance can be more difficult • Meeting changing and tighter regulation can be costly • Some areas now have planning constraints for new HMOs – critical to know if your purchase of a property to convert into an HMO is in one of these restricted areas • Know about article 4 directions where you may have to apply for planning permission,[34] before you buy your large house for conversion to an HMO. Also, ensure any HMO you're planning to purchase is legal and has permission • During a period of high energy costs, your profits will be squeezed, if not disappear completely. Cost control and rent reviews will be required

For example, in Liverpool as of 17 June 2021, planning permission must be obtained in 11 of the city's wards for properties being converted into an HMO for three or more people. If you're looking to convert a large house to an HMO, in whatever city or town in the UK, you must know about any restrictions before you buy.

Student house in multiple occupation

There has been an explosion in the higher education sector over recent years, with more young people attending university and college than ever before. In terms of student accommodation, there are many options ranging from halls of residence and self-catering to renting a house with a group of friends, as well as the new city-based 'pod flats'.

34 An article 4 direction is a direction under Article 4 of the General Permitted Development Order, which enables the Secretary of State or local planning authority to withdraw specified permitted development rights across a defined area. Department for Levelling Up, Housing and Communities and Ministry of Housing, Communities & Local Government (2023) 'Guidance: When is permission required?' Available at: www.gov.uk/guidance/when-is-permission-required, accessed 5 January 2026.

The main advantage of student letting is that the property you buy works hard for you. Aim to find a location that's popular with students near the university or college and possibly entertainment spots, with as many bedrooms as possible and/or rooms that could convert to a bedroom. This type of property needs to be licensed and comply with HMO regulations.

Students rent rooms on an individual basis, which means the combined income can be much higher than if the property were let as a whole. Including facilities such as Wi-Fi and a television in a communal area can increase demand for your property, helping to ensure it remains fully let throughout the year.

You can expect a student let to be more management-intensive. Be sure to base your cash flow calculations on a 10 to 11-month year, with July and August usually a void period. Increasingly, landlords charge a retainer fee for the summer months of perhaps 33% of the monthly rent to help combat lost income during these periods.

For student HMOs, consider the following:

- Student population size: bigger is better
- Is the university sector growing or contracting?
- Does the university/college have a large or small supply of (competing) halls of residence?
- Are there plans to build more student accommodation, either by the university/college or a private company?
- Are rents stable, increasing or decreasing?
- What's your unique selling point – why would students rent your property rather than another?
- Have you considered renting to university/college employees, mature students or students accompanied by their families, many of whom are from overseas?

It's worth considering the factors in Table 6.

Table 6: Factors to consider with student lets

Advantages	Disadvantages
• Higher rental return through letting individual rooms • No need for expensive kitchens, bathrooms or gardens • A steady, self-renewing stream of tenants as each new academic year brings new potential clients • In cities with popular, high-achieving universities/colleges, expect good capital growth over the long term • Some overseas students will pay their rent 12 months in advance	• Competition from universities/ colleges, private companies and other landlords can be strong • Management-intensive • Letting for 10–11 months of the year • Unknown impact of changes in government policy, such as the effect of increasing tuition fees on student numbers in less popular universities/colleges

Holiday lets and Airbnb

I have considerable experience owning and managing holiday lets in the Lake District. We first bought in 1999, which has proven to be an excellent long-term investment idea (Figure 18).

It was purely by chance, as at the time I was in the army and away a lot. When I came back to Britain, I wanted somewhere peaceful and tranquil to hang out – that's literally how it started. Instead of paying huge hotel bills, I paid a mortgage and then had the idea to get other people to pay the mortgage and start a lettings business.

Then we bought another and another…

Figure 18: 365 days-a-year market in the Lake District

Many areas would be devastated without the holiday lettings business. We employ a housekeeper who looks after several properties, not just for us but others too. Gardeners, tradespeople and local shops, restaurants and pubs get business for holidaymakers who would rather have an Airbnb than a hotel room.

As economies grow and people become wealthier, there is a tendency to buy second homes at home or abroad. In England, popular areas for second homes are the Lake District, Cotswolds, Devon and Cornwall, to name just a few.

Second-home buyers should be clear from the outset what their strategy will be:

- No letting – second-home use only
- Live and let – a mixture of private use and rental
- Entirely rented – no personal use.

At the time of writing, the definition of what constitutes a holiday home for tax purposes is that the property must:

- Be in the UK and available for holiday letting on a commercial basis for at least 210 days in the tax year
- Be commercially let as furnished holiday accommodation to the public for at least 105 days in the year
- Not have individual lets exceeding 31 days
- Not be let to the same person for more than 31 days in the year.[35]

The rules on what constitutes a holiday let and the specific tax breaks available are likely to change, so do research the rules of any buy-to-let strategy at the time you begin your research. Governments change, and with them so do policies.

A good place to start for holiday let regulations and tax breaks is your accountant. As with the other examples in this chapter, it's key to consider the pros and cons (Table 7).

Table 7: Factors to consider with holiday lets

Advantages	Disadvantages
• Helps pay for your second home • High weekly rents compared with a standard buy-to-let • Some tax breaks • If bought correctly in an area in high demand, strong capital growth over the long term • Many marketing options through sites such as Airbnb, Booking.com and Vrbo.com	• Needs to be fully furnished • Requires a hands-on approach to market and let property over 52 weeks year • Can be seasonable – choose your area well • Distance away from your main residence may be an issue if something goes wrong and needs immediate attention • Can be more difficult to obtain finance than a standard buy-to-let • Government legislation in England, Wales, Scotland and Northern Ireland frequently changes, so research the latest rules before you are tempted to buy

35 HM Revenue & Customs (2022) 'Guidance: HS253 Furnished holiday lettings (2022)'. Available at: www.gov.uk/government/publications/furnished-holiday-lettings-hs253-self-assessment-helpsheet/hs253-furnished-holiday-lettings-2022, accessed 5 January 2026.

Warning!

Talk with an accountant before you buy a holiday let. Rules on council tax are changing, and owners are required to pay more than the standard council tax in parts of the UK. You may also wish to discuss incorporation and opting to pay business rates, if this makes sense for your personal circumstances and the specific property.

Key points

- Problem properties provide opportunities for the astute auction buyer seeking value.
- Ensure you have a strategy for buying properties, so it's not a random walk in the dark.
- If buying leasehold, ensure your solicitor reports on the lease. Do not under any circumstances buy without this.
- Ensure you research any constraints or increased taxes, if you're following a serviced accommodation, short-let path.
- Blocks of flats give you options, particularly to pay back investment or pay off a mortgage while retaining some completely unencumbered.
- There is nothing more important than fire safety – LACORS.
- Remember: ground rents increase over time, as do service charges.
- Right to manage is an option to remove poor management companies that might be overcharging you.
- Freehold two-up two-down houses are the workhorse of buy-to-let.
- HMO conversions – look up the legislation before you buy.
- Commercial property has many different uses.
- De-risk a property with buying well, insurance and a good managing agent.

Chapter 10
Development Opportunities at Auction

This chapter – even a library of books – on the topic of renovation and development won't make you the next big thing in property development. Instead, it points you towards the key professionals who can help and gives you an idea of some of the questions to ask. Very rarely do you come across books which actually give substance and practical advice beyond the ubiquitous 'fit a new kitchen and bathroom', as if that's the whole story about renovation, refurbishment and developing – all of which mean roughly the same thing (although I always think of 'developing' as much larger scale projects).

It's also clear that many people who offer advice on property developing have never done it to a meaningful level, which explains both the huge gaps in content and superficial advice that anyone who owns a home or rents a property could tell you.

This chapter gets into some of the detail, as property developing isn't quite as straightforward or easy as some might suggest.

TV programmes, exhibitions and magazines

There has been a proliferation over the years of TV programmes and glossy magazines depicting budding property developers tackling their projects with varying degrees of skill and success. No doubt some viewers and readers think they can turn up to an auction, buy a property, renovate and make loads of money.

Surely it's that easy? Well, it's not. Property development and refurbishment should carry a government health warning: it isn't a one-way route to a fortune, but we rarely hear about people's huge failures as it doesn't make for great TV or copy.

However, it's these failures that some of us buy at auction, sort out and then sell on.

Case Study
Distressed Assets property

I have a project which I bought at auction and banked. It's a shop and accommodation above which a 'property developer' from outside of the city purchased and converted at great expense (the specification is incredible) into three flats with no planning permission or building regulations certification.

Indeed, I understand that they used two different builders, as they felt at some stage that the first one ripped them off. Eventually, after a lot of expenses, they gave up and sold the property to me!

The land is leasehold, but we have an offer from the freeholder's agent to sell it to us for £2,900 plus their legal fees – a steal by anyone's definition. We will fix the permissions and, with the freehold, add significant value.

Lesson

This is a salutary lesson in property developing. Don't get out of your depth, and ensure you have an A-team that you can trust, reinforced with contracts and insurance.

The A-team

Your success or failure will be determined to a large extent by the team you employ. You don't want second-rate 'journeymen' (to borrow a word from boxing), but those who are fresh and on top of their game. It's better to spend a bit extra at the start of a project than a whole lot more at the end because big mistakes have been made.

In sport, the military and indeed in most walks of life, surrounding yourself with an A-team makes the difference. When you recruit the best, you have a fair-to-good chance of making a few quid, as well as not injuring or killing a contractor in the process. (As we'll see, health and safety on-site is one of the issues you have to understand and be across because, if you're not, the repercussions are severe.)

Task, team and individual

The army emphasises:

- **Task** – the actions you take to achieve a mission
- **Team** – your actions at the group level, to encourage effective teamwork and group cohesion
- **Individual** – actions that address each team member's specific needs.

Figure 19 very simply illustrates the interdependence of the three elements.

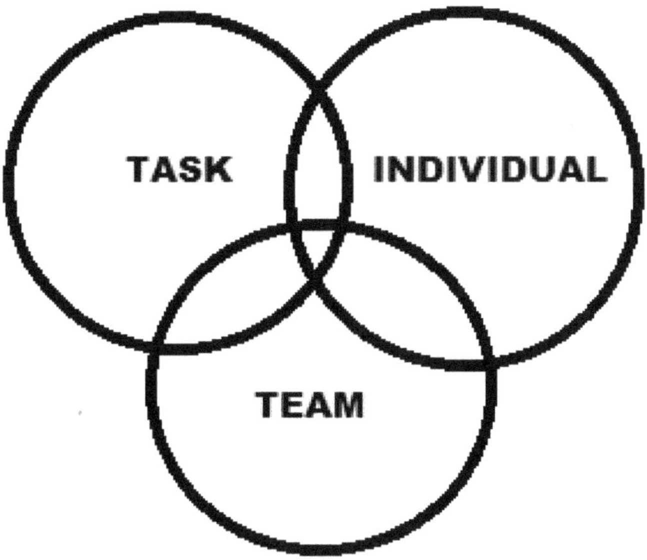

Figure 19: Task, team and individual

Of all the opportunities at auction, renovation and development require leadership and teamwork across many disciplines: every individual must be brought along and psychologically buy into the project. Indeed at times, people may need to be nurtured and encouraged, particularly if some things don't go to plan.

Key A-team members

As well as your solicitor, mortgage broker, insurance broker and accountant, you'll need some or all of the following.

Architect

The architect is the ideas person. They have considerable experience working to a client's wishes and advise on the feasibility and cost of the project you have in mind. As with all of the professions, try to go with a recommendation. If that isn't possible, research thoroughly and ask to see examples of what they've done at a similar scale to the project you're considering.

The term 'architect' is protected by the Architects Act 1997. Only qualified people registered with the Architects Registration Board can practise as architects. The same services can be provided by people who aren't architects, but they cannot use that title.

Roles performed by an architect might include:

- Carrying out feasibility studies and appraisals
- Advising on the requirement to appoint other professionals to your A-team
- Advising on buying and procuring materials
- Adding to the project brief
- Preparing the concept and detailed design
- Making planning applications
- Arranging tender documentation and their evaluation
- Checking designs prepared by third parties
- Acting as contract administrator

- Inspecting the works as necessary
- Advising on rectification of defects.[36]

This list is far from exhaustive as architects can – and often do – get involved in all aspects of design and construction. (I was fortunate to work with an outstanding architect in the past who had a passion for what he did and was always trying to improve the project with innovative suggestions for materials, as well as a sharp eye on costs.)

Planning consultant

A planning consultant is just that: someone who helps with all things to do with planning and the local authority. They also help with retrospective planning applications and the Lawful Development Certificate. Their role may include:

- Preparing and submitting planning applications
- Contributing to assessment of potential development projects
- Negotiating and nurturing relationships with the local planning authority and others
- Advise on planning appeals
- Advising on local planning policy
- Advising on issues related to transport traffic and infrastructure
- Advising on neighbourhood planning issues.[37]

Building surveyor

A building surveyor is your sergeant major, for want of a better analogy. They should be all over the project and lead with most of the issues. They coordinate, set deadlines, map out the project, hold weekly site meetings, ensure the Construction (Design and Management) Regulations 2015 are adhered to (more about this later in the chapter), and many more key roles. This is the appointment you don't want to get wrong.

---

36 Designing Buildings (2023) 'Architect'. Available at: www.designingbuildings.co.uk/wiki/Architect, accessed 5 January 2026.

37 Designing Buildings (2023) 'Planning consultant', 17 October. Available at www.designingbuildings.co.uk/wiki/Planning_consultant, accessed 5 January 2026.

The job of a building surveyor includes:

- Doing property surveys
- Producing reports and recommendations
- Pinpointing defects and advising on corrective works
- Giving advice on planned changes and enhancements
- Preparing budgets and timetables
- Advising on environmental and safety concerns
- Liaising with clients and contractors throughout the project
- Offering guidance in relation to planning and legal matters.

Quantity surveyor

To continue the military analogy, the quantity surveyor is the quartermaster, also sometimes known as a 'commercial manager'. Their role is to ensure that correct quantities are factored into the project at the correct prices. Effectively, they are the on-site or project accountant.

Where required, they:

- Advise on the project's feasibility
- Produce valuations during the project for the client to pay the contractor
- Manage the split of the project into its various elements, then contract subcontractors after tender (if required)
- Deal with contracts and legal issues
- Manage the budget.

Warning!

It's important to understand a contractor's financial muscle. If they're living hand to mouth, you don't want them anywhere near your project. You need to do as much due diligence on your contractors as you did on purchasing your project. Your quantity surveyor can help with this, and it will be established anyway during the tendering process.

Valuations are also key. On an office-to-residential conversion project I did, valuations would be every fortnight on a Friday, when everyone was paid.

As the client, you must walk around the site yourself with the main contractor and project manager or quantity surveyor, to satisfy yourself that works are being completed according to the schedule and budget.

Structural engineer

Structural engineers design, evaluate and inspect structures to ensure they're effective and stable. We have used a structural engineer on every development project, as their expertise is invaluable.

They:

- Run and provide calculations
- Advise on what's required to ensure the construction is safe
- Advise on necessary compliance with building control requirements.

On a smaller scale, you will use a structural engineer if you're building an extension or knocking down any walls to open up a space. They assess the structural situation and integrity of the building, and the steel reinforcement required to ensure it doesn't fall down. (Incidentally, I've helped contractors in the past with fixing steel in place. Unless you've arms like Arnold Schwarzenegger, pass on it!)

These engineers take on many other roles, including:

- Demolition assessment
- Foundations safety assessment
- Walls assessment
- Risk assessments
- Site appraisals.

They're a key component of any development or refurbishment project.

Contractor and/or builder

Depending on the size of your project, you might put your contract out to tender. Your project manager or building surveyor can do this for you and provide the specification to several companies. Some will respond, while some won't, depending on their workload, size of projects and companies they feel comfortable with taking on.

The range in quotes can be quite large, so careful analysis and advice are crucial at this point, as well as assessing the contractor's track record and financial standing. Cheap as well as expensive are different sides of the same coin – both are not necessarily what you require.

In-house team

For a long period, I had my own in-house construction team that went from project to project. They would finish a project on a Friday and start another on Monday. (The examples in this book under case studies are only a fraction of what I've done over the years. As you gain more experience and the projects become more complex or frequent, this is something for you to consider.)

Building control

National building standards were only introduced in the UK in 1965, which may surprise you. Now known as building regulations, they state:

- What qualifies as 'building work', and so falls under the remit of the regulations
- What types of buildings are exempt
- Reporting procedures that must be followed at all stages of construction work
- Requirements for specific elements of building design and construction.

Building regulations require a project's compliance to be independently validated. This includes new buildings, modifications, installations and extensions.

Building control are the police of property development. They take the architect's plans and provide written guidelines on what you must do to ensure that construction meets the current regulations, and normally, they are very helpful people who know their profession well. You deal with them at the start of the project: they visit site throughout to ensure everything is going to plan (from a building control perspective).

You can either use the local authority building control team, or a private sector company. (I have used the latter, as I've found them easier to speak with on the phone. They appear to be more available, at least in my case.)

Warning!

We have bought (also you see in newspapers) developments, houses and garage conversions which have not had building regulations certification.

- If someone undertaking building work breaches building regulations, the local authority can prosecute them. An unlimited fine can be levied (sections 35 and 35A of the Building Act 1984). Prosecution is permissible for up to two years after works have been completed.
- The local authority can also serve an enforcement notice on the property owner, requiring alteration or removal of work which breaches the regulations (section 36 of the 1984 Act). If the owner doesn't abide by the notice, the local authority has the power to do the work themselves and recover costs.[38]

Acoustic consultants

These are not sound engineers who ensure that building site ghetto blasters are set to maximum! They're professionals who advise on meeting current sound transmission requirements within a building. Sound insulation testing assesses the performance of party elements: i.e. separating walls and floors between residential dwellings.

There are two categories of sound insulation testing:

- **Airborne** – this assesses the performance of separating wall and floor elements due to noise transmitted through the air, e.g. conversations between people or television noise.

38 HM Government (2022) 'Building Act 1984'. Available at: www.legislation.gov.uk/ukpga/1984/55, accessed 5 January 2026.

- **Impact** – this assesses the performance of separating floors due to noise transmitted through impact, e.g. footsteps on the floor above.

Acoustic engineers advise on the materials to use to pass these tests. Note that this is a building regulations requirement – you will not get final sign-off without it.

The 10 stages of property development and renovation

This isn't a recognised '10 principles of…', rather, my interpretation based on experience. Other lists and sequences exist elsewhere that are valid.

1. Selecting property from auction
2. Market analysis and feasibility study
3. Professional advice
4. Set maximum bid at auction based on the outcome of Stage 3
5. Appoint the A-team if successful at auction, after completion
6. Design and planning application, or go to the next phase of building regulations if planning is in place and no alterations are required
7. Tendering and contracting
8. Construction
9. Snagging (i.e. checking and rectifying minor faults after building work), building control and sign-off
10. Sales (if not off-plan) or lettings and property management.

We won't go through all the stages in sequence here; instead, just highlight some of the critical areas. (Remember, this short chapter won't make you the next rock star property developer, but it arms you with insight and questions to ask your A-team!)

Before we start, let's look at land development.

Land development

Of all the development projects open to you, this is actually the simplest. I can assure you, from developing derelicts or near-derelicts, with land development there shouldn't be many unknowns. Whether you would want to cut your teeth on a large project is questionable, but smaller projects such as a house or two are well within the competence of a new property developer with excellent advisors.

You have to start somewhere – and with your A-team supporting you, it shouldn't be too onerous.

Warning!

If you go back to Stage 2 of property development, market analysis and feasibility study, then at the beginning you will have assessed the project's viability in terms of sales value and construction cost. This is where an appreciation for the wider economy is important for property developers and investors.

As we've seen previously, in a falling property market and a high level of general inflation and construction inflation, your property development project may not be feasible, even only after a few months in the planning. In a rising market situation with controlled inflation, the outlook is very different.

Remember: your project does not sit in isolation from the wider market and economy.

Developers usually use this type of 'rough-and-ready' calculation when appraising a potential project:

Sales Value – Cost of Construction + Land = Profit

You will commonly hear and read the term 'Gross Development Value' (GDV). The GDV of a development project is an estimate of the open market capital value or rental value the development is likely to have, once it's complete.

Residual method of appraisal

The residual method of valuation is a development appraisal that incorporates the GDV calculation. There are a couple of ways of using it.

Method 1:

Land = GDV – (Construction + Fees + Profit)

Where Land = Purchase price of land or property, Construction = construction costs, Fees = Fees and other transaction costs, and Profit = Required profit.

Method 2:

Calculating Property Developers' Profit

Another way to use the residual appraisal is to reconfigure the equation to calculate the property developer's profit:

Profit = GDV – (Construction + Fees + Land)

Case Study
Distressed Assets: Liverpool L6 – 2013

We purchased a fire-damaged, four-bedroom house for £55,000 after auction, as it didn't sell, being another property in the 'too difficult' bracket for property investors. It was in a very lettable road, a few yards from one of the main arterial routes into Liverpool city centre, with frequent public transport.

We spent about £31,698 converting it into a six-bedroom HMO with an additional bathroom and double kitchen. We also dealt with the fire damage in the budget and other general improvements. In the same year we sold it for £156,000.

Lesson

The lesson is repeated in all of the real-world examples throughout this book. Always ask yourself: 'How can I add value, rectifying issues in properties many investors will not buy?'

Further, ensure that the property you buy to convert to an HMO is in a permitted development zone, or investigate the probability or otherwise of obtaining planning permission. The photo of the property, pre-development, is below (Figure 20). From the outside it looked OK, but clearly the fire damage inside and at the back of the property put a lot of potential bidders off.

I didn't think 'fire damage'. I thought 'opportunity'.

Figure 20: A fire-damaged house is an opportunity

Project spreadsheet

One of the first things you should do before setting off on your property development journey is to create a spreadsheet which can focus your thoughts on costs and sales. Use this as a basis to populate a much bigger, more comprehensive spreadsheet bespoke to your requirements.

Table 8 provides a breakdown for an idea of what's entailed in a small development project, many of which you will still find in auctions today. You can adapt and amend it for your own circumstances: for example, you might have an inclusive contract price where some of the headings aren't relevant.

Table 8: Sample project spreadsheet

		Costs	Sales	Remarks
Property	Purchase price			
	Freehold purchase			
	Rent arrears where applicable			
	Stamp duty			
	Property insurance			
	Indemnity insurance			
	Commuted sum[39]			
	Survey			
Professional fees	Architect's fees			
	Planning application fee			
	Building regulations			
	Project manager			
	Building control			
	Acoustic engineer			
	Acoustic engineer certification			
	Structural engineer			
	Specialist advice (damp, etc.)			

39 A commuted sum is a contribution in lieu of affordable housing agreed between the developer and the local authority.

	Construction, Design and Management coordinator			
	Building surveyor (Health & Safety)			
	New energy performance certificates (EPCs)			
Legal fees	Buying			
	Selling			
	Creation of new leases			
Auction fees	Auction fees, including Special Conditions of Sale			
Finance costs	Valuation fee			
	Arrangement fee			
	Interest			
Refurbishment				
External	Windows and external doors			
	Bike storage			
	New timber fence			
	New/repair wall			
	Drains			
	Render/brickwork			
	Damp-proof course			
	Waste and water drainage			
	Driveway			
	Front gate			
	Metal staircase			
	TV aerial/satellite dish			
	General repairs			
	Scaffolding			
	Loft insulation			
	Fascia, soffit, gutters, etc.			
	Painting			

Heating	Gas central heating, including boilers			
	Night storage electrical heating			
	Water pumps			
Electrical	Rewire			
	New consumer unit			
	Sockets			
	Switches			
	Certification, including Electrical Installation Condition Report (EICR)			
	CCTV/intruder alarms			
	Access control			
Fire safety	Fire risk assessment			
	Fire alarm panel system or interlinked smoke/ heat detectors where applicable			
	Fire doors			
	Fire-resistant door frames			
	Closures, smoke seals and signage			
	Fire doors fitting			
	Automatic opening vents			
	Emergency lights			
	60-minute fire-rated cupboards, housing meters and supply			
	Signage			
Bathrooms	New suite			
	Mixers, taps, general			
	Basin and toilet package only			
	Wall and floor tiles			
	Compliant lighting			
	Mechanical extraction			

Kitchen	New kitchen			
	Replace work surfaces and doors of old kitchen			
	Integrated hood, oven and cooker			
	Mechanical extraction			
	Flooring			
	Lighting			
	Taps			
	Mechanical waste			
	Compliant lighting			
Labour				
Internal	Blinds			
	Carpets			
	Flooring in general, laminate/wood			
	Plastering			
Miscellaneous	Welfare container/office			
	Waste removal (skips)			
	dB matting (for underfloor noise reduction)			
	Insulation			
	Other building materials			
	Selective licensing			
	HMO licence			
	Total			
Utilities				
	Electricity			
	Gas			
	Water			
	Internet			
	Sales value			
	Total costs			
		Profit		**Margin**
		Freehold value		
		TOTAL VALUE		

Essential issues

Here are some issues you must think about and take appropriate professional advice on before you start.

Construction (Design and Management) Regulations 2015

The Construction (Design and Management) Regulations 2015 (CDM) are the main set of regulations for managing the health, safety and welfare of construction projects. CDM applies to all building and construction work, including new build, demolition, refurbishment, extensions, conversions, repair and maintenance.[40]

A commercial client is an organisation or individual for whom a construction project is carried out in connection with a business, whether the business operates for profit or not. Examples of commercial clients are schools, retailers and landlords. The client must make suitable arrangements for managing a project.

This includes ensuring that:

- Other duty holders, such as designers and contractors, are appointed
- Sufficient time and resources are allocated
- Relevant information is prepared and provided to other duty holders
- The principal designer and principal contractor carry out their duties
- Welfare facilities are provided.[41]

On projects which are derelicts or near-derelicts, you need to factor into your costings welfare facilities, including running hot water, toilet facilities and somewhere for site staff to have a break.

40 HM Government (n.d.) 'The Construction (Design and Management) Regulations 2015'. Available at: www.legislation.gov.uk/uksi/2015/51/contents/made, accessed 5 January 2026.

41 HM Government, Construction (Design and Management) Regulations 2015.

There are well-known companies which can literally drop a welfare container, or office, on your site which covers the key requirements of CDM welfare. Figure 21 shows one of our sites to give you an idea of the size of the thing. It does take up a bit of space, particularly if you double up on the containers.

Figure 21: On-site welfare facilities

Speak with your A-team about your responsibilities as a client and their responsibilities as principal contractor and principal designer. There is a lot of health and safety compliance to meet in property development and refurbishment – ignore it at your peril.

Contracts

Depending on the project, you will have either a Design and Build, or Standard Form contract (Joint Contracts Tribunal, JCT); I've used both.

The Design and Build contract gives the entire project to a single entity and says 'build that', so they take it from conception to completion (I did an office-to-residential project in this way). Alternatively, you might decide to use an architect for the design phase before tendering out and contracting with another party.

No matter what the size of your project, you must have a contract in place. My wife is a lawyer: she says verbal contracts mean nothing when things go wrong and a situation has to go to arbitration, dispute resolution or court.

Stage payments (valuations)

On larger projects, the contract determines when the first payment is made and the frequency. It also has a retention rate, which is the percentage you retain until all work has been done satisfactorily. Progression of the work is 'valued' and expressed in terms of the percentage of the overall work until completion.

For example, after Valuation 1 you might see 20% of the electrical works completed, and eventually after, say Valuation 10, 100% complete. You pay as you go: it isn't a foolproof system, but it's not bad.

Schedule of Works

On smaller projects, do not pay your contractor in advance. You must use a system similar to the one outlined earlier for larger projects: be sure to pay as you see results. Have your builder/contractor break down the costs in a Schedule of Works according to headings, such as electrical, plumbing, etc., and detail what you're getting for your money. You can then work out what you'll need to pay them as the work progresses.

Clearly this will be a discussion, but if the contractor requests large payments in advance of work, you've instructed the wrong one. If your project warrants it in terms of scale, it would be wise to appoint a professional project manager.

Contingency fund

Contingency can be defined as a future event or circumstance that's possible, but can't be predicted with certainty. As we've seen previously, you should always earmark funds for issues and problems which can arise on a renovation project, be it a large or a small development.

Examples include:

- Changes in interest rates, and so the cost of funding the project
- Structural issues – for example, we had a wall collapse because there were no foundations, and had to build a two-bedroom bungalow from scratch
- Legal disputes – e.g. party wall issues, boundaries and contract disputes with the contractor
- Corruption and theft
- Change of plan, or if the estimates are wrong.

I can't emphasise enough that even for the smallest project, you must consider professional security including steel entrance doors, steel sheets on windows and a portable alarm system with a response facility. (We use a system where the security company can see any intruders and talk to them. We have never had a breach of security while using these systems.)

For comfort, earmark 25% of the build costs to contingency. You may wish to be lower or even higher but, as ever, be sure to have a plan B.

Insurance

By insurance, I don't mean accessing a comparison site on the internet and buying a generic policy for the works and risks you're taking on. Instead, talk with a qualified and recommended insurance broker who specialises in construction. (We've had the same insurance broker based in London for many years, who understands what we do and need.)

Make sure that you, and the team who work for you, are fully covered.

Permitted development rights

Permitted development rights allow the improvement or extension of homes without the need to apply for planning permission, where that would be out of proportion with the impact of the works carried out.[42]

42 Department for Levelling Up, Housing and Communities and Ministry of Housing, Communities & Local Government (2019) 'Permitted development rights for householders: Technical guidance'. Available at: www.gov.uk/government/publications/permitted-development-rights-for-householders-technical-guidance, accessed 5 January 2026.

What is and isn't allowed should be studied in detail. Just to whet your appetite, here are a few examples to consider when flicking through auction lots and wondering how to add value and make a profit.

Extension to the rear:

- Must not extend beyond the rear wall of the existing house by 3m if attached, or by 4m if detached
- Uses similar building materials to the existing house
- Takes up less than 50% of the size of the land around the original house
- Is less than 4m in height (or less than 3m, if within 2m of a property boundary)
- Has eaves and a ridge that are no taller than the existing house.

Extension to the side:

- Covers less than 50% of the size of the land around the original house
- Uses similar building materials to the existing house
- Takes up less than 50% of the width of the original house
- Is less than 4m in height (or less than 3m, if within 2m of a property boundary)
- Has eaves and a ridge that are no taller than the existing house.

Two-storey extension:

- No windows in wall or roof slope of side elevation in additional storeys
- Takes up less than 50% of the width of the original house
- Takes up less than 50% of the size of the land around the original house
- Uses similar building materials to the existing house
- Has eaves and a ridge that are no taller than the existing house
- Terraces to be no more than 3.5m higher than the next tallest terrace.

Loft conversion:

- A volume allowance of $50m^3$ additional roof space for detached and semi-detached houses
- Uses similar building materials to the existing house
- The development must not include a window in any wall or roof slope forming a side elevation of the dwelling house
- The roof pitch of the principal part of the dwelling must be the same as the roof pitch of the existing house
- Has windows that are non-opening if less than 1.7m from the floor level.[43]

The government's joint venture Planning Portal (www.planningportal.co.uk) has a helpful interactive tool that allows you to quickly find out which project might be allowed under permitted development rights, or would require planning permission.

Warning!

As with any development and construction, be sure to take professional advice. Permitted development doesn't mean you can put anything up: you still need a quality contractor, and to adhere to all the points made here.

You also need to comply with:

- Building regulations
- Party wall legislation
- Right to light, and many others.

Having said that, as a property developer you are looking for opportunities at auction, and this might be an area of interest to you. You may even decide to specialise in these types of developments.

---

43 Department for Levelling Up, Housing and Communities and Ministry of Housing, Communities & Local Government, 'Permitted development rights for householders: Technical guidance'.

Auction opportunities

As we've seen previously, excellent development opportunities are available at auction and for sale for various reasons such as bankruptcy, no contingency fund for when plan A ran into trouble, or the new, amateur developer just had enough. Indeed, some developments don't even get off the ground, and these end up at the auction too. There are two types of property and/or land: within date, current planning permission and without planning permission.

Properties and/or land within date, current planning permission

These properties can be lucrative but carry differing amounts of risk. Property and land with planning is a straightforward calculation of build costs and an analysis of both the rental and letting markets, depending on your strategy.

For this type of development, you'll need to ensure that planning permission doesn't expire before you start the project – if so, consult a planning professional for advice. In many cases, planning permission can be extended.

Case Study
Distressed Assets: Wirral – 2015

This was a freehold, residential redevelopment opportunity with planning permission for change of use from a residential care home to 13 apartments. The lot comprised a large, detached, double-fronted former care home arranged over the ground, first and second floors, together with a lift and gardens (Figure 22).

We took the plans, looked over them with our architect and made some changes. It was a reasonably large project requiring extensive changes internally, and the structural engineer made some excellent suggestions. There were no utilities for the site, so to comply with CDM requirements, we hired office and welfare containers form a well-known national supplier. It was a great base to hold meetings and get a hot cup of tea on a cold day.

As we've seen previously, it's key to have an A-team you can trust. We did the construction work as we had a full-time team, and hired in the relevant trades and professionals. I also appointed a building surveyor (RICS) project manager, who was invaluable.

Again, these projects are not without issues: we found ourselves having to rebuild part of the property from scratch, as the foundations were non-existent.

We also had to revert to plan B and construct a new build from the slab upwards. Today it's a very fine, adapted bungalow providing a long-term home for a wonderful tenant.

Lesson

Converting a near-derelict property into 13 apartments is not without risk. But doing the initial planning, sourcing materials and understanding the constraints imposed by the utility supply were the key success factors.

We sold the entire development off-plan prior to commencement of works, which also gave us an exit.

Figure 22: Near-derelict to 13 apartments

Properties and/or land without planning permission

Purchasing land or a property without planning carries additional risk to the other option. What if permission is refused?

It's important to take professional advice on the probability or otherwise of obtaining planning permission in a particular local authority area. Buying this type of lot at auction is at the higher end of the risk spectrum, and anyone other than a seasoned professional should avoid it.

Case Study
Distressed Assets: Liverpool L13 – 2014

There are some projects as a developer that I have enjoyed, and others I haven't. This project in L13 falls into the former category and was a property we bought at auction configured into three apartments. It was in a bit of a state internally, but generally the exterior was fine, the basement dry and we knew the road well, having another block across the road.

We applied for planning for eight apartments, which was refused. We then resubmitted for six apartments, which was accepted. We did the construction ourselves and hired in our A-team.

It was a very successful project: there was definitely a feel-good factor about bringing the building back into use.

Security

I've referred to security in this book, and Figure 23a illustrates this well. We use a professional security company and, on exchange of contract, have the building secured with the owner's permission. If this isn't forthcoming, although it has never happened, we do it on completion. We also have a mobile alarm system with a response team.

You may find that the property is already 'tinned', so you can take over the contract from the seller.

It's prudent and good for insurance purposes to do this (some insurers insist on it). A tinned property isn't necessarily a sign that the area is a 'war zone'; rather, of a professional team that knows what they're doing. To date, we have had smooth running sites with no losses.

Figures 23a and 23b illustrate the point. Once developed, with good, integrated security, the tins can be removed.

Figure 23a: A secure, tinned property

Figure 23b: Completed project

A remedy to no planning permission: Lawful Development Certificate

We have bought a number of these types of properties over the years, and there are still a lot of them out there. Essentially, they are flat conversions which have no planning permission or building regulations.

The four-year rule: note the changes

The four-year rule (i.e. four years of continuous property use) is often used to legitimise properties where a council has failed to enforce planning regulations. By providing evidence, such as council tax bills and utility statements that the property has been in continuous use, the council, via a Lawful Development Certificate, must confirm the dwelling is deemed to have planning permission.[44]

On 11 May 2022, the government introduced the Levelling Up and Regeneration Bill to Parliament. It announced that the four-year rule would be phased out, with a time period of 10 years for all such planning exemptions.[45]

Case Study
Distressed Assets: Liverpool L9 – 2012

This was an exceptional purchase during the Credit Crunch from an auction house in London. It was a freehold house divided into two large apartments that didn't have planning permission or building regulations. In addition, it was a former cannabis farm, so all in all, that put everyone off.

I was the only bidder and bought the entire lot for just £20,000.

We used a planning consultant, and the four-year rule, and legitimised the situation.

44 Department for Levelling Up, Housing and Communities and Ministry of Housing, Communities & Local Government (2014) 'Guidance: Enforcement and post-permission matters'. Available at: www.gov.uk/guidance/ensuring-effective-enforcement, accessed 5 January 2026.

45 Department for Levelling Up, Housing and Communities (2022) 'Levelling Up and Regeneration Bill', 5 July. Available at: www.gov.uk/government/collections/levelling-up-and-regeneration-bill, accessed 5 January 2026.

Property and land banking

Many years ago, I land banked on a large scale, only to be 'Credit Crunched'. This hasn't put me off, but now I bank properties for future development. Currently, I have a number of projects banked and scheduled to start shortly: some we purchased before the lockdowns of 2020 with a view to developing them before now, but the world changed and those developments are still in the bank.

You will see from this case study why we aren't in a hurry.

Case Study
Distressed Assets: Wallasey CH44 – 2018

New clients are always interested in what we've done over the years and, as stated elsewhere in this book, ask property sourcing agents for evidence of what they've done for themselves and for clients. As mentioned previously, the only evidence I accept are solicitors' completion statements: once you have those, you can do your own due diligence on them.

In our case, I have a spreadsheet of a sample of deals we've done over the years – some of which are reproduced in this book, while others are not. With the numbers and prose, I send solicitors' completion statements, as some of the deals border on the unbelievable. That is why I do it.

Here's one such example.

This project was a freehold block of a studio apartment and a three-storey, four-bedroom maisonette with a small outside space on a popular road with shops and amenities. It didn't sell at auction, and I didn't have it on a list. But as I always do, I looked on the internet at what didn't sell and booked a viewing the next day. Outside of the 24-hours' notice period, the tenants were very helpful. They're still there to this day, which is one reason we have yet to develop it – they're nice people, great tenants, and we can wait.

What's the big deal? We bought it after auction below the guide price, and some way below the reserve. The owner wanted out and wasn't prepared to wait. Remember: a lot of sellers at auction have psychologically spent the proceeds of the sale. They have it in their heads that the cash is forthcoming and, when it's not, some may have mixed emotions.

In 2018, we bought the entire lot for just £45,000 – that's not a typo! I could see how we could add value immediately. The property was in a reasonable condition, the tenants were happy and the rent was £10,200 per annum. As we managed it ourselves and it was freehold, the gross yield was a 23% on the purchase price. The net was just minus the insurance and two gas certificates a year. Even since then, there have been very few repairs (Figure 24).

Once the tenants in the larger property decide to move on – and there is no sign of that yet – we'll convert it into a six-bedroom HMO and keep the studio as is.

Once we do that, the numbers will be off the scale.

Lesson

The fact that a property doesn't sell at auction doesn't necessarily mean it's a bad property, or there is something wrong with it. It could be the time of the year. Just before Christmas and the summer holiday season can be slow for some regional auction houses. It can also be that no one else spotted the opportunity – you would be surprised how often that happens.

Keep your eye on properties which don't sell at auction and, if they tick your boxes, move quickly to exchange contracts and pay the deposit. That's the only way you'll be sure to get it.

Completion Statement (Buyer)

Relating to the Sale of
Wallasey, CH44

Monies received :

Sale price of the property	£	45,000.00
Add		
Buyers Contributions to sellers legal fees	£	660.00
Searches	£	201.00
Land Registry Official Copy Entries	£	21.00
Sub-total gross price and additions	£	45,882.00
Deduct		
Deposit paid on exchange	£	4,500.00
Balance required	£	41,382.00

Figure 24: Completion statement

Risk management

Hopefully, this chapter will have quashed any idea that property developing at whatever scale is a walk in the park or a route to untold wealth and happiness. Many in the media don't address the pitfalls and the 'What ifs?'

Risk management – whether health and safety, financial, the original due diligence when purchasing the property or land – must be the number one priority. Without it, you're effectively driving a car blindfolded at 70mph on a motorway. Approach property developing in a serious, businesslike manner, with a professional team supporting you, then whatever level you are at now, you'll be a huge success.

As Lao Tzu said: 'The journey of a thousand miles begins with a single step.'

Key points

- Don't underestimate the challenges of property development. You tend to see the huge successes in the media – not the many howlers that astute developers buy to sort out, and then sell on or keep.
- Appoint an A-team of advisors. Go for the best, as also-rans will only give you second-division advice.
- Keep in mind all three components of a project: Task, Team and Individual.
- Approach all stages of development, from acquisition to final sale, in a competent and professional manner.
- Cut your teeth on a manageable project.
- Understand the maths – Gross Development Value (GDV).
- Always keep a contingency fund.
- Ensure you're adequately insured for development works.
- Take advantage of permitted development rights to add value.
- Use the Lawful Development Certificate, where appropriate.
- If the moment arises, seize your opportunity and bank it.

Chapter 11
How to Buy Bargain Properties at Auction

In my view, there is no better method for buying genuine, below-market value properties than at auction. Many of the reasons are apparent but, just to recap, here's a few:

- A more transparent market than private treaty
- Motivated sellers – distressed assets
- Problem properties which you can fix
- It's immediate exchange of contracts, which stops gazumping and other issues, such as a last-minute increase in the asking price from a seller, who may take advantage of your commitment and that you have already invested cash (legal fees and possibly a survey) and psychologically into the process
- All the information for the property is available to all buyers, but local knowledge and research may unearth a greater insight, such as the rental value is too low, or an infrastructure project is planned nearby.

There are three phases to buying property at a traditional or online auction:

1. Pre-auction
2. Auction day
3. Post-auction.

This chapter follows the process to get to the stage of either making an offer prior to auction, on the day or after the auction.

Property auctions

Every year I put up a wallchart, find the auction dates of the main houses I follow on the internet, then mark them on it. These are specific to me; you'll find that they aren't necessarily the ones that you follow, as they may not cover your area or region. There are some based in London that cover many regions (we've purchased properties in those in the recent past, as we will see later in this chapter).

Once armed with the dates, I begin looking at the lots two to three weeks prior to auction. Auctions usually have closing dates, so you may find that one scheduled for 1 September may close to new lots on 10 August. This allows for administration and creating the legal pack (which we will discuss later in this chapter).

Jim Slater: The Zulu Principle

Jim Slater is a well-known stocks-and-shares investor who designed a specific method to select growth shares. His original book on the subject, *The Zulu Principle: Making Extraordinary Profits from Ordinary Shares*,[46] was a bestseller and explained the 'Zulu Principle'.

Slater named his approach to investment when he noticed that after reading an article about Zulus, his wife was better informed on the topic than he was. He went on to think that if his wife were to read all the books she could find on the Zulu people, accompanied by a visit to South Africa to meet them, in a short period of time she could become one of the leading experts on that 'clearly defined and narrow area of knowledge'.[47]

46 J. Slater (2008) *The Zulu Principle: Making Extraordinary Profits from Ordinary Shares*, Harriman Modern Classics.

47 Slater, *The Zulu Principle*.

This Zulu Principle can be applied to property auctions and specific types of properties, where you become the expert. Once you've learned about auctions and won and lost a few, your level of expertise becomes much greater than someone walking in off the street. Moreover, if you decide to become an expert with a particular type of lot, you're doubling down on your expertise and creating a competitive advantage:

A competitive advantage arises when, through research, specialisation and experience, you're ahead of any potential competition.

You could become an expert in:

- Renovation and/or refurbishment projects
- Repossessed property – 'mortgagee in possession'
- Probate sales
- Houses in multiple occupation (HMOs) – both operating and converting
- Blocks of flats
- Leasehold issues
- Freehold issues
- Land development
- Land improvement and gaining planning permission
- Land break-up – such as selling garden extensions to adjacent properties on land where planning permission isn't possible
- Commercial properties
- Industrial properties
- Commercial-to-residential development
- Serviced accommodation
- Ground rent portfolios.

The list is endless, but the point remains – become an expert!

Pre-auction

At Distressed Assets, we have specific requirements at auction. As this book has illustrated, we look for problem properties that we can fix. For a large part of the past decade, we've bought blocks of flats and created leasehold titles, sold some and retained some with the freehold. Some of the blocks had problems while others didn't, other than there was a motivated seller and some works were required.

Strategy evolves, as we've seen from Chapter 3, and we now look at anything we can fix, not just blocks of flats.

Phase 1: Internet search

First, look online at the available lots and immediately reject:

- Specific locations – there is nothing like local knowledge of an area where 500m can mean the difference between success and failure
- Prices (overpriced lots)
- Leasehold in very large blocks where it would be difficult to gain management through right to manage (RTM)
- Developments with a history of criminality or antisocial behaviour – you have to ask why, all other things being equal, certain apartments in particular blocks are always at auction at significantly reduced prices. Again, local knowledge gives you an edge
- Structural issues requiring underpinning, and anything else where the price of fixing it is an open chequebook.

The first rule of renovation is to control costs.

The second rule is that sometimes,
there are easier ways to make money.

Block viewings

Having made a list of properties that tick your boxes, call the auction house to arrange viewings. In some cases, they will be advertised on the website as open house viewings that you can attend at specific times: these are known as 'block viewings'.

You may see lots that don't have viewings. This may be for a variety of reasons, for example, tenanted property that is sometimes difficult to access or the seller doesn't want to alert tenants and others to a sale. This may happen with corporate sellers who, for their own reasons, are selling a large number of properties and want to remain as anonymous as possible in the short term.

It is not unusual to see documents (Office Copy Entry, OCE) in the legal pack redacted to remove the seller's details and original purchase price. They even go as far as redacting their name on the Assured Shorthold Tenancy agreement, should the property be occupied.

Another issue is that sometimes the OCE document is out of date. For example, currently I'm bidding on an online auction and the OCE was printed nine months ago: a quick search at the Land Registry reveals a very different OCE than the one in the legal pack. The new one shows a different owner, that the property was only purchased six months ago and that there are no charges on the register.

Tip

The Land Registry will give you an unredacted and current version of the OCE for a small fee.

Opportunity

These situations present an excellent opportunity for the astute and experienced auction investor. The fewer potential buyers the better, as properties with a lot of competition seldom provide the best opportunities for buying at significant value.

Many people will point out to you: never buy a property that you haven't been able to view internally. I disagree. Sometimes you have to make a reasonable and thought-through judgement call.

In Chapter 9, we saw an example where we bought six flats unseen. This may sound like the plan of a fool, but the seller was a well-known housing association with excellent standards, including Vaillant boilers, excellent fire safety provision, commercial flooring and the like as standard.

I know the area well, already having properties on the road, and the building was in good order from the outside with external insulation. It was a great buy, but only because the risk was minimised with experience and knowledge.

Case Study
Distressed Assets: Liverpool L4, L9 and L21 – December 2022

A corporate was selling a considerable number of properties at a hybrid property auction. A hybrid is where the auction is live in the room, with both traditional telephone and proxy bidding, as well as online bidding. Prior to Covid-19, I would have taken a train to London for the auction and possibly stayed overnight, as the lots I was interested in were towards the beginning and end of a large auction.

I looked at all the lots of interest online and was able to discount some due to location. I did find it amusing, on the day, watching the auctioneer online introducing a property and saying what a cracking property it was in an excellent area, when I knew better.

After narrowing the list, I drove to the various properties to undertake an external inspection and was able to speak with a few tenants – this is where you have to use your charm and be a detective. There are no internal viewings, but you can gather a lot of intelligence from the tenants on the doorstep and by the condition of the exterior.

When researching the property on the doorstep, ask the tenant:

1. Is your rent up to date? Their reaction will tell you more than what they say.
2. How long have you lived here? Do you want to continue to live here?
3. Are there any issues with the neighbours?
4. Are there any problems in the road/street?
5. Are there any problems with the property?
6. Any leaks from the roof?
    a. Any damp?
    b. Does the boiler break down?

c. Any strange smells?
d. Do the white goods work OK? How old are they?

At this stage some tenants will invite you in, but this is a great opportunity to ask the end user the questions you need to make an informed decision.

We were successful at auction with three terraced properties in excellent rental areas. Having reduced the options to four, we only wanted three, as each client in this case wanted one each. All three clients are building a portfolio, and it would be the third property for all three of them.

I held property four in reserve, should we fail with any in plan A. All four properties had things in common:

- Good areas and no signs of any issues in the locality. Others were rejected after the drive-by, as I could see issues in the street such as a broken window and rubbish. This is an element of property due diligence that you cannot miss – you, or your professional advisor, must see the property from the outside, as well as assessing the building and the locality. The property could be at auction for this reason.
- Either a fairly new roof or existing roof was in an excellent condition. No missing tiles, level and no sign of sagging.
- An excellent exterior. Bricks pointed, uPVC double glazing looked well fitted, good main doors and generally well looked after.

I made the assessment that given what I had seen externally, and given what I knew about the seller and its standards, it was worth bidding.

Remember, the energy performance certificate (EPC) gives you a lot of information about the property too. It's not just the size but whether there is insulation, double glazing and a heating system among other things.

Additional factors

I have the experience and knowledge to make the call, so clients trust my judgement. Rightly, many investors would be deterred from bidding, as they don't have that confidence that only years of doing property auctions gives you. Even at very attractive guide prices, I knew the bidding would be slow.

However, we didn't get one of our lots because someone paid far too much for it. As it was, we had a reserve property that the client switched to instead.

The results from this auction were:

- Two-bedroom terrace, Liverpool L9 – purchased 23% below our maximum bid, yielding 11.7%
- Three-bedroom terrace, Liverpool L21 – purchased 20% below our maximum bid, yielding 9.3%
- Two-bedroom terrace, Liverpool L4 – purchased 37.3% below our maximum bid, yielding 11.2%.

Phase 2: On the road

Sometimes, you can be the first to request viewings and the lots can be seen in one day; but most of the time they will be spread throughout a week or longer. Empty properties are the easiest to gain access while the tenanted ones are more difficult, as a minimum 24 hours' written notice is required.

Warning!

On some occasions, tenants refuse entry into the property. This may be an indication of a problem that needs resolving, if you were to purchase the property. It could be a dispute with the landlord, or something to do with the tenants.

The risk is increased significantly if you haven't seen the interior of the house or flat, plus the rent arrears dilemma discussed earlier in this book can be a real risk.

This is, of course, contrary to the point above. It's all about experience and a judgement call.

What to look for: property inspection checklist

On arrival at a property, be sure to look at the following.

Roof:

- Condition – missing tiles, slope, bowing, sagging, chimney tilting, pointing.
- Is there a flat roof on an extension or outrigger (i.e. a small extension normally found in terraced houses which contains a kitchen and/or bathroom) with felt? Check their condition.
- Internally, look for evidence of water ingress on top floor ceilings, such as discoloration, patches and cracks.

Structure:

- Is the property leaning – any sign of subsidence, cracks, movement, problems with bay windows?
- Any movement around doors, floor levels or windows?
- Has any render or paint been applied to hide anything?
- Is it fully double glazed (some particulars have been incorrect in the past).
- Are the window frames fitted well – are the seals still intact?
- Do the windows open, or are they corroded (a big issue in coastal locations) –and are restrictors fitted to limit how far they can open?
- Are there any drain smells – this might be either a blocked drain or debris.

- Is there a basement? Is it damp? Be careful using any wooden stairs leading to the basement if the property has been empty for a considerable time, as they might collapse. Bring a torch with you.
- Are the utilities supplied from the street or road to the basement – if so, what is the condition of the pipes and equipment?

Damp/rot:

- Any sign of a damp-proof course? (These are small round holes a few feet above ground level.)
- Internally, is there any sign of rising damp, or damp from blocked gutters? They are very different, and the costs of fixing the problems are very different too.
- On entering the property, is there any overwhelming smell? This is more noticeable in empty properties – wet rot – like a musty, earthy smell. Dry rot is more like a mushroom smell. It's also worth stamping on the corners of rooms to test the soundness of the flooring, also inside a bay window.
- Does the roof on the bay window leak?
- Has any furniture been moved to hide damp?

Electrics:

- Is the consumer unit metal or plastic? Is there an Electrical Installation Condition Report (EICR)? This is a legal requirement to let the property: generally, they are valid for five years.
- Are there enough sockets, or are extension leads overloaded?
- In older properties, is the cooker hardwired? (I have seen one on an extension lead!)

Gas and plumbing:

- Is there a gas boiler? Is it old and likely to be replaced in the near future? Is there a gas safety certificate? (This is a legal requirement for letting.)
- How old is the boiler, and has it been regularly serviced? How often does it break down?

- Is the flue legal? Regulations prevent a boiler flue from being situated within 30–60cm of a window or door. This is to prevent harmful gases from exiting the flue and re-entering the property through an open door or window.
- Is there a stopcock?
- Are the drainpipes and soil stack(s) (which take waste water from the property to the sewer) in working order?

Internal:

- Does the kitchen or bathroom need replacing? If not, what can you do to freshen them up?
- Are any white goods in the sale? The auction office can advise you on this, but it's highly unlikely that white goods won't be included at auction.
- Is the property insulated?
- Is there any asbestos present? (This was used extensively in the 1960s and 1970s.)
- Is there scope to increase value by dividing bedrooms which have two windows, roof space or to the rear?
- Any sign of rodents – traps, gnawed carpet or droppings?

External:

- Is everything you see in terms of land around the property in the sale? You might be surprised. Check the plan in the legal pack.
- Familiarise yourself with what Japanese knotweed looks like. It's a hazard and requires professional clearance.[48]
- Are the boundary walls and fences in good repair?
- Is there off-street parking or residents-only parking?
- Any signs of local trouble, antisocial behaviour, boarded-up windows?

48 Knotweed Help (2023) 'Japanese Knotweed UK Law'. Available at: www.knotweedhelp.com/japanese-knotweed-law, accessed 5 January 2026.

Case Study
Distressed Assets: Liverpool L13 – 2017

We bought a couple of properties in Liverpool L13. Both had three one-bedroom flats, but the middle flat had two windows and the bedroom was large. Turning it into a two-bedroom flat was very easy and inexpensive, but added £15,000 to £20,000 to the value of each at the time (Figure 25).

Figure 25: A way to add value: increase the number of bedrooms

For apartments, in addition to the above:

- What are the communal areas like, including the outside? The legal pack may let you know if there is a management company or it may not. If you're bold enough, ask the current owner or occupiers; but there is usually signage or notices which give you a clue.
- Is there a working fire alarm panel and signage?
- Is the block secure?
- Where is the refuse point?

That's a lot to get through in possibly 30 minutes maximum, maybe shorter. The more times you do it, the better you become and the quicker it takes. I take a phone with me for photos of everything – this is particularly important if you're viewing many properties. I also take a torch as well as the one on the phone, and collapsible ladders to poke my head into the roof space. It's incredible what you can find up there!

Surveyor and builder

If you're new to property development, look at paying for a building surveyor to accompany you. Do the initial property visits yourself, as many properties can be rejected by most people, then once you've eliminated the non-starters, organise a second viewing with a surveyor. Many do this for a relatively small fee, which can give you the reassurance you need while honing your choices.

Alternatively, if you know any builders, they are equally capable of helping you – with the added advantage of giving you a rough idea of any repairs or renovation costs at the time.

Phase 3: Narrow the list of target properties

The viewings are the key filter for me: I can view for a day, maybe 10 properties, and not want to move forward on any of them. For every 10 to 15 properties, we find a potential purchase.

Legal packs

The next stage is a quick look at the legal pack, which you can download from the internet: all of the instructions are there for you, it's just a question of registering for it.

Many auctions just have the following documents:

- Contract of sale
- RICS *Common Auction Conditions* 4th Edition (2018) RICS
- Special Conditions of Sale
- Energy performance certificate (EPC)
- Official copies of the title register and title plan
- For tenanted properties, a copy of the Assured Shorthold Tenancy agreement.

Others provide more information, including:

- Search information, including local authority searches, drainage and water search and any other searches application to the location
- The property information form (TA6)
- The fittings and contents form (TA10)
- If the property is leasehold, an official copy of the lease and the leasehold information form (LPE1)
- Where applicable, documentation relation to planning permissions and building controls
- For commercial properties, relevant Commercial Property Standard Enquiries forms.

Addendum

You must check the Addendum before the start of the auction. The Addendum represents any amendments or additions to the preprinted information in the catalogue or online. It can be updated right up to the start of the auction, so it's important that you check this information before placing any bids.

Warning!

Remember: many properties in an auction have problems. Some will be legal problems, issues with the lease or service charge. In terms of the lease, there might be restrictions about which you should consult a solicitor. Additionally, there may be entries on the title, such as a unilateral notice (which has happened to us in the past).[49]

Note: This book is not a law book. If you are unsure about anything, you must consult legal advice.

49 A unilateral notice is an intention to hinder a sale, which can be a competitor tactic. 'A unilateral notice may be entered without the consent of the relevant proprietor. The applicant is not required to satisfy the registrar that their claim is valid and does not need to support their claim to the interest with any evidence.' HM Land Registry (2025) 'Practice guide 19: notices, restrictions and the protection of third-party interests in the register', 16 June Available at: https://www.gov.uk/government/publications/notices-restrictions-and-the-protection-of-third-party-interests-in-the-register/practice-guide-19-notices-restrictions-and-the-protection-of-third-party-interests-in-the-register, accessed 5 January 2026.

As noted previously, when a legal pack is 'thin' it could be a sign of an issue, such as excessive service charge. This is one reason many leasehold flats don't sell at private treaty and, when a buyer completes at auction, they are shocked to find that the service charge and ground rent equate to seven months' rent.

Be warned, and research beyond the legal pack. There is plenty of open-source information on the internet, in forums and so on.

Phase 4: The final cut

Having viewed the properties and narrowed the options further by looking at the legal packs, it's time to analyse the numbers. This gives you a batting order of one, two, three and so on.

The example below is real and was purchased for a client at the height of the post-Credit Crunch crisis. As stated earlier, the best times to buy are at 'peak pessimism'. Today, this property would sell in the region of £400,000 to £450,000.

For your proposed purchase, you would complete something like this. Clearly, some of the numbers (such as service charge) won't be available in the legal pack, so some personal investigations might be necessary – this could be a call to the auction house. If they don't know or can't find out, a visit to the development can be the answer, by speaking with one of the owners or occupiers.

Case Study
Distressed Assets: Bethnal Green, London E2 – 2009
Buying costs

Purchase price	£165,000
Auctioneer's fees	£350
Stamp duty	Nil (up to £175,000 at the time)
Legal fees	£1,050
Survey (optional)	None

Mortgage arrangement fees	£1,870 (rolled up into mortgage)
Mortgage broker's fee	£300
Valuation fee	£300
Deposit (25%)	£41,250
Total cash required to buy	£43,250 (NB: not including mortgage arrangement fee)

Cash flow

Amount borrowed	£125,620 (25% plus £1,870 arrangement fee)
Mortgage costs (pcm) (based on 75% loan-to-value mortgage at 5.49% interest-only)	£575
Mortgage costs (per annum)	£6,897
Buildings insurance	Nil (covered by service charge)
Annual service charge	£789
Annual ground rent	£250
Letting agent fees @12% (per annum)	£1,560
Total annual costs	**£9,496**
Rental income per annum	**£13,000**
Annual cash flow	**£3,504**

Property investment ratios and calculations

Income and costs

Returns on this and that look very academic and businesslike, but the maths for buy-to-let is relatively simple. Let's look at an example.

Case Study
Distressed Assets: Liverpool L4 – March 2024

This was a two-bedroom, freehold terrace house recently refurbished with a new roof, attractive kitchen and bathroom, gas central heating and double glazing. The property is also registered as an EPC C. In terms of location, the client has the option to provide serviced accommodation, as the house is a two-minute walk to the Liverpool FC stadium in Anfield.

Valuations vary and are subjective – but we consider it to be about £90,000, given its excellent condition; we secured it with a pre-auction offer of £65,000. The property was considerably under-rented, which impacts its attractiveness for potential buyers who don't fully understand the area and rental values. This is a good thing for those of us who do.

This is a point worth dwelling on, and during our property investment and sourcing workshops it leads to healthy debate. Chapter 4 deals with market value and how to calculate it; my personal preference is to look at the income, then work out what the property is worth to me or a client: the income capitalisation model.

For cash buyers, this is a good approach. For mortgage buyers, you must stick more rigidly to the methods used in Chapter 4, as the RICS valuer for the lender will use the comparable evidence method and their experience.

Purchase price before costs = £65,000 (costs are stamp duty, legal and auction fees, approximately 6%)

Purchase price, including costs = £68,900

Rent after review = £7,800

Gross yield on purchase price = 12%

Gross yield on total costs = 11.3%

The property was purchased for cash, so no mortgage costs.

Table 9 shows the indicative costs and net yield.

Table 9: Indicative costs and net yield at £65,000 cash purchase price

Total rental income at market rates		**£7,800**
Insurance (rebuild value)	(£600)	
Letting fees at 8%	(£624)	
Gas safety certificate	(£85)	
Total operating expenses	(£1,309)	
Net operating income		£6,491
Before-tax cash flow		£6,491

Net yield or return on cash invested:

£6,491 as a percentage of £68,900 (total costs) = 9.4%

Clearly, the above example doesn't take into account any repairs, but we don't know them yet. However, the figure of 9.4% gives us a comparator for other properties we are looking at and can help us rank our options.

To 'compare apples with apples', we need to know either actual or projected costs when analysing the viability and attractiveness of a property investment.

The income capitalisation model

To continue the earlier point, and using this case study as an example of the income capitalisation model, let's see what this property is worth based on the income it generates.

Currently, the average gross yield in north-west England is 7.4%.[50] To purchase an income of £7,800 before costs would mean having to pay £105,405 (income is capitalised by dividing it by the average yield).

50 Rightmove Rental Trends Tracker Q3 2025.

We don't want the average here, but 9% is fine – so the value of the property is £86,666.

The above is useful as it illustrates that you're effectively buying an income stream. However, to finesse it you would have to look at net yields.

Freehold house

Typical freehold house annual running or operating costs are as follows:

- Mortgage payments (if applicable)
- Building insurance
- Letting fees (if applicable)
- Repairs and maintenance
- Annual gas safety certificate (if applicable)
- Voids
- Council tax (when the property is empty)
- EICR, EPC and landlord selective licence (but these are not annual costs).

Leasehold flat

If the property is a leasehold flat, service charge would be added to the cost base, which should include building insurance, communal repairs and maintenance, fire safety, cleaning and so on.

There is also the potential for Section 20 works:

> A section 20 notice (S20) is a notice to tell leaseholders that the freeholder (via the management company) intends to undertake work or provide a service that leaseholders will have to pay towards. A S20 must be served on any leaseholder who will be affected by the work or receive the service.[51]

51 Section 20 of the Landlord and Tenant Act 1985 (as amended by the Commonhold and Leasehold Reform Act 2002). HM Government (n.d.) 'Landlord and Tenant Act 1985'. Available at: www.legislation.gov.uk/ukpga/1985/70/contents, accessed 5 January 2026.

In other words, as the freeholder you may have to contribute to significant communal works affecting the building, such as a new roof, new windows, etc.

Warning!

When a leasehold flat is sold, the management company or freeholder supplies an LPE1 which sets out various information about the property. In addition, the management pack includes details of past, present and future service charges, the block insurance policy, fire risk assessment and other documents where applicable.

The LPE 1 has a section which says: '4.8 Within the next 2 years, are any Section 20 proposed to the Property?'[52]

This property may be at auction because the leaseholder is aware of a substantial Section 20 notice that would not have to be declared at auction, as caveat emptor applies. Be on your guard.

After careful analysis and visiting the property, we are now ready for auction day!

But first, is it worth putting in a pre-auction offer?

Pre-auction offer

There is never any harm in placing a pre-auction offer, as it doesn't need to be the maximum bid you would make at the live auction. It's speculative and could reap rewards.

In my experience, a property being sold by a 'mortgagee in possession', receiver or administrator would normally 'go to the room' – these days, on the internet as well as or instead of it. This gives maximum transparency to the sale, as well as potentially receiving a higher price.

52 The Law Society (2023) 'Leasehold forms: LPE1 leasehold property enquiries form'. Available at: www.lawsociety.org.uk/topics/property/leasehold-forms, accessed 5 January 2026.

However, some private sellers – particularly those who don't want to risk sitting on an unsold lot – may take a pre-auction offer.

The same rules of the live auction apply. You will need to deposit 10% of the sales price and the auctioneer's fee. Making this offer requires certified proof of ID and address: a passport or driving licence, and a utility bill or bank statement not less than three months old.

Case Study
Distressed Assets: Pre-auction offer, Liverpool L3 – November 2022

This was a studio apartment in Liverpool, guiding at £25,000 and in vacant possession. The leaseholder was selling a number of properties to raise cash for other purposes. I knew he wanted to sell, and estimated the reserve price would be £30,000 – it could possibly sell for £35,000 or more.

We manage and own some apartments in the block, and understand that the low capital values are a direct result of the poor block management and huge fees that we are addressing through RTM.

We made a pre-auction offer of £20,000 on behalf of a retained client, which was rejected – but £25,000 was accepted. The apartment is in a prime Liverpool city centre location and will rent at £5,700 per annum.

As a long-term investment, with a new management company reducing excessive service charges and improving the aesthetics of the building, overall rents will rise. This will prove to be a very smart investment, as capital values return to where they should be.

Both pre- and post-auction you can negotiate with the owner via the auction house. (We'll look at post-auction later in this chapter.)

Auction day

Prior to Covid-19 and lockdown in the UK, I looked forward to auction day and made an occasion of it, whether we were successful or otherwise. It wasn't unusual to take along my pre-school children, then go out for a family lunch afterwards.

I would also look forward to seeing friends I've made on the circuit over the years, some of whom were direct competitors for the types of properties we targeted. It was a great day out, successful or otherwise, and everyone remains friends.

Some auctions, particularly in London, are back to normal in big rooms while others in the provinces are not. Some are online only, while others are a hybrid model of room and online.

Key auction terms to know

Guide price

A guide price is an indication of where the reserve price is currently set. It isn't necessarily what the auctioneer expects to sell the lot for, and shouldn't be taken as a valuation or estimate of sale price. The reserve will not exceed the guide price by more than 10% if it's a single-figure guide price, and if a guide price range is quoted, the reserve will fall within that range.

Reserve price

The reserve is the current minimum figure for which the auctioneer is authorised by the vendor to sell the property. Note that the reserve is liable to change throughout the course of marketing. An auctioneer reserves the right to lower the reserve during the auction to a level that matches the existing highest bid. In the event that there are no further bids, the highest bidder is declared the purchaser at the end of the auction process.

Tactics in the room

It's worth looking at the routine of auction day and tactics: I like to be early, have a coffee and read the Addendum. You then have to register to bid. You will need ID, as mentioned previously, and may get a paddle or card with a number on it.

Generally, I watch a few lots to get a feel for prices, then have a chat with a few people. As my lot approaches, I stand at the back of the room, because I feel I have a full view of it and the participants. I also make sure that I have eye contact with the auctioneer.

Once the lot starts, I remain silent. If the lot goes above my maximum bid, that's it. No one would ever know I had an interest. When the bidding slows down and it's obvious, I wait to enter. It could be a lot going up in £5,000, £2,000 or £1,000 increments down to £500. As the auctioneer says, 'Is that it? Going once, going twice!' my paddle goes up and I make myself known.

With my maximum bid firmly in my head (I have never exceeded this), I rapidly increase the bidding if the original person is still in: no hesitation as they bid – straight back. Sometimes, people are taken aback by the shock of almost being the winner, only to see someone else bidding the property up. I assure you, this tactic works.

Once your bid is successful, a member of the auction team shows you to the contracts desk. There, you sign the contract, pay the deposit and auctioneer's fees, and inform the clerk of your solicitor's details.

As we've seen previously, most auctions have a 28-day completion. I have seen shorter and longer periods, and sellers do this for multiple reasons – you will know prior to auction via the auction pack.

If you don't complete within the contractual period, you will be served a 'Notice to Complete'.

Notice to Complete

The RICS *Common Auctions Conditions* 4th Edition state:

> G7.1. The SELLER or the BUYER may on or after the AGREED COMPLETION DATE but before COMPLETION give the other notice to complete within ten BUSINESS DAYS (excluding the date on which the notice is given) making time of the essence.
>
> G7.2. The person giving the notice must be READY TO COMPLETE.
>
> G7.3. If the BUYER fails to comply with a notice to complete the SELLER may, without affecting any other remedy the SELLER has:
>
> > (a) terminate the CONTRACT;
> > (b) claim the deposit and any interest on it if held by a stakeholder;
> > (c) forfeit the deposit and any interest on it;
> > (d) resell the LOT; and
> > (e) claim damages from the BUYER
>
> G7.4. If the SELLER fails to comply with a notice to complete the BUYER may, without affecting any other remedy the BUYER has:
>
> > (a) terminate the CONTRACT; and
> > (b) recover the deposit and any interest on it from the SELLER or, if applicable, a stakeholder

The Notice to Complete is unambiguous. If you do not complete, there are severe penalties.

Alternatives to in-person bidding

Telephone bidding

When bidding by telephone, you need to register with the auction house in advance and have sent over the relevant documentation already discussed, which include a deposit for 10% of your maximum amount, plus auctioneer's fees. Many people are rightly reluctant to do this as it reveals your maximum bid; thankfully, an increasing number of auction houses take a credit or debit card.

Once you've filled in the forms and registered, the auction house will phone you a short while before bidding on your lot starts, and take your bids. The disadvantage with this method is that you cannot judge the room, but it is convenient if you can't travel on that day.

It goes without saying: if you're on a mobile phone, ensure you have enough battery charge and a good signal. (I've seen auctions where the telephone bidder has just stopped!)

Proxy bidding

There is also the option of proxy bidding, where the auctioneer bids on your behalf to an upper limit. I have never liked this method as the control element is lost: I'm inherently suspicious of someone bidding the lot up (it does happen), but some less confident investors may choose this method.

To register, simply follow the similar process to telephone bidding described above.

Third-party bidding

You can employ an expert in your area who sources the property, provides a detailed analysis and then bids on your behalf up to a pre-agreed maximum. You will need to provide this person with written authority to bid on your behalf, also for your records, written confirmation of the lot number, address and maximum bid.

As I tend to bid on multiple lots in the same auction and at times, two online auctions at the same time, I place a sticky note with the lot number and maximum bid on my computer monitor.

Once the lot is completed, I remove the sticker and replace it. This isn't something you want to get wrong!

Post-auction offer

As we've seen in previous chapters, some properties don't sell at auction. The reasons some lots don't sell are obvious, such as being overpriced, but for others it's not. We take it on a case-by-case basis.

Why would you buy post-auction when the property didn't make your original list?

In one word, negotiation. The seller has put the property into auction for a reason. It could have problems (which we like), or they just need some cash quickly for another reason – which provides an opportunity. You can still view the property, as most auctioneers will show you around: they're keen to sell, as this is one way they make money; but they also want to keep their 'sold' statistics as high as possible.

Some buyers base their entire strategy on buying after auction: they're in a strong position, because the seller has failed to get a quick sale and the cash they need. Many are open to an offer – and reasonable, low ones at that. As with the pre-auction offer, you haven't time to delay and ruminate as another astute buyer might beat you to it.

If you have done the due diligence and have the finance in place for 28 days-or-less completion (auction conditions apply), go for it.

Case Study
Distressed Assets: Liverpool L20 – December 2023

This was a three-bedroom terraced house with new Vaillant boiler, fully insulated external walls, second-generation roof and energy rated as EPC C (Figure 26). It was under-rented, with good tenants on a statutory periodic tenancy. The house was large at 1,055 sq. ft and in excellent order throughout. It was part of a portfolio of properties being sold by the same company, and we were successful prior to auction in acquiring a number of them.

After the auction, we secured this property for a long-standing client for just £65,000 – an excellent bargain and at a market rent, yielding about 14%.

There are many psychological pressures on vendors after an auction when properties haven't sold. It's a great time for buyers who can move quickly in terms of time, space and due diligence.

Update 2025: 46% capital growth in six months without refurbishment or renovation.

A BRRR, without the second R

This mentee (JR) had bought a number of auction properties since 2021, and leveraged them recently. This property, without any refurbishment or renovation, was conservatively valued after six months for mortgage purposes at 46% higher than the purchase price. In my view, the difference was much greater, but mortgage valuers rightly are extremely cautious. By anyone's standards, that's a fantastic acquisition and the result of listening, absorbing and putting into practice the principles of this book, with many phone calls along the way.

In addition to this property, JR has acquired significant income and equity over the past four years, recently adding a £68,000 house in January 2025 with a 13% yield, and another in late 2024 at £60,000 with a 17% yield. The portfolio overall is a case study in building equity and income from distressed assets and securing your financial future.

These types of acquisitions can be attained only through wholesale property investment: all three of the examples above were bought at auction using very specific tactics.

I get immense personal satisfaction from guiding and assisting my mentees with their goals, and sharing in their joy when the results are spectacular.

If you wish to get into the nitty-gritty, please join us on one of our workshops in London or live online (for details, see the end of this book).

Figure 26: Unsold lots – bargains are to be had after the auction

After the auction

As noted previously, if successful, once the auction concludes you must ensure that:

- You insure the property for its rebuild value, not the price you paid or what you believe is its market value.
- Put in place any necessary professional security – which can include 'tinning' the windows and doors and/or a mobile alarm system. This is something your insurer may insist on if the property is empty, depending on its location.
- Inform your solicitor to expect to receive the contract and other documents from the auction house.
- Celebrate – whether with champagne, a soft drink or coffee, mark the occasion. I've always been a great believer in celebrating success – and over time, I'm pretty certain that this has positive psychological impact on us as a company, leading to more success.

The next stage

Treat tenants with respect

As we've seen, most residential auctions complete after 28 days or less and move straight to the property management stage, as the property is already tenanted. If you aren't going to be managing the property yourself, you will need to instruct a lettings agent. Whether it's you or them, on the day of completion, be sure to introduce yourself to your tenants and formalise the relationship.

It's good practice to forewarn the tenants by posting a letter of introduction straight after the auction. Believe it or not, some tenants don't know their homes are being sold, particularly if it's being done under the radar by a private individual or corporate. (Personally, I don't understand this, although I guess they want the tenant to continue to pay rent. Often, when I knock on doors – when there are no formal viewings – the tenant isn't aware of this, which I must admit doesn't sit well with me.)

For some people, tenants are a means to an end. They pay rent, that money goes on a spreadsheet and percentages and cash flows are calculated. Accounts are produced and at the corporate level, bonuses are paid according to their criteria of success. Some forget that tenants are people with real lives, with the same aspirations as themselves, working hard and often looking after partners and families. Treating them with basic respect and dignity isn't asking much – without them, there are just a lot of empty, soulless properties.

Management

We often take over several properties on one day. Recently, we took over four properties on 21-day completion from an auction a few weeks ago. The procedure is as follows.

Make contact

After the letter of introduction we make contact for an appointment, so the day of completion isn't a surprise for the tenant.

The first thing we ask is about any necessary repairs and maintenance. This is a good way to start, as the tenant is reassured that you are one of the good owners or agents, not the bad. In most cases we know what the issues are, as we have either viewed the property, or knocked on the door to speak to them prior to auction. Having found the issues, it's important to rectify these quickly.

Don't increase rent straight away

We don't increase rents to market level on day one. It's our choice, while many do otherwise. As discussed in this book, a lot of properties we buy or source for clients are under-rented, which is one of their attractions, making them a target in the first place.

In a recent case, the rent was an incredible 50% below the market level. We ease tenants into rent rises, particularly those who have lived in their home for many years. We will have a new Assured Shorthold Tenancy with a new rent, but at a negotiated level and with a plan to achieve market level without making it financially painful for the tenant. This is how we elect to do it.

Serve new documents

Remember: issuing a new Assured Shorthold Tenancy is a new tenancy, so other documents must be served too, including:

- The EPC
- Gas safety certificate and/or EICR
- How to Rent booklet (ensure you have the current edition)[53]
- Prescribed information on the Deposit Protection Scheme[54]
- Contact information.

We also check that the smoke detectors are in working order, correctly fitted and positioned, and that the tenant signs to agree that we have done it.

Depending on how old the inventory and check-in report is, it also can be a good idea to do a new inventory.

Arrangements must be made to transfer the tenant's deposit from the previous owner's protected scheme to yours.

There is nothing difficult about taking over an auction property, but it's important to get it right – both in terms of the documentation and the relationship with your new tenant.

Key points

- You can buy before, during and after the auction. All three have advantages.
- Become an expert, gain a competitive advantage.

53 Department for Levelling up, Housing and Communities and Ministry of Housing, Communities & Local Government (2023) 'Guidance: How to rent', 2 October. Available at: www.gov.uk/government/publications/how-to-rent, accessed 5 January 2026.

54 Tenant deposits belong to them and must be lodged with a government-approved scheme. Tenants are entitled to receive details about the deposit, where it's held and as prescribed information. HM Government (n.d.) 'Deposit protection schemes and landlords'. Available at: www.gov.uk/deposit-protection-schemes-and-landlords, accessed 5 January 2026.

- Don't be deterred if you're prevented from viewing the property. This means others are too, and lessens the competition.
- Don't be afraid to speak with tenants. They are the real experts about the property you are intending to buy.
- You can learn a lot from external viewings and the EPC.
- Have a property inspection checklist – tick items off.
- Take professional advice from a building surveyor or builder, if you're new to property investment.
- Read the legal pack and take legal advice.
- Read the Addendum.
- Do the maths – include all of your costs.
- Don't buy a leasehold property without legal advice on the lease.
- Think about your auction room tactics, or online tactics before the auction.
- Don't disregard lots that didn't sell – there are great opportunities for negotiation after the auction.
- Appoint a managing agent or make contact with the tenants on the day of completion, or the very next day.
- Finally – good luck!

Chapter 12
Online Auctions: The Covid-19 Innovation

The preparation, research and due diligence outlined in this book apply to traditional auction, whether in the room or online.

Post-Covid-19 lockdown online auctions have been a huge success, with many advantages for both auction house and client. The auction house has lower costs by transferring everything online, while the buyer has fewer costs, including travel to the auction and maybe an overnight hotel.

Online auctions have a larger audience as they're a level playing field, whether bidding from Manchester, Mauritius or Melbourne. The hybrid model – where the auction is live, and bidding takes place both in the room and online – opens up much larger participation, as those who, for one reason or another are deterred from telephone bidding and proxy bids, can take part over the internet.

For the buyer, the emotion and competitiveness of the auction room is gone, as you sit with a drink in a room with internet connection and watch the price go up on-screen. In some cases, you can even place a bid at your maximum, which means you don't have to do anything other than watch – the computer does it all for you. There is also less danger that the auctioneer might miss your bid, although in my experience, I have never seen that happen.

For those who have bid at auction before in a packed room, the online version is much less stressful when you can preset the proxy maximum bid. However, in the hybrid auction, ensuring that you can click 'bid' and then 'confirm' has stresses of its own.

The main disadvantage, ironically, is technology itself. It can break, freeze, experience outage or another glitch. But overall, online auctions are here to stay – and I'm a fan. However, in some auction houses, the actual room still remains king while online plays a supporting role.

Tip

If you're bidding online at a live-in-room auction, per the hybrid model, ensure you don't leave it too late to bid. This isn't a case of brinkmanship per the tactics of the auction room, as technology isn't always quick enough to bid at the 'Going once, going twice…' stage. I've seen many online bidders fail due to bidding too late, and they had been warned by the live auctioneer on the stream.

You might also wish to investigate the online proxy bid, as discussed in this chapter. I've found this very useful too.

Some auction houses have returned to the big room, in-person auction, while others remain solely online. Recently, I had a chat with a director of an auction house I know well and have bought a lot of property from over the years. They have no plans at the moment to return to a large-room format. I guess if your sales or sold numbers are strong, and your data suggest that participation is high, why revert to in-person when all it does is increase costs and takes additional staff time?

Here are definitions of the various online auctions.

Types of online auctions

Modern method of auction (conditional)

This is an online form of the established property auction: it's been around for a while and gives estate agents another route to market. Potential bidders have much more time than the traditional auction to allow both mortgage as well as cash buyers to participate. This makes the potential market for the property much bigger than the more traditional unconditional auction.

Properties are marketed prior to auction on the popular property portals. Hopeful buyers can bid online at any time and, at the end of the auction, the highest bidder wins. The winning bidder pays a reservation fee of about 5%, which is in addition to the purchase price; they have 28 days to exchange contracts and complete 28 days after that, making it 56 days in total.

For my purposes and strategy, and that of my clients, traditional online auction suits better, but I have bought through the modern method of auction.

In Chapter 14, you will see a comprehensive comparison of the two methods from the seller's and buyer's perspectives, illustrated with two comparable properties I purchased in 2024 using both methods. The numbers are very different, and provide considerable food for thought.

Traditional online auction (unconditional)

This has the same rules as the traditional, in-person, in-room property auction. When the hammer hits the gavel, the auction concludes: exchange of contracts takes place and the buyer pays a deposit plus the auctioneer's fees, with completion 28 days later or less depending on the Special Conditions of Sale.

The online auction process

Registration

For this, you need to open an online account to bid at the auction. Once you've done this, you can 'watch' – i.e. observe the properties or lots – that are of interest to you, as well as access and download the legal packs.

You will need to provide certified photo ID (driver's licence or passport) and proof of address (last three months) to the auction house for anti-money laundering checks to be run. The house may use online apps such as Credas (https://credas.co.uk).

Terms and conditions

You'll be asked to read and accept the auction house terms and conditions. There also may be particular documents concerning the sale of the property you're targeting that you'll need to read and accept.

Register credit or debit card

You'll need to register a credit or debit card, and the auction house will take a holding payment. This is a non-refundable deposit payable if you're successful, deducted from the 10% deposit due on exchange of contracts. On the fall of the virtual gavel, the winning bidder's card is debited while payments are returned to the unsuccessful participants.

Online auction bidding from anywhere in the world

When the auction opens, you can place bids in line with the predetermined bid increment levels, using the '+' and '–' buttons on-screen. Depending on the lot price, increments might increase by £1,000, £3,000, £5,000 or more.

Every time you submit a bid, you will see whether you're successful or not. If successful the screen will be green, informing you that you're the highest bidder.

Proxy bids

Some auction houses have slightly different software, so it's important to log in well before your lot to look at what it can or cannot do. Some allow proxy bidding, which I personally like, as it allows you to set your maximum bid: no one else can see it. Then as the bids go up, you will automatically be the highest bidder until your maximum bid is exceeded. If the bidding stops short, then you win at that price, not your proxy bid.

In the real-life example in Figure 27, I set the proxy bid at £92,000. Every time someone else bid, mine was automatically increased so that I could continue to be the highest bidder. Also note, the software tells you when the reserve price has been met, as well as the number of bidders watching the lot – in this case, 10. (If you're wondering, we did win the auction.)

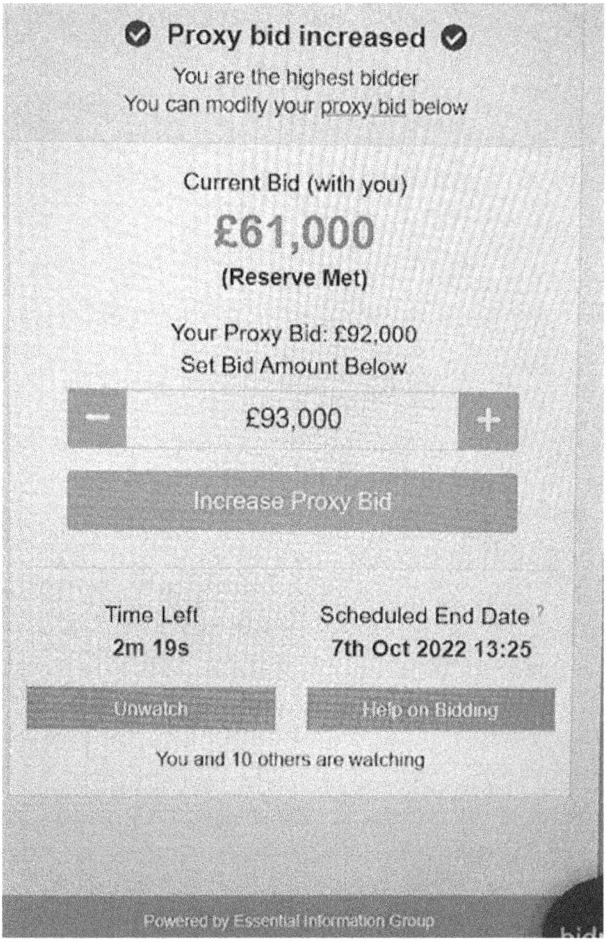

Figure 27: Online auction screen

Interestingly, many people use the proxy function as it gets around any temporary technical issues you might have, including not clicking the increment button in good time.

If prior to auction you set your proxy bid, and find yourself the highest bidder some way north (in price terms) of the reserve (usually within

10% of the guide price), there is a fair chance you will get it – as all of the proxy bids on that lot have been taken out. Clearly, this doesn't account for the manual bidder or a proxy who changes their bid, but it's an interesting phenomenon of online auctions.

Reserve prices

Almost all lots have a reserve price (the minimum price that the owner will accept at the live auction. Note that this reserve price is negotiable after the auction, should the lot not sell). Usually, it's about 10% higher than the guide price.

Hypothetical scenario

At online auction, the reserve price has been set at £105,000 and the current bid is £95,000.

Investor G wants to bid and the minimum is £96,000, but they decide to place a maximum of £99,000. This is below the reserve, so the online system places a bid for Investor G at their maximum bid amount, and they become the highest bidder at £99,000.

Investor H enters the fray. The minimum bid is £100,000, but Investor H places a maximum bid of £110,000. The online system automatically increases their bid to meet the reserve, and they are now the highest bidder at £105,000.

Note that the bid only goes to the reserve price, not Investor H's maximum £110,000.

Investor G is informed that they have been outbid. If no further bids are placed, Investor H wins the lot for £105,000.

Bidding extension window: 'bid sniping'

Unlike eBay, bid sniping (an online auction tactic that places a winning bid just before the sale ends, preventing any counter-bids) is not possible in online property auctions. Auctions close at their allocated time, but if a bid is placed within the final 30 seconds, the time is extended by an additional 30 seconds. This is known as the 'bidding extension window'. The auction only ends when a full 30 seconds passes, with no further bidding.

In the auction shown in Figure 28, the bidding window was extended five times.

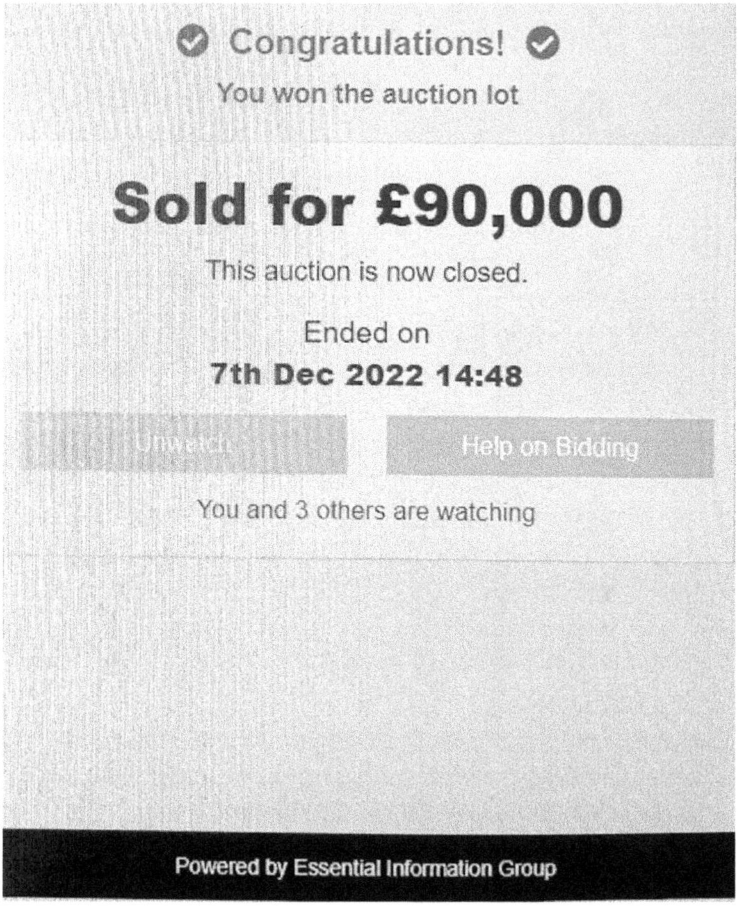

Figure 28: Another real-life example

The winning bid exchanges contract

As I've mentioned already, I'm a fan of the online auction. As someone who has spent many years travelling to auctions and, in some cases, staying overnight, I like the convenience of being able to bid anywhere there is an internet connection. Of course, telephone and proxy bidding have always been available – they still are – but they haven't been something I wanted to do. Online is very different, at least for me.

Ensure that you've ticked all the auction house's boxes prior to auction day, as some do require more detail than others. Some auction procedures are different, so it's important to familiarise yourself with the specifics for the auctions in which you are bidding.

Key points

- Buyers can bid online or by phone.
- Like traditional auctions, the highest bid before the auction closes, wins.
- The buyer is committed to buy the property.
- Exchange of contracts, with a 10% deposit, is within 28 days. If you don't exchange contracts, the reservation fee is forfeited.
- Online auctions are here to stay, whether conditional or unconditional.
- Ensure that you register at least the day before the auction – preferably earlier than that, should there be any issues that need to be resolved.
- Check that your internet connection works!
- You might be able to set an automated online proxy bid, or you may have to click.
- Don't leave it too late to bid, as you can miss the lot.
- There is 30 seconds' additional time after each new bid, which avoids 'bid sniping' at the end of the auction.

Chapter 13

Repossessions and Law of Property Act Receivers

Sadly, during normal market conditions, many individuals, companies and developers can go bust for myriad reasons. As we've seen in this book, they might be overleveraged, as interest rates rise sharply, or there can be other factors meaning they can no longer meet their mortgage or loan commitments.

During a recession, the number of bankruptcies and insolvencies increases. In the post-Credit Crunch period, we managed to source some incredible opportunities for ourselves and clients, some of which are below.

It's worth highlighting that, at times, you can purchase a property before it's sent to the auction house by approaching Law of Property Act (LPA) receivers. As a private individual you may find this difficult, so may wish to instruct a company to do it on your behalf.

What is a Law of Property Act receiver?

An LPA receiver is appointed by a lender or mortgagee who has a fixed charge over property under the statutory power given to that lender in Section 109 of the Law of Property Act 1925. The LPA receiver works entirely for the lender, not the borrower.

Why are they appointed?

Source: Shutterstock (reproduced under licence)

An LPA receiver is appointed where a borrower has defaulted on a mortgage for a specific property by the powers in the legal charge. The LPA receiver's role is to take control of the property and recover cash for the lender by selling it.

While the LPA receiver is obliged to obtain the best price for the property, this does provide an opportunity for an astute investor to get significant value.

What are the risks?

Purchasing a property from an LPA receiver comes with several risks for a buyer.

Lack of information

Often, the LPA receiver has no personal knowledge of the property, and sells on that basis. They won't reply to enquiries at the beginning, and it's unlikely that their solicitors will have any more information – or be able to provide replies to anything – beyond the documents they actually hold. Moreover, the receiver doesn't accept any liability or give any representations or warranties as to any outstanding matters.

As we've seen, while for non-receivership transactions the usual rule is caveat emptor – which places the onus firmly on the buyer to carry out as much due diligence as they can – in receivership sales, the buyer's position is weakened further due to lack of information or seller representations or warranties.

In this situation, a buyer must inspect the property with a fully qualified surveyor, and carry out as much independent investigation as possible to try and reduce risk.

Title guarantee

The LPA receiver doesn't have title to the property, as they aren't its registered owner: they're only acting as the seller's agent and give no warranty on title. Your solicitor will be able to reduce this risk.

Environmental and planning

Typically, LPA receivers exclude any liability for environmental risk: they will try and place this entirely on the buyer. There may be room to negotiate this, so at minimum a buyer should seek to leave all historic liability with the seller.

In this situation, searches and surveys are vital, as this is the only way the necessary information can be obtained.

Management contracts

Where the property has management or other service or maintenance contracts, the LPA receiver won't be unable to confirm if these have ceased or varied. Again, a buyer needs to consider this during due diligence.

Funding

These risks can also affect how the property purchase can be funded. Some lenders are reluctant to lend where title to the property can't be verified.

Opportunity

Many of these risks can be offset by thorough legal due diligence, carrying out appropriate searches and making the necessary enquiries of local authorities. Overall, purchase from an LPA receiver does carry a greater risk in terms of the information available to any buyer, but this should be reflected in the purchase price and may be outweighed by commercial factors.

Case studies

There are some excellent opportunities during economic recessions. Sadly, some developers and private individuals can no longer pay monthly interest on their debts. The examples below were purchased, either for us, or a client, from the LPA receiver and therefore were not placed at auction. For brevity, I'm only illustrating the point with two cases, but there are more in London, Liverpool and Yorkshire.

Case Study
Distressed Assets: Eight two-bedroom leasehold apartments, East London – 2010

In the example below, the properties were purchased for cash and only six months later, in a market where surveyors regularly undervalued, were refinanced by a bank 17% above purchase price. In anyone's books this is a sound investment.

Purchase price (2010)	£1,793,000
Market value official valuation (January 2011)	£2,100,000
Discount	17%
Mortgage deposit	N/A
Rental income	
Per month	£9,666
Per annum	£115,992

Letting agent fees	
Rate:	10%
Per month	£967
Per annum	£11,604
Buying costs	
Stamp duty (4%)	£71,720
Legal fees	£8,000
Mortgage broker fees	N/A

Costs		
Per month		**Per annum**
Mortgage	N/A	N/A
Letting Agent Fees	£967	£11,604
Service Charge	£1,350	£16,200
Ground Rent	£200	£2,400
Total	£2,517	£30,204

Cash flow		
Per month		**Per annum**
Rental Income	£9,666	£115,992
Costs	£2,517	£30,204
TOTAL INCOME	£7,149	£85,788

Case Study
Distressed Assets: Freehold 12 x two-bedroom/two-bathroom apartments, Liverpool – 2012

This is a fantastic development in its own grounds with private parking in a prestigious area of Liverpool. The development was sold by a receiver unbroken, and remains so today (Figure 29). It had recently been developed to a very high standard.

In 2012 it was purchased for £1 million, or £83,333 per apartment. If the value of the freehold were realised at the time, it would have been £78,000.

Comparable apartments within a few minutes' walk were selling at the time for between £123,500 and £189,995, but the majority were in the £128,000 to £130,000 range. The value of this particular development is plain to see.

The property was under-rented, although the gross yield was 9.3%

Today, an individual apartment would sell for about £285,000, a significant uplift in 16 years.

Figure 29: Unbroken freehold investment via an LPA receiver

Using a military analogy, there is significant value if you can ambush a development before it is sent to auction. Even given the caveats about buying through a receiver, the risk/reward ratio, for those who do thorough due diligence, significantly favours reward.

Key points

- There are excellent opportunities for the astute buyer, not just in periods of economic shock or when sentiment is low, but in all market conditions.
- Distressed assets are not without risk, but thorough due diligence, with the support of professional advisors, is key to minimising it.

Chapter 14
Selling Property at Auction

In a book devoted to buying bargain properties at auction, it's almost counter-intuitive to start this chapter by saying that auctions are a terrific way to sell property. How can they be both a great place to buy and sell?

It's a fair question, so this chapter will show you why both statements are correct – and why indeed you may find yourself trading: buying at auction simply to put it back in the next one, or in another auction house in a different part of the country.

I have sold properties at auction, both for myself and clients. There are many reasons why you might choose to do this, rather than through private treaty with an estate agent. You might be a property trader looking for a 'quick turn', or a receiver wanting to demonstrate transparency.

We will look at each in turn, but first it's worth mentioning again the difference between unconditional and conditional auctions, as this affects the timing and legalities of a sale.

Selling property at unconditional auction: traditional method

As discussed in Chapter 12, the unconditional auction is the one we are all familiar with: when the hammer hits the gavel (or virtual gavel), the auction concludes with exchange of contracts and completion 28 days later, or as stipulated in the Special Conditions of Sale.

All things being equal, a seller can expect the proceeds less costs, shortly after completion.

Selling property at conditional auction: modern method

A conditional auction doesn't have the same certainty as the traditional method, because the buyer can pull out – albeit losing their deposit. Additionally, many of these auctions have a process where the buyer has 28 days to exchange contracts, and 56 days to complete (which we'll look at below).

Why sell property at auction?

Speed

One of the best reasons to place a property into an auction is the speed of the transaction, from marketing to receiving the cash in your nominated bank account. As a late lot in a traditional auction (missing the extended marketing period), it's feasible to have the whole transaction wrapped up in six to seven weeks. As a standard lot, eight weeks would be a reasonable expectation.

For example: if there is a new government, you believe it will change the legislation or tax regime relating to investment property, and you are already considering selling in the short term, it might be sensible to consider selling quickly to lock in the current rate of, say, capital gains tax or to avoid new onerous regulations. A quick calculation can help with your decision-making.

Alternatively, you may wish to release cash quickly to invest in another property or project. Again, this is a simple calculation of the costs and benefits.

If speed is your aim, choose a traditional auction over modern method.

Certainty

Traditional auctions give sellers certainty of sale. As the hammer falls, contracts are exchanged and buyers can't pull out without penalties. If they do, they will lose their deposit and fees, and may be subject to legal action.

If you need to liquidate real-estate assets quickly for any reason, a traditional auction would be a good option.

Transparency

Auctions offer transparency for sellers who require it, such as local authorities, receivers, mortgagees in possession, proceeds of crime and so on. The market decides the price in an open and fair way.

Often, many of these lots 'go to the room', as this is the most transparent and open part of the auction process. Only if the lot doesn't sell can you usually make an offer, which will be examined on its merits. I've had considerable success over the years, for myself and clients, making post-auction offers in these sorts of circumstances (examples of which are in this book).

Competition

As a buyer, one of the considerations I have when filtering lots is potential for competition. Only recently, I looked at a lot and understood that there were 27 other people looking at it. That was enough for me to drop out without any further due diligence, as competition drives prices – however, this is exactly what you want as a seller. The more bidders, the more likely you are to achieve a decent price – sometimes above market value.

Over the years, I've seen many auctions where a sense of competition and winning has taken over from sound, rational and coherent decision-making.

In a recent online traditional auction, I was guiding one of my mentees with the bidding: they were in London and I was in Liverpool, but with modern technology we were both 'in the room'. After extensive due diligence, we had decided and agreed on a ceiling price or maximum bid, and programmed the software to automatically bid. Our maximum bid was exceeded, and we dropped out – discipline and sticking to the game plan are key success factors with auctions.

Then two bidders went head-to-head, and my mentee couldn't believe what they were witnessing – but after years of property auctions, I'd seen it all before. It was like two punch-drunk boxers slugging it out with both fists, in the middle of the ring: win at all costs. Eventually, the winner paid 35% above our maximum bid, which was a fair price at auction. However, in reality they lost, because they would have been better off buying through private treaty at a lower price.

A classic example of why it's important not to get carried away, and to stay calm and composed.

As a seller you want competition, so the marketing and guide price of your property are crucial, as well as selecting the right auction house.

Online bidding with or without a live auctioneer

The auction process changed after the Covid-19 pandemic lockdowns (see Chapter 12), and hasn't returned to the pre-2020 model in most cases.

Now, traditional online auctions are either led by an auctioneer via a live stream, or just over computer screen. In my opinion, the live auctioneer does have a role in assisting the seller (experience and intuition suggest that they squeeze out the last pound for sellers). Remember: that's their role. Some are highly skilled at whipping up buyers – which is exactly what sellers want – and the auction house aims to get the best possible price for their clients, the sellers!

No time-wasters: serious buyers and investors

I've not come across many time-wasters, whether buying or selling at auction. Many of the tyre-kickers occupy the private treaty space, as the property auction world is more complex and less easily navigated than popping into an estate agent's office.

Additionally, serious auction buyers have their finance in place prior to bidding, whereas a lot of private treaty sales depend on mortgage finance that isn't certain and, in some market conditions, is difficult to obtain.

Internet marketing to large national and international markets

With the advent of online auctions, lots attract investors and bidders from around the globe, and indeed many of my clients live overseas. Overseas buyers have always bought at auction, but the digital revolution seems to be attracting more investors (certainly, that's my experience).

I recently purchased a property via online auction while sitting round a swimming pool on holiday abroad. As I've mentioned elsewhere in this book, I'm a great fan of traditional online auctions, as they open up a whole new world for people who can't get to the auction's physical location. Whether you live in Manchester, Madrid, Mumbai or Melbourne, it's a level playing field; we have people from all over the world attending our workshops live online, as well as in person in London.

Property in the UK has a global appeal – it's one of the factors that support it as a solid, long-term investment.

Selling 'as seen'

Unless you're a property trader who may wish to add value to a property before selling it on, you don't have to do anything with a property prior to selling at auction. I've bought properties in all sorts of condition, from derelicts to five-storey, tenanted city-centre office blocks: a lick of paint here and there wouldn't have increased what I would have paid.

Don't spend money that you don't have to:
it's not necessary to sell successfully at auction.

Legal protections

Here's a summary of key legal safeguards for sellers to note.

Binding sales contract

As mentioned previously, once the hammer falls, the buyer exchanges contracts with the seller. It's binding, with penalties for breach of contract. The buyer must pay a deposit immediately – if they fail to complete the purchase, the seller can retain the deposit and pursue legal action, if they so wish.

Reserve price

The seller can set a reserve price: this ensures the property isn't sold for less than a minimum acceptable amount. It's crucial, in consultation with the auction house, to set a realistic reserve price, but not one that undersells the property – it's a judgement call.

Auction houses are in the business of selling property, and might not agree with you about your reserve price. It's situations like these where advice from a company like mine, which specialises in buying and selling at auction, would be sensible (for further details, see the end of this book).

Caveat emptor ('buyer beware')

Again, properties at auction are sold 'as seen', which limits the seller's liability for defects or any other issues.

Right to withdraw

The seller can withdraw the property before the auction begins, if they so wish. It's important to read the contract you have with the auction house, to be fully aware if there are any penalties or not for withdrawing your lot.

Problem or unusual real estate can be sold

If you have a problem property or other real-estate asset and a private treaty sale isn't viable, you can look at traditional auction.

Problems may involve:

- Leasehold issues
- Length of lease

- Excessive service charges
- Missing freeholder
- Subsidence
- Boundary disputes
- Flooding and environmental issues
- Title issues
- Derelict property

– and so on.

Other auction lots can be:

- Ground rent portfolios
- Land with or without planning permission
- Garages
- Toilet blocks
- Other properties more suited to traditional auction.

Little or no hassle

Traditional auctions are hassle-free, and obviously quick. Once you've decided on an auction house (we can help you) which best suits your property and will result in a better sales price, the main legwork is done.

The auction house produces the particulars, which you're advised to assist and scrutinise (you'll have to agree to them in any event); and your solicitor, the legal pack. The auction house undertakes the viewings. It's a simple and straightforward process.

Here's a side-by-side comparison of both types of auction (Table 10).

Table 10: Comparison of traditional and modern method auctions

Unconditional: traditional method	Conditional: modern method
Bidding and offer process	
The property is sold 'as seen'. Once a bid is accepted, the buyer is legally committed to purchase the property and must complete the sale within a specified time, as stated in the Special Conditions of Sale (usually 28 days). There is no option to pull out. The buyer pays a deposit (often 10%) immediately after auction, with the balance on completion.	When a bid is accepted, the buyer doesn't immediately purchase the property. Instead, they sign a reservation agreement and pay a non-refundable deposit (usually 4–5% of the sale price). This effectively gives them an option to buy, not a commitment. The buyer has a set period (usually 28 days to exchange contracts, and 56 days to complete) to conduct any further due diligence, including obtaining mortgage finance.
Completion times	
Completion is usually 28 days from the auction date, with no conditions attached. I've had shorter and longer completions of 14 days and six weeks, and this information is found in the Special Conditions of Sale and the contract. The buyer must be ready to proceed immediately.	Completion typically happens within a 56-day period after the reservation agreement is signed. This gives the buyer time to secure a mortgage, undertake a survey, and decide if they wish to proceed.
Risk	
The buyer assumes more risk, because they commit to the purchase immediately after winning the bid. If they can't complete the sale, they risk losing their deposit and may face legal action. On exchange of contracts the buyer must insure the property, unless it's a leasehold property covered by the freeholder's policy.	There's less risk for the buyer. They don't exchange contracts immediately, and the reservation form they complete is more of an option to buy – a period where they have exclusivity to undertake due diligence, raise finance and ensure they are completely happy with the transaction. The reservation fee, subject to a minimum, can be viewed as an option premium that is lost if the buyer withdraws.

<table>
<tr><th colspan="2">The market</th></tr>
<tr><td>Traditional auctions attract more experienced investors or buyers who are prepared and able to make quick decisions.

TV programmes and books like this have made traditional auctions more accessible to new and old property investors and buyers alike. It's a huge market: if you get the marketing material right, a realistic guide/reserve price and choose the most suitable auction house for your lot, you'll do well as a seller.</td><td>A larger potential market of buyers who want the extra time and flexibility that this method allows. It opens your lot to buyers who require mortgage finance, and for one reason or another don't want to use bridging finance.

(Interestingly, I don't think bridging finance is widely understood by many wishing to buy at auction, so the modern method is their preferred choice.)</td></tr>
<tr><th colspan="2">Marketing</th></tr>
<tr><td>Usually, these auctions are more fast-paced, targeted at those who want to secure a quick deal without the risk of protracted negotiations and gazumping.</td><td>Typically, properties are marketed with the option to proceed under the condition that the buyer confirms their decision within the given time – usually, exchange of contract at the 28-day point.</td></tr>
<tr><th colspan="2">Price expectations</th></tr>
<tr><td>If you get the reserve price right, and the marketing goes to plan to ensure many potential investors view your property and download the legal pack, with a fair wind and lots of competition you can expect an excellent price for your property.</td><td>Prices may be lower, given that the speed of transaction is much slower and fees are higher – the final price you pay is significantly higher than the reserve price.

In the example below, I paid £14,000 for the property, but the fees were £6,900.

For a tenanted property in excellent condition, £20,900 yielding 34% (29% net) is certainly one of my top 20.

I have no problem with the fees, and have paid similar amounts at some traditional auctions over the years: I look at total, not notional, costs.</td></tr>
<tr><th colspan="2">Seller's view</th></tr>
<tr><td>Sellers looking for a quicker, more straightforward sale might prefer this route, as it ensures the buyer is committed once the hammer falls and contracts are exchanged.</td><td>Sellers might use a conditional auction to attract a larger pool of potential buyers who wish to use traditional mortgages, and/or are risk averse.</td></tr>
</table>

Case Study
Distressed Assets: Liverpool L13 – October/November 2024

These are some real-world examples of both traditional and modern auction methods in the same block, achieving similar rental returns and purchased within weeks of each other (Table 11). The chances of this scenario are extremely rare, but they provide food for thought for both buyers and sellers when choosing options for auctions.

The results below are indicative only in so far as these transactions were undertaken by me, but without doubt they demonstrate a difference between two methods of auction, at the same time, with good comparables.

Table 11: Examples of traditional versus modern auction methods

	Apartment 1	**Apartment 2**
Auction type	**Modern method**	**Traditional method**
Details	• One-bedroom top-floor apartment • Tenanted • No arrears • Excellent condition	• One-bedroom ground-floor apartment • Not tenanted • Required minor refurbishment
Price paid at auction	£14,000	£40,000
Costs including: Special Conditions of Sale additions Auctioneer's fee Stamp duty (where applicable) Legal fees	£6,900	£6,284
Total acquisition cost	£20,900	£46,284
Gross yield at market rent based on purchase price	51%	18%
Gross yield at market rent based on total acquisition costs	34%	15%
Average cost per apartment	**£27,000**	**£27,000**

Average total cost per apartment	£33,592	£33,592
Average net (after costs) yield	18%	18%

Comment

I bought the apartments because I know the block well: it's in an excellent rental area, and we own the freehold. I always say in my workshops that you must be careful buying leasehold properties at auction, because often service charges aren't disclosed in the legal pack, management companies vary significantly, and some leases carry onerous terms.

That hurdle was already jumped, as we owned the freehold; if we hadn't owned it, I would have asked my solicitor to obtain a copy of the lease (if not in the legal pack), and we would have made enquiries about historic, current and future service charges, as well as information about the management company, freeholder, cladding and any ongoing disputes.

Acquisition can simply be sitting in front of the TV with the kids watching Harry Potter for the umpteenth time and deciding to look on your phone at auction properties that fit your strategy. That's what happened with Apartment 1. I was stunned to see the guide price, so immediately registered with the auction house and bid for it. It was a Saturday night, but the technology allowed me to do it after uploading ID checks and other information.

The auction was due to finish on the Monday at 2pm – at the same time that I was presenting to the management of an auction house based in north-west England, but with national reach. I stopped my presentation, held up my phone at the finish time, and said 'I've got it!', then a discussion flowed from this.

About a week later, I received an email from a completely different auction house to Apartment 1, letting me know that Apartment 2 was in the next sale date. It was an unconditional auction, and I became aware that the owner wasn't accepting pre-auction offers, instead going to the room.

I know the auction house well, and prepared for the live online sale. Bidding was brisk, and it was clear there were two of us battling it out. I had my maximum bid, which was heavily influenced by the fact that I'd just bought the penthouse (top-floor flat) for just £14,000, plus costs. I was prepared to go higher, as I would pound cost average both apartments (see below). As it was, the other bidder dropped out at the stamp duty threshold, leaving me to acquire the property at £40,000 (plus costs and £2,000 stamp duty).

Although the property required some work, I was delighted with the outcome.

Pound cost average

When I averaged out the cost of the two apartments, each one was £27,000 before costs, and £33,592 with a gross yield of 21%. Taking it a stage further after service charges, the net yield was 18%.

Flipping properties for profit

In terms of a private-treaty sale, I would put both properties on the market now at £59,950 and accept £55,000, so after costs my net profit would be:

£110,000 – £67,184 – £2,000 legal fees = £40,816

On a return-on-investment basis, this would be 61% over a very short period – which by any standards is excellent.

Any investor undertaking due diligence will note that a similar apartment, albeit it a two-bedroom unit (converted from a one-bedroom apartment, using a large living room with two windows) sold for £65,000 in March 2023.

A net yield of 11% is incredibly attractive to a buy-to-let investor

At £55,000, the net yield for an investment buyer at a private treaty sale, where they can undertake all the required due diligence on an apartment purchase, would be 11% – which is attractive. This type of transaction gave me options. As it is, the properties won't be sold but held for the long term, enjoying the income.

You may ask yourself, why would someone sell a property at auction below what they could expect in a private treaty sale? We considered the possibilities earlier in this chapter, with many wanting speed and certainty for whatever reason – divorce, debt, health, unpaid taxes and so on.

Aborted private treaty sale

This may happen when a property has been under offer for some considerable period, the sale falls through and the seller decides to go to auction instead, having been fed up with the process and length of time it's taken. Sometimes I see estate agents' boards lying on the ground in the yards or gardens of properties with a 'Sold STC' sign across the top.

This clearly indicates an aborted private-treaty sale, so for the buyer it's essential to find out the following. Did it fail:

- the survey?
- on the searches?
- for any other legal reason?
- on the buyer's inability to obtain mortgage finance?

Crucial questions, the answers to which will determine if the auction buyer proceeds.

I hope these real-world examples give you something to consider when selling, but also buying at auction. In summary:

A seller of property at auction wants competition, while a buyer does not.

The sales process

Whichever auction method you choose, the process as a seller is the same, although do note the differences outlined in Table 10. For illustrative purposes, the process described below is for a traditional auction.

1. Decide why you're selling at auction and not via private treaty at an estate agent.

2. Seek advice from an auction specialist, or directly with an auction house. At Distressed Assets we can help you sell through both types of auctions, and the service is free (the auction house splits their fee with us. You pay nothing extra for our assistance).

3. Research the market, using the tools and techniques outlined in this book to determine market value. Having done that, you'll be in a more informed position to instruct an auction appraisal or valuation. It's also important at this stage to understand all the costs involved in selling. Some auction houses charge you a fee (often 2–2.5%), but others are 'free' as the buyer pays – which is stipulated in the particulars and contract. You may wish to instruct your solicitor to include your auction and legal fees in the Special Conditions of Sale, for the buyer to pay on completion.

4. If you're happy with the auction valuation then proceed. If not, negotiate and if necessary, obtain another opinion– I've done this, and you'd be surprised at the difference in price.

5. Once ready to proceed, you'll receive a contract (often for electronic signature). It's important that you read the contract and fully understand what you are signing up to, as surprises

further down the road can be costly. It's also important to understand if there are any tie-ins post-auction, as this limits your options to find other routes to market, should your lot not sell and no acceptable post-auction offer is received.

6. You will be asked to complete anti-money laundering checks.

7. Once the contract is signed, you should instruct a solicitor to prepare a legal pack. Some auction houses offer this service for a fee.

8. Work with the auction house to create the particulars which, combined with photos and video (in many cases), are the hook to lure buyers and create a sense of competition. If you know anything about the property or locality that might be of interest to an investor, make sure it's in the particulars of sale:
   a. Is planning permission (or even lapsed permission) in place to add value?
   b. Is there potential for an HMO or serviced accommodation?
   c. Is there potential for an extension?
   d. Is there potential to split a large bedroom with two windows into two?
   e. Is the boiler new?
   f. Is the property under-rented? If so, what yield could a new investor expect at the market rent? This will influence their maximum bid.
   g. Are transport links nearby?
   h. Are any local schools highly rated?
   i. Are there any excellent shops, restaurants or pubs within walking distance?

   These are just a few examples, but packing your particulars with information to enable a buyer to make an informed choice is essential for success.

9. There will be a deadline to have the contract signed: usually, three to four weeks before auction day or days, as some auction houses have them over more than one day.

10. The auction house will have published block viewings for your property, or arrange viewings according to demand. Either way, you may receive pre-auction offers well in advance of the auction. It's a judgement call whether to accept a pre-auction offer, but remember: you don't have to respond instantly.

    The auction house can tell you about the number of viewings, and how many people have downloaded the legal pack. This gives you an idea of the popularity of the lot. If you have several interested parties, you might decide to take the lot to the room and hope for competitive bidding to drive the price.

    If you have just one expression of interest for an unpopular lot, and the offer is attractive after negotiation (you don't have to accept their first offer), then maybe don't take it to the room if you want certainty, as speed is essential. If the property doesn't sell in the room, it will be marketed as unsold and emails will be sent to regular buyers, as well as a general mailshot for post-auction offers.

11. If the property sells at any stage, the buyer will pay a deposit (usually 10%), and the auctioneer's fee and contracts are exchanged. The legal process now begins in earnest.

12. After 28 days, or the time stipulated in the Special Conditions of Sale, completion takes place. You will be required to sign a TR1 form for your solicitor, which requires a witness, then completion takes place.

13. If the buyer doesn't complete on the contractual date, your solicitor may advise you to issue a Notice to Complete, which gives them 10 working days to fulfil their obligations. This carries a fee for the buyer, which should be stated in the Special Conditions of Sale.

14. After completion, you should receive the proceeds within a few working days.

Tip

A mentee purchased a property at auction in 2024 for £75,000: the market value in the road was about £110,000. At £75,000 and market rent, the gross yield was 12%. The property is in an excellent rental area, where they let quickly.

I viewed the property with my mentee, and was pleased to see it in excellent condition, with a new roof, external insulation and a new boiler. The tenants were nice, having lived there for more than six years; there were no rent arrears. It had an EPC E.

Given the focus on environmental issues and the government target of EPC C by 2030, undoubtedly an EPC E would have discouraged less savvy investors from even viewing the property, if they were undertaking a filter with EPC as one of their criteria. It was easy to identify on the viewing that the property was an EPC C, given the works undertaken, particularly the external insulation.

Prior to selling, be sure to check and update the EPC. In this case, for the sake of £60 or so, marketing with EPC C rather than EPC E would have benefited the sale. As a buyer, the EPC E helped us, as there may have been less competition.

Key points

- If you're unsure whether selling at auction is right for your property, take advice.
- Unconditional auction gives you certainty and speed, as the sale is 'as seen'.
- Conditional auction gives you a wider market, as the completion date is usually 56 days. It can attract mortgage buyers, but buyers can pull out if they wish.
- Increase competition from your lot by including as much information as possible that may be of interest to a buyer or investor.

- If you have an old EPC and you've undertaken improvement works, update it.
- Ensure you choose the most appropriate auction house for your lot.
- Agree guide and reserve prices with the auction house, to attract potential buyers.
- Instruct a solicitor who regularly undertakes auction-related work. Remember: you don't have to include everything in an auction pack, and sometimes it's to your disadvantage if you do.
- Consider pre-auction offers, but only if interest is very low. If not, go to the room.
- If your lot doesn't sell, you may receive post-auction offers that might be below your reserve price. It's a judgement call, depending on your need for speed and certainty. If these aren't crucial factors, you may wish to go again at the next auction.

Chapter 15
Critical Success Factors: The Property Auction Checklist

I hope you now have better understanding of how to be successful at property auctions than before you read the book. As mentioned in the Introduction, what you have read here is a result of extensive, full-time experience of property auctions acquired over the past decade and more.

Here are some final points to think about.

Keep an eye on the economy and its direction

We don't buy property or invest in a vacuum, so we need to keep an eye on the economy and where it's going, to adapt our strategy and evolve with changing circumstances. This could be in a period of rising inflation and rising interest rates, or a deep recession, falling prices (deflation) and falling interest rates. We must be nimble in our approach and adapt to changing circumstances.

Don't get carried away with the latest trend

We must keep abreast of the latest trends in property, deciding whether to go along for the ride or sit it out. If sitting it out, when will the opportunity arise? For example, recently I've seen many student-type 'pod' properties selling for a fraction of their original price. The question is: do they now present an opportunity at much lower prices, or not?

Avoid the noise

It's important to avoid the noise of the media and some other less experienced and informed property investors you may meet in-person or online. Auctions are a niche and there are many people out there who claim to understand them, but have little or any experience, other than watching TV programmes or reading books. Make your own decisions, based on your own experience and research, and ignore the noise.

Buying at auction: the 'to-do' list

Strategy

1. Sit down, relax and decide why you are doing this, what you want to achieve and what your ultimate goal is. It could be to provide a monthly income to supplement your salary or pension, or develop and sell to make a profit. Only you can decide, by involving your partner and/or your family, friends, colleagues or A-team. This initial session, pondering your aims and strategy will pay off handsomely, providing you with spearlike focus. Success is to a large extent about commitment and focus. Write it down, and refer back to it as you move forward.
2. After that, decide how you will do it. Become an expert in one type of distressed asset, such as the freehold house: the two-up two-down engine room of UK buy-to-let. Only by becoming an expert, whether in sport, business or property are we able to move to the next level – from gifted amateur to professional. You will find opportunities are plentiful, once you're an expert.
3. Where will you do it? Near home, or go to where the yields (ratio of rent to property prices) are high? If the latter, research the area and if you are time-poor, employ an expert to source the property for you and buy into their A-team. This shortcuts the process, but there is no reason why you can't do it yourself. You must ensure that in the area you've chosen, you have a foot on the ground: someone who will look after your interests. In this case, it would be a good lettings and property management agent.

Research

4. Once you have decided on all that, you're good to go. Subscribe to an information provider, such as the Essential Information Group (see Chapter 6). Search for your target properties in your target area and set up email auction alerts that will save you significant time in research.
5. Seek human intelligence (HUMINT) on the ground. Talk with estate agents and lettings agents.
6. Visit your target area during the week and at weekends, as well as during the day and night.
7. Conduct desk research, including reading the legal pack, to eliminate properties from your list. Use the framework of the Intelligence Cycle. Work out market values based on the comparable property method. Are any properties under-rented? Have any got additional points for a new roof, new boiler, conservatory, off-street parking?

Risk

8. Limit your risk through research and due diligence, and by appointing professional advisors.

Finance

9. Concurrently, decide on how you will finance your first purchase and speak to a recommended mortgage broker.
10. Ensure the property you're bidding on is bridgeable or mortgageable, if that's your refinancing solution.
11. Stress-test your borrowings.
12. Gearing or borrowing magnifies gains and losses. Don't be a forced seller because you haven't done the numbers.

The auction process

13. Have a reserve in case you don't get the property that interests you. You might initially find six properties that do, but you're only going to buy one.
14. Remember, auctions sell problem properties as well as distressed assets. Ensure you aren't buying a property that you can't fix.

If in doubt, take professional advice. If you get it wrong, that fee for advice will seem very cheap in comparison with dry rot, subsidence or a defective lease.

15. View the shortlist. Keep in mind the issues raised in Chapter 11. Take a builder or surveyor with you on your second viewing, if necessary. Seek HUMINT from the tenants: they know the property and its issues better than anyone else.
16. Have a chat with the neighbours if you can. Look for the unusual, any signs of antisocial behaviour in the street.
17. If you're new to this, ignore what other viewers are saying about the property. Some think they are being clever by trying to put you off, mentioning non-existent issues as they walk round. I just smile and say, 'Are you sure?'

Legal

18. When you've narrowed down the options to just two, ask a solicitor to report on the legal packs. Negotiate the fee based on success: if so, you will instruct them to complete the transaction.
19. Do not bid on a leasehold property without seeing the lease, and preferably the service charge account. A solicitor must report to you on the lease. When an apartment is in an auction without lease and management arrangements detailed in the legal pack, this is a red flag.

Set your maximum bid

20. Once you're satisfied with the legal pack and the numbers, you're ready to set your maximum bid. Decide what the property is worth to you: it may be a calculation based on the rent or comparable data alone; but generally, it will be a combination of the two. If it's a development or renovation property, work out the Gross Development Value (GDV), which will inform you the maximum you can pay for the property and/or land. Ensure you factor a reserve into your calculations, as well as a 20% plus profit margin.
21. Consider a pre-auction offer.

Bidding

22. You're ready to bid. If it's online, gather together photo ID and proof of address and, ideally, register a couple of days before the auction. If you're bidding in-person in a live room, take the ID with you as well as a credit or debit card to pay the deposit and auction fees, should you be successful.
23. Check that the lot has not been withdrawn (which happens) and read the Addendum.
24. Position yourself at the back of the room, so that you can see both the auctioneer and the competition. If online, login and ensure you have a secure and strong connection. You can set a proxy bid to make the process easier, which allows you to do other things. If the connection is lost, your bid will still be active.
25. Before you bid, ensure you have the funds to complete.
26. Never go above your maximum bid. Don't see it as a competition that you must win. You only obtain value at auction by being dispassionate and calculating. Don't get carried away in the moment.
27. If you're in the room as the auctioneer says, 'Going once, going twice…', put up your paddle. Remember your maximum bid: every time the other bidder raises their bid, go straight back without hesitation and raise yours. In many cases, you will win.
28. If you don't, you still have your reserve property. If you fail to get that, there will be unsold lots to look through. And if all else fails, it's simply meant to be – so just look forward to the next auction.
29. If successful, an auction room staff member will take you to the contracts desk. Here, you pay the fees and deposit, and the contract is either given to you or posted to your solicitor. If online, you'll receive the documents from the auction house by email or post, depending on the current policy.

Insurance

30. You must insure the property. Many people forget, even those who have done this for a while.

Common sense

31. It's a cliché but true that money is made when you buy the property, not when you sell.
32. Above all else, use common sense. Most of us can tell if a property is OK and if we can't, there are people who can help you. But common sense gets you a long way in property, as it does in life.
33. Enjoy it, and remember it's not rocket science – anyone can do it. What's stopping you?

Property auctions are a great way to buy genuine, below-market properties (distressed assets) which you can either rent, renovate or sell for profit. Many people think property auctions are risky, but those who say that have either never done it or aren't good at it. The key is to define what you want and become an expert.

Do thorough due diligence and appoint an A-team of professional advisors who know their stuff. Be modest with your aims and build on success that allows you to become bolder and more confident with experience.

I hope you have enjoyed the book and if you want to get in touch, please do; it would be great to have a chat.

Distressed Assets

Thank you for buying this book.

The astute investor buys distressed assets because that's where the best value is found. They understand the difference between retail and wholesale property investment. This is as true now as it was in 2008 and further back, during the economic depressions and recessions of the past.

Currently, we buy almost exclusively by auction as it's the best, quickest and most transparent way to buy genuine below market-value properties with further potential to add value, either by managing up rents, developing or flipping.

We do this for ourselves and our clients. We also have access to exclusive off-market deals.

Distressed Assets services

At Distressed Assets we offer several services:

- Dominic Farrell's 12-Month Fast-Track Mentoring Programme
- One-day intensive Distressed Assets Property Auction Workshop four times a year in central London and live online. Check the website for dates
- Advice on selling property at auction and achieving the best price
- Mortgages and bridging finance
- Legal conveyancing and advice
- Lettings and property management in north-west England
- Refurbishment and renovations in north-west England
- Right to Manage services across the UK.

Free Distressed Assets property investment newsletter

If you'd like to stay updated on Distressed Assets' property auction news and acquisitions, please sign up at our website: www.distressedassets.co.uk

Dominic Farrell's 12-Month Fast-Track Mentoring Programme

Tell me and I forget, teach me and
I may remember. involve me and I learn
Benjamin Franklin

THE PROPERTY AUCTION PROFESSIONAL

Property Auction Professional Mentorship – Mission Statement

Our mission is to transform amateur and novice investors into competent, disciplined, and independent property auction professionals.

Buying below market value, including at auction, is a process, not an event. Success comes from preparation, due diligence, patience, and decisive action, not luck, bravado, or following the herd.

What we will do for you - Our mentorship programme will teach you how to consistently buy property below market value through auctions, distressed assets and genuine off-market opportunities, using process, evidence, and professional judgment. Our mentorship programme is unique because we show you how to put the theory into practice, guiding you throughout the acquisition process, until you feel ready to act independently. We achieve this by building your confidence, motivating you to succeed, and training you to think and act like a professional.

How we do it – Dominic uses leadership and motivational skills finely developed as a decorated infantry officer during his extensive military career in the British Army. He will help you become a confident, motivated, and – crucially - independent investor equipped with the skills required to source, analyse, and execute deals anywhere in the UK, in any market conditions.

In particular, you will learn how:

- To assess risk accurately
- To understand seller psychology and legal nuance
- To execute with confidence in live, pre-auction and post-auction environments
- To operate ethically, compliantly, and for the long term

We value discipline over excitement, process over emotion, and results over opinions.

The Programme

This document sets out the formal framework of the mentorship. Direct communication includes one-to-one engagement and a structured monthly seminar with Dominic Farrell, and, from time to time may include contributions from selected external specialists, including mortgage, legal, and insurance professionals.

The Property Auction Professional Skool Community

In addition, mentees join the private Property Auction Professional Skool Community, which provides a structured online environment for the exchange of information, insights, opportunities, and peer support. The Skool community also hosts supplementary resources, session recordings, and a weekly digest summarising activity and key updates.

Details of the programme structure are set out below and may be subject to change.

Foundations of Auction Mastery (Modules 1-3)		Outcome
Onboarding	• Complete an online risk profile - The DISC Profile • One-to-one Zoom with Dominic Farrell	Identifies individual strengths and development areas, along with the goals and fears that typically motivate behaviour Establishes personal goals, aspirations, and desired outcomes for the mentorship
Module 1 **How Property Auctions Really Work Based on 18 Years of Experience**	• The winning mindset – based on proven military principles • Securing a competitive advantage • The auction ecosystem (auction houses, sellers, buyers) • Wholesale v retail investing • Conditional v unconditional auctions – which is best? • Why many amateur investors overpay for property at auction • Auction psychology and crowd behaviour • Choosing the right auction strategy for your goals and available capital	Dispels most common misconceptions about auctions and equips you with a personal auction strategy framework, and a clear understanding of what it takes to succeed
Module 2 **Finding Profitable Deals Through Professional Research and Analysis**	• How to use professional software to find bargain properties • Types of auction stock • Selecting locations that work (Liverpool case study – principles applicable UK-wide and overseas) • Identifying “missed by the market” opportunities – a key auction strategy • Desktop due diligence • Risk management **Live demonstration of software and filtering processes** • Understanding how mortgage valuers assess market price and security for the lender • Targeting grants (free capital) **In-person group visit to a live auction – London (optional)**	Enables you to identify your own deals using professional software, quickly eliminate those that don’t work, and focus on the most promising opportunities

<table>
<tr>
<td>Module 3

Legal Packs & Risk Management</td>
<td>• The conveyancing process
• Special conditions of sale, completion timelines, hidden fees, rent arrears clauses, notice to complete
• Title issues, leases, restrictions, charges, mortgages
• Common red flags and deal-killers
• Common green flags that others may miss – opportunity
• Selecting and working effectively with solicitors/conveyancers
• When to walk away immediately, and when to pay for legal advice
• Indemnity policies to reduce risk
Live online Q&A session with a solicitor:
Legal pack walk-through using real auction examples</td>
<td>Builds familiarity with a legal risk checklist and solicitor briefing template, enabling you to identify major red flags and avoid costly mistakes that catch many amateur investors out</td>
</tr>
<tr>
<td colspan="2">Numbers, Finance & Execution (Modules 4–6)</td>
<td>Outcome</td>
</tr>
<tr>
<td>Module 4

The Numbers That Matter</td>
<td>• Acquisition costs at auction
• Stamp duty, auction fees, and hidden costs
• Yield, net yield v capital growth
• In-built equity at auction
• What return on investment (ROI) means
• Exit strategies:
○ flip, BRRR, hold, develop
• Stress-testing deals and cashflow
Live online: follow and discuss a live online auction</td>
<td>Provides you with a realistic understanding of total costs using completed deal appraisal templates, ensuring there are no hidden surprises after acquisition</td>
</tr>
</table>

Module 5 **Finance & Funding**	• Raising finance from non-standard sources • Credit ratings and how to repair them • Cash v bridging v buy-to-let finance • Auction timelines and funding risks • Structuring deals to stay liquid • Common finance mistakes at auction **Live online Q&A session with a bridging and mortgage broker:** **Bridging finance, mortgage finance, and BRRR strategies**	Your personal funding route mapped out, including alternative strategies you may not have encountered elsewhere
Module 6 **How To Undertake Auction Viewings (Live in Liverpool)**	• Group property viewings • Street-level analysis • The key issues – roof, subsidence, damp, heating, and electrics • Refurbishment cost estimation • Rental demand assessment • Evening group debrief **Dinner and group networking for those staying overnight (optional)**	A shortlist of live auction opportunities for discussion and analysis This module converts theory into practical, real-world execution that can be implemented immediately
Deal Pressure & "Deal Defence" (Modules 7–9)		**Outcome**
Module 7 **Preparing to Bid**	• Set-up process • Anti-money laundering requirements (AML) • Final due diligence • Bid limits and discipline • Calculating the maximum bid • Avoiding emotional and reactive bidding • Tactics for pre-auction offers	Positions you to bid independently and confidently in-person or online auctions, avoiding "paralysis by analysis" and missed opportunities

Module 8 ***The Deal Den panel Presentation* (Online)**	Each mentee presents one real deal to the group and Deal Den panel: Each presentation must include: • Property overview • Purchase price and strategy • Legal risks • Full financials • Exit strategy • Downside risk (A *Deal Den* presentation template will be provided) • Challenging questions • Stress-testing assumptions • "Would you bid – yes or no?"	Participants learn more effectively by doing than by theory alone This module provides real, live auction experience through the structured compilation and presentation of a transaction at the Deal Den Based on the Deal Den panel presentation, the opportunity will be conditionally approved or rejected
Module 9 **Live & Post-Auction Strategy**	• Bidding tactics • Reading the auction room and online bidding • Post-auction negotiation • Securing unsold lots • When to walk away	You are equipped with a live bidding and post-auction negotiation plan, preparing you for every eventuality
Acquisition, Completion & Scale (Modules 10-12)		**Outcome**
Module 10 **Trading and Selling Property at Auction**	• Trading property – profit is made on purchase, not on sale – margin is crucial • Assessing wholesale and retail demand • Use of estate agents • Use of property sourcing agents • Overall transaction costs and tax	Understand the mechanics and due diligence required to trade property at auction for short-term profits
Module 11 **Completion, Refurb & Letting**	• Managing refurbishment risk • Regulatory compliance • Letting strategy and rent reviews • Property management and the law	Understand how to estimate refurbishment works and instruct contractors with confidence, ensuring clarity on total project costs

Module 12 **Review, Scale & Next Steps**	• Review of acquisitions • Structured review of lessons learned • Building systems for repeat purchases • Market outlook and future strategy	You'll identify what worked well, your true strengths and weaknesses, and receive a tailored plan for Year 2
The Deal Den panel	***Deal Den*** Session: mentees present: • Biggest learning experiences • What they bought or nearly bought • Their next 12-month acquisition plan	This module helps position you for future success at auction, having been out in the field, rather than providing purely theoretical knowledge

Figure 30: Mentoring

Source: Shutterstock (reproduced under licence)

What do mentees think?

46% capital gain in 6 months with no refurbishment

"I've been with Dom and his team since 2021, and have been extremely pleased with his advice, guidance, and property expertise. I've made four property purchases through Dom so far, with more to come in due course, the best so far being a purchase for £65,000 valued during raising a mortgage a few months later at £95,000, a 46% capital gain, with no renovation being required!

All my investments have been successful.

Dom has a killer combination of skills.

He has very strong knowledge, strong academics (and, more importantly, years of subsequent practical experience of successful property investment), which has led to successful investments for me. He has a way of cutting through the noise and speaking plainly and with focus, and he has been a real pleasure to work with.

My fourth property deal is another clear win acquired post-auction for just £60,000 with an initial yield of 18%"

J. R. Guildford, Surrey

60% capital gain in 8 months with no refurbishment

Today I got a survey on my first property bought through working with Dominic. I paid £75,000 and my goal was to do a "no money left in" deal. To achieve my goal, I needed the value to come back at £100,000 (borrowing 75% against a £100,000 valuation means I would get my original £75,000 investment back).

Well to my surprise the surveyor came back with a valuation of not £100,000, but £120,000. That means I'm now able to borrow £120,000 x 75% = £90,000 from the bank. Put another way I'm getting all my original £75,000 back plus an extra £15,000.

Put yet another way I'm getting all my original £75,000 back, paying for my mentorship fee in full, other costs, such as stamp duty, plus getting cash back on a property that I didn't refurbish, has been paying me rent, has had no issues with tenants, and got a free EPC upgrade. But if you want to know the truth, that's not what I paid the fee for.

The real value for me is the countless meetings, phone calls and text messages where I was told what was wrong with the property I was looking at, what to look for, and the major pitfalls to avoid in property, so I can position myself for success, which comes as part of the mentorship.

That's what I can take with me for the rest of my life. The £15,000 cash back is just confirmation (not that I needed it) that I chose the right guy. As with anything in life the "price" is what you pay, and the "value" is what you get. Those who can only see price will never benefit from the value. Thank you, Dominic."

C Gallagher, London

For further details on Dominic Farrell's 12-Month Fast-Track Mentoring Programme, contact him directly by email or telephone.

Contact details for Dominic Farrell
Dominic Farrell
Email: dominic@distressedassets.co.uk
Tel: 07888 867333

Distressed Assets: https://www.distressedassets.co.uk/
LinkedIn: www.linkedin.com/in/dominic-farrell-property/
YouTube: www.youtube.com/@DistressedAssets
Facebook: https://www.facebook.com/distressed.assets/
Instagram: https://www.instagram.com/ukpropertyauctions

One-day intensive Distressed Assets Property Auction Workshop

Discover the world of buying distressed assets on our one-day intensive workshop in London or live online. Once you buy wholesale, you will never again buy retail. See the brochure for further details. We are all looking forward to meeting you.

PROPERTY AUCTIONS WORKSHOP

How Professionals Buy — and Amateurs Overpay

A one-day, intensive workshop on selecting and valuing auction properties, and buying them significantly below market value utilising professional strategies and tactics.

Led by **Dominic Farrell**

Property Auction Specialist | Investor | Author

Most auction buyers fail before they even bid

- Guess the value
- Follow the crowd
- Overspend on refurbishments
- Bid emotionally, not strategically

Television programmes and poor advice *create confidence without competence.*
This workshop is designed to correct that — fast.

What you'll learn in one focused day

- How professionals value property before auction
- How to set a maximum bid — and stick to it
- How to navigate legal packs for opportunites
- Why spending less on refurbishment often produces better returns
- Discipline, patience, and decisiveness at auctions
- Raising bridging and mortgage finance

This workshop is for you if:

✓ You want to **buy below market value**
✓ You want repeatable results
✓ You want to think like a professional investor
✓ You want to gain a competitive advantage

Full day only £97

In-Person / Live Online Workshop ☑ One-Day Intensive ☑ Booking Required

"Discipline beats enthusiasm at auction — every time."

www.ingramcontent.com/pod-product-compliance
Lightning Source LLC
LaVergne TN
LVHW050928210926
848482LV00013B/564